CW01188480

My Life
in Jewelry

My Life in Jewelry
A Memoir

Azza Fahmy

Translated by Sarah Enany

The American University in Cairo Press
Cairo   New York

This book has been translated with the
assistance of the Sharjah International
Book Fair Translation Grant Fund

منحة الترجمة
Translation Grant

First published in 2024 by
The American University in Cairo Press
113 Sharia Kasr el Aini, Cairo, Egypt
420 Lexington Avenue, Suite 1644, New York, NY 10170
www.aucpress.com

Text copyright © by Al Dar Al Masriah Al Lubnaniah
Except where otherwise stated, all illustrations are copyright © by Azza Fahmy
Published in Arabic in 2021 as Mudhakkarat Azza Fahmy: *ahlam la tantahi* by
Al Dar Al Masriah Al Lubnaniah
English translation copyright © 2024 by Sarah Enany

All rights reserved. No part of this publication may be reproduced, stored in a retrieval system, or transmitted in any form or by any means, electronic, mechanical, photocopying, recording, or otherwise, without the prior written permission of the publisher.

ISBN 978 1 649 03289 8

Library of Congress Cataloging-in-Publication Data

Names: Fahmy, Azza, author. | Enany, Sarah, translator.
Title: My life in jewelry : a memoir / Azza Fahmy ; translated by Sarah Enany.
Other titles: Mudhakirat Azza Fahmy. English
Identifiers: LCCN 2023020890 | ISBN 9781649032898 (hardback) | ISBN 9781649032904 (epub) | ISBN 9781649032911 (adobe pdf)
Subjects: LCSH: Fahmy, Azza. | Jewelers--Egypt--Biography. | Women jewelers--Egypt--Biography. | Jewelry making--Egypt--History. | Art metal-work--Egypt--History. | LCGFT: Autobiographies.
Classification: LCC NK7198.F256 A34 2023 | DDC 739.27092 [B]--dc23/eng/20230606

1 2 3 4 5   28 27 26 25 24

Designed by Adam el-Sehemy
Printed in Egypt

Contents

Introduction   1

1. My Early Years   5
2. Among the Craftsmen   79
3. Business and Motherhood   147
4. Inspiration and Adventure   199

Epilogue   281
Glossary   285
References   289
Index   291

To my mother, from whose experience I learned how to do the best you can with what you have without disgruntlement and with good grace; to my father, the wonderful person who gifted me a fairytale childhood that gave me deep Egyptian roots that strengthened my love for my homeland (I wish he had lived long enough to see my success!); and to the two blossoms of my life, Fatma and Amina. I've laid a heavy burden on your shoulders; I hope you continue what we've started. And to Thuraya Moussa, my granddaughter, who I hope will jump onto our bandwagon.

Azza Fahmy, aka Zuzza Kazouza

Introduction

I've never stopped to think of me. All I do is charge on ahead, hurtling like a train out of control. There were always things to be done and a to-do list that needed to be checked off every night before bed. I always had a notebook with me full of lists and a red pen to mark off what was done. The day the idea for this book was born, we were just celebrating the fifty-year anniversary of the Azza Fahmy company. The girls in the office were busy planning the celebrations, and I panicked. "Goodness," I thought, "fifty years gone? Where did the days and years go?"

It was like this was the final chapter, the final scene of the play. I'm like, "Girl, you need to cool it and settle down. You need to talk about Azza Fahmy the person. You've got to know yourself." Maybe the reason I wanted to know myself was this story I'm going to tell you:

In early July 2016, I was chosen by UN Women to go on a short trip to Japan with a group of distinguished Egyptian women from different fields to attend a grand conference in Tokyo about women. I made friends with Dina Sherif, and we sat next to each other on the bus, with her pumping me and asking me questions and me telling her my life story. She looked at me and said, "You know, these are things the next generations need to know." I laughed at her; I couldn't see anything important about it. I'm nothing but a woman who worked really really hard at something she really really likes, and that was it. What I want to say is, Dina was talking about Azza Fahmy's career, and her journey with jewelry, and the different facets of this woman's personality as they related to her career. She began to cut into what I said with comments: "Now this is the Egyptian Azza!" she'd say, and "Now this is Azza the mother!" and "This is the Azza who can take a stand when she needs to; Azza the fighter!" These things she said made me rethink and review my life. And she made me wonder, too, why I'm this way. It had to come from somewhere. It came from things that shaped me into what I became.

This business of self-discovery was something I felt was important for me to know just then. Maybe I woke up to it later in life, but as they say, "it's never too late." I must scratch the surface, ask myself all sorts of questions, find out what makes me tick. How did I turn out this way?

After all this journey and all these years, I'm finding that, after all, I need to spend some time with myself. Who is this Azza? That's what I need to think about. It's not just a professional success story with a craft that used to be relatively unimportant in the field of art and creativity; it was that it worked so well that I managed to put it on the map of the region, and now the world map too.

Part of this career, the steps and stages it took, I already see clearly—university, then my government job, the craft district of Khan al-Khalili, the process of forming my company. These steps I know like the back of my hand, and I've given so many interviews I'm sick of them. What I need to think about now is the personal part, what makes me who I am. My upbringing, who I am, where I came from, why I am what I am, who influenced me as a person, my family history and how it affected me, the characteristics that have become part of me. Now I'm a brand called Azza Fahmy.

There was so much. A father; a mother; different sets of circumstances; the friends around me; what Egypt was like back then; the general atmosphere of Egypt that I experienced that existed back then; that long history, and all the elements and events that affected me. There was a story behind the story that I felt needed to be told. My story had to be written by me, myself, the way I feel it and remember it (you know, most of the stories out there never found anyone to write them). I wanted to do it like talking freely on a psychiatrist's couch. I made myself the little girl again who lived in the beauty of Upper Egypt and Helwan—the Egypt that used to be. I tried to remember this and go down into the storehouse that we call memory, which you think is all but erased—but when I began to remember and write things down, my life started to take shape in front of me like a movie. I saw myself facing myself: sometimes I'd push the button and the whole thing would come spooling out.

I was worried about language as well. I'm no writer. How shall I write? In Egyptian or Classical Arabic? I decided to write whatever came to mind, this or that. To write from the heart, and there'd be time enough for editing later. I tried to squeeze my memory like an orange, to squeeze out more than fifty years of events. It wasn't easy, but sometimes, each image would unravel many things.

The first stage, calling back the distant past from memory, was hard! Everyday details, family customs, my upbringing—all this was important to remember: My childhood and the social atmosphere of that era around a Cairo family that lived in Upper Egypt, in Sohag, then moved to Helwan, and also the Cairo of the 1960s and 1970s. The Sagha, or goldsmiths' and silversmiths' district; Khan al-Khalili; historic Cairo from the Fatimid era. I asked the world what it had been like fifty years back, how the craft used to be, the traders, the master craftsmen and their apprentices, and their habits in this important neighborhood that brought together craft and trade. How were things run there? I lived these long years with them—what mark did it leave on me? What did it create inside me? What were the major traces they left behind? I found that this *was* important for people to know, being part of Egypt's craft history, and its cultural and social history as well.

Images, images, images. They began to fill my head and my thoughts from the moment I felt the urge to rewind the tape from the start. A history I'd forgotten, which I'd never brought to mind. With every image, I would pull out the little pad and pen I always kept in my handbag and jot down whatever occurred to me before it ran away. Because my days and my life are pretty busy, this tended to happen when I calmed down—in Azza Fahmy's few moments of calm. They do happen, after all—on vacation, waking up extra early, the odd sleepless night, trips abroad, long transit times in airports—and the result was memories and situations that popped into my head, which I rushed to record.

> I am Egyptian, like the earth, intimate and glorious. Like the sun, old and yet young, I am Egyptian.—George Jordac.

1
My Early Years

Roots
I'm a bit complicated. Egyptian–Sudanese on my father's side, Egyptian–Turkish on my mother's. I was raised in Upper Egypt in my early childhood and have become a Cairene since middle age. What people call "the old Upper Egyptian stubbornness" comes out in a lot of what I do; there's also the traditional side that I acquired, which comes out in many of my reactions. That comes from my upbringing and the time I lived in the district of Helwan, south of Cairo. I still have a very special corner inside me where a little craftsman nestles, born of my work in the craft district of Khan al-Khalili and the Sagha, the goldsmiths' and silversmiths' district, and the master craftsmen, or *ma'allimin*, with whom I spent my youth. These were all stages, and the people I came to know in my life, some of them just passing through, but many of whom left imprints on my mind and soul, although I see my life before my eyes as interlocking links that formed the main characteristics of my personality.

What is very clear to my mind now is that my father and mother and Upper Egypt played the main part in forming my childhood. Their images are the first things that come to mind whenever I remember that place.

My Father
My father was Abdel Moneim al-Subki, or "Subki," as his friends called him. I've heard that it was the name of a famous African soccer player at the

A portrait of my father by artist Sanad Basta, 1944.

My mother, Zubeida Mahmoud, 1955.

start of the last century. His skin was the color of chocolate. I remember him from photographs as looking like Morgan Freeman. Although he died early and left us behind, the short time I spent with him, until I was thirteen, was very rich. He managed to gift me a great storehouse of knowledge on every level. This storehouse never ran out; I still have it. It always affected me and accompanied me in every stage of my personal and professional life.

My father led me to live in a fairytale world that's really worth writing about now. I thank him for his insistence that we, as a family, share this world with him. It was a world full of stories and details that he'd tell and take us along for the ride, details about every corner of life. It furnished me with new dimensions for my love of this dear country of mine. I see these stories now as a magical world, like images from the famous book *Description de l'Égypte*. My father was quite something with us, his kids. He talked about history, geography, agriculture, and people. He had a story for every occasion. He told us these stories hoping to convey information; he wanted to give to us everything he had learned in his life that he felt was useful for us to know. For everything that happened, every situation, everything we saw, he had a piece of information or a story. I grew to love geography and history from his stories that made them fun. I appreciate this even more now, having found myself using the same method of telling stories and explaining things. (You know, the new generation is different. My children often get impatient when I'm telling them things. It shows, so I get embarrassed and stop talking.)

My father was a special man. It's hard to find all these things together in a single person. With simple people he was free of pretense; with his friends, he was charismatic, the life of the party; and with his extended family, he was their role model and their guiding light. He was very sociable and could get along with anyone, rich or poor, learned or ignorant. That's why everyone liked him. Over time, I acquired part of his personality: I like to ask a lot of questions, and I'm never shy to ask again if I don't get it. I like to find out things and understand them.

He was Egyptian to the bone, Egyptian even in the sense of being influenced by Western culture, as his early education was in foreign schools and his work was with the British. My father was my first teacher. I never really got to know him properly till long after his death. The older I grew, the more I appreciated the store of things in my consciousness and my personality thanks to my father. I know that the reason for my powerful love for Egypt and my strong sense of belonging here is that I learned about its smallest details at a very young age. Always, when I think and ask myself now, "How did I become what I am?" I find that the key is my father, and all the knowledge and interests that he opened up to me early on. It was in the way he implanted in me, indirectly, the passion for knowledge and the love of my country. I suppose you could say that our childhood with my father in Upper Egypt was like a chapter in a book about our homeland, a chapter where we became deeply and spontaneously acquainted with life's every detail.

I got to know my father better through his choice of reading material and books, and the furniture he preferred—I still have his Asyut-style chair with the wooden arms that he kept in his room; I use it in my home and I'm very fond of it, and of the lifestyle he practiced. I wish he had lived longer so I could have enjoyed more of his company. I think we'd have been good friends. The way I am was shaped by my father since childhood, and much of what he imprinted on me has become central to my life, the most important being my deep roots in my beloved country, Egypt. The way I see its plants and trees, villages and towns, houses of worship and monasteries, people and their differences, jewelry and fashions, food and customs and traditions—all of this is "homeland" to me.

I'm older now, and I've gained a different perspective. When you're in the thick of things, you can't really make an informed judgment, especially if you're still young. You feel this is normal and that everyone is the same as you and living like you. The fact of the matter is, I was growing up, but my parents were growing older too. Only now do I appreciate the childhood I had with my father, as now I have the awareness to value the parts of my character he implanted in me. I'm this way today because a large part of me is thanks to him; he is always at the forefront of my memory, alongside everything I learned from him.

My father never wore a necktie on special occasions, only a bowtie; I don't know why. His shoes were an English brand called Churchill—the same classic style in different colors. I know he had his shirts made at a tailor's in downtown Cairo; I can't remember where. He bought his pajamas from a store called George's—I think it's the same store that's still in business on Talaat Harb Street. For shirts, they always made him two extra collars and two extra pairs of cuffs from the same fabric. My mother would take the shirts to the tailor's in Sohag when the collar wore out to get a new one sewn in. Nobody threw their shirts out back then; these patterns of consumption are new to us.

My father's refined taste was reflected in everything around us, not just his appearance; you could see it in his way of thinking, the way he interacted with people, our lifestyle, and the details of our house: the furniture, lighting, paintings, and colors. After he graduated from the Higher School of Commerce in Cairo, he started to work at a British cotton company called Bell, whose main office was in Sohag. It had other, smaller offices in Upper Egyptian cities such as Maragha, Abu Tig, al-Balyana, and Girga. The company's business was buying cotton from farmers in the surrounding areas and packing it into sacks, then moving it to offices and branches from where it would be transported to the main branch in Sohag. That's where my father worked, at the company headquarters, which had a cotton gin. Ginning cotton involves separating the fluffy cotton from the seed, producing thousands of bales of cotton, enough to fill vast spaces inside the compound walls. To the side were the sacks of seeds, a by-product of ginning, from which an edible oil was extracted that they called "French oil." It was famous for the fact that you could fry food in it more than once. The husk of the seed was used for animal feed.

The company had both Egyptians and Europeans working there. Most of the latter were Greeks who specialized in classifying and categorizing cotton and assessing its quality. This was done by the length of the staple: fine or extra-long. High-quality cotton textiles using extra-long-staple cotton made up only 5 percent of the world's cotton, 70 percent of which was produced in Egypt.

Later, I found out that the different varieties of cotton were named after the research centers that produced them, according to the name of the seed. The Cotton Research Center in Giza was the biggest of these, and they were responsible for breeding new varieties of cotton seed, all of which were numbered, from Giza 1 to Giza 96. The best varieties, the ones that proved their worth, earned names instead of numbers, such as Amoun, Ashmouni, and Menoufi.

I remember M. Valisar, or Uncle Valisar, as we called him, the master selector of the company. He was a Greek. An assistant used to walk one step behind him, following him around everywhere. The assistant carried a metal bucket full of blue-black ink, with a brush in it, and Uncle Valisar had an extremely sharp knife hanging at his waist by a chain. Sometimes Ali and Omar, my brothers, and I would trot along behind him as he passed by each giant bale and cut a slit in the burlap with the knife. Then he would get a piece out of the bale—a sample—and pull strands out of it repeatedly, bringing it up close to his eyes, then making his decision. After that, he'd have his Upper Egyptian assistant carrying the bucket of dye draw a mark on the bale of cotton in the blue-black ink. This mark represented the class of cotton: long-staple, short-staple, Giza cotton—each had its own mark: X, XX, XXX, and so on. The more complex the mark, the higher the cotton quality. All these details were part and parcel of my childhood and my relation to the world of the white gold we call cotton.

I remember, too, Uncle Petrax, the Greek foreman responsible for shipping the bales to Alexandria. One summer, we went on a trip he organized to Cyprus and had a wonderful time with the Greek Cypriots. By the way, my father also spoke a smattering of Greek.

The season for ginning, classing, and exporting cotton—now that was a special occasion we all shared. It was a monumental event in Egyptian life, especially in Upper Egypt. The family would come together for lunch at 1:15 p.m., at which time we kids would be back from school and my father was on his lunch break before heading back to work. The butler would sound a brass gong they called a *dingi* in the dining room; at that, everyone would come out of their rooms and sit at the table. At 2:00 p.m., my father absolutely had to turn on the news on the radio to hear the latest closing price for cotton, broadcast daily from the Alexandria Cotton Exchange, which announced its final price at 2:00 p.m. The price changed numerous times daily, and closed at 1:30 p.m., to be broadcast at 2:00 p.m. We would hear "Good Fully Good," "Good," "Giza 50," "Karnak," and "Menoufi," all of which were important research centers for cotton in Egypt.

In summer, because of the heat—especially in Upper Egypt—my father, like most of the Greek officials, would go to the office in a pair of khaki shorts and a short-sleeve shirt in cotton or linen, and an extremely light oval cork hat. I used to see this outfit in the movies, worn by jungle explorers, or in the swamps. He wore this suit while overseeing the cotton ginning and the company's work in the fields and farms. (We kept this hat a while. My father bought a new one every year, from England, I think.)

The company headquarters overlooked the Nile and the docks; in Upper Egyptian, people called it al-Muwarrada. Next to it was an absolutely massive sycomore fig tree, and next to that was a waterwheel with a cow always turning it, bringing up water. I used to go to watch the waterwheel and the village women on the Nile filling up their clay pots. This memory prompts me to wonder, when I'm faced with an ancient Egyptian mural depicting a sycomore fig tree: how did our marvelous ancestors manage to embody the beauty of this tree with such professionalism and accuracy, such simplicity and loveliness? Sycomore figs were a popular fruit in Upper Egypt, but unfortunately I've never tasted them.

My father came by his employment at that company through my grandfather's contacts with the British businessmen who worked in Egypt. These contacts started in Sudan. Mr. Olton, an important British cotton merchant, was friends with my grandfather, Fahmy Bey, and through him, my father found his way into the business of cotton, or "white gold," as they called it.

My paternal grandfather Mohammad
Bey Fahmy Ibrahim, 1940.

It was the number one source of hard currency at the time and an important source of GDP. My father got a bunch of promotions, and eventually became the manager of the company.

As a child, I learned about this important side of Egypt; my brothers and I found out about it through my father's visits to every town, village, and hamlet of Upper Egypt, on which we accompanied him. With him, we grew to know Upper Egypt and the details of the white boll from the moment it was harvested until its export to England, returning eventually to Egypt in the form of fabrics and textiles. One of the most prominent pictures in my head from that world is the season for the cotton harvest, seeing groups of girls, blooming with youth, loaded onto the great lorries on their way to work in the fields, wearing brightly colored gallabiyas, both plain and floral-patterned, their hair bound up in scarves with multicolored bobbles, clapping and singing songs about cotton, and how pretty and how dear it was.

> Cotton seed, with your leaves,
> Cotton boll, little bell

Cotton boll, rattle and swell
Cotton boll, in my bosom dwell"

There was always a hiring manager responsible for gathering these young girls from the villages to work at collecting cotton. I remember that this man always wore a traditional *libda,* a kind of felt cap, and carried a thick cudgel—useful for busting an enemy's head open in a fight—and collected boys and girls in a movement called a *tarhila.* I want to say something important here: most of the villagers and poor people at that time went barefoot. It was normal for people to walk barefoot, and the streets in the villages were unpaved. Something else is stuck in my memory: the image of the Upper Egyptian kids doing their homework together under a streetlight, all together, in the evenings because there was no electricity in their homes. It was the same for most villages in that time.

Harvesting cotton requires a large workforce. That's why they bring in young girls; it's cheaper to hire them for the day. Each girl collects the cotton bolls in the lap of her gallabiya or in the breast of her dress, as the song goes. I used to see the cotton fields of Upper Egypt dotted about with dozens of girls in their bright gallabiyas—small multicolored pops of color scattered about the green expanse, collecting Egypt's white gold while singing happily: "Collect the goodness; it's all we have, white and bright on the stalk!"

This living painting will never be erased from my memory. The radio used to play a lot of songs about cotton as well in those days, one of which was "Cotton of the Nile, you light up the world. Lovely cotton, collect it, Nile girls." This was the season of plenty for everyone, eagerly awaited from year to year. When the cotton harvest season was over, you would find the village women and the young girls wearing gold of every type: half-moon earrings, and on the older women heavy gold necklaces and bracelets. The amount of gold was greater or lesser depending on the profit from the harvest. Gold wasn't for ornamentation or bragging rights: it was a way to save up money for use when needed. Money was saved in the form of jewelry, flaunted with pride by women and girls; but when the family was in need or on hard times, it was sold. It was the farmers' bank. At the same time, this was the season for engagements and weddings in the countryside, and traditional songs were famously sung. I was made acquainted with this popular tradition by the documentaries of my friend, the Egyptian documentary maker Atiyat al-Abnoudi. "He's come to you, girl / He's come to you, girl / Tomorrow he'll wrap bands / Of gold on your arm / And make up for what you've been missing."

But I have to tell you, women in Upper Egypt—even those who have nothing—like to wear something that suits their budget: a necklace of imitation amber that a woman threads herself, or red beads to look like rubies, anything. A woman without any jewelry was called *'atla*, or "on the shelf." The markets were piled high with glass beads of every shape and form. The Bohemia region in Central Europe was one of the major producers of beads worldwide, and I'm going to come back to that again when I talk about my time in Khan al-Khalili—I remembered all these details when learning the craft there, and I remember seeing the farmers and the merchants filling the place after the harvest was sold, their traditional, familiar leather wallets fat with money to buy gold. These wallets were fastened to the inside of the waistcoat with a chain, always in dark brown leather, studded with snap fasteners in white metal in attractive patterns. I was very fond of the traditional wallet design, so much, in fact, that I sought out—and finally found—the manufacturers who made them for the farmers. They were tradesmen from Sharqiya in the Delta. I had them produced and sold them in the first gallery I opened in the smart district of Mohandiseen, in Cairo.

Cotton was transported on Nile barges from Upper Egypt to Alexandria for export—long crafts made of iron loaded with rows and rows of cotton bales, piled high, since lorries or large trucks weren't widely available at that time. The loading dock for the cotton bound for Alexandria was right outside the company headquarters; I always heard my father repeating the name "Onsy Sawiris," the Sawiris family patriarch, as one of the people who had a private deal for moving cotton to Alexandria, I think. I don't really remember all the details.

My father's office at the company had a kind of simplicity that was hard to achieve; it was the height of good taste, done in a British design: the desk, the chairs, the brown leather couch with buttons, the glass lamps standing on the desk, and the magnificent glass ceiling fixture of moderate size. Through a wide window, the office overlooked a garden with climbing vines on trellises made especially to reach the gorgeous windows, divided into square panes of glass. The outside of the building resembled a mansion in the English countryside.

I'd like to mention an incident to do with my father's office, twenty-five years after we left Sohag and went to Cairo. The handweaving of textiles from the town of Akhmim became one of my interests, and I wanted to develop this craft. Akhmim has been famous since the Coptic era for hand-woven textiles, especially in silk. Their silk was popular for shirts among the well-to-do of the towns and villages. There was an especially costly silk called *sakrouta,* heavier than raw silk, used to make luxurious gallabiyas worn by village mayors and fine folk that rippled when they walked. At this time, we had opened up Al-Ain Gallery, Cairo's first showroom for folk crafts made by young artists. I was visited in Cairo at the time by the Khatib family, the most famous of the families that made handwoven textiles in Akhmim. They asked me to help them develop their industry and add a new range of colors to their product.

My visits to Akhmim, on the eastern side of the Nile, opposite Sohag, multiplied, to work on the looms, as well as designing and introducing the new colors to the Akhmim fabric. I always stayed at the home of Hajj Hussein al-Khatib, the family patriarch, who owned the greatest number of looms in Akhmim. I remember enjoying meals prepared in traditional earthenware tajines, and the famous Upper Egyptian cuisine. They would always send me back to Cairo laden with bulgur and traditional bread. These visits made me nostalgic for Sohag and my childhood, and at one time I had the strongest desire to visit the place where my father worked and see his office and the house where we had lived such a happy childhood. The Khatib family provided me with a car and drove me to the company offices, which had been taken over by the government. We arrived at the site and saw the gin. I walked through the great door and headed straight for my father's office. I knew the way perfectly well, even after thirty years. I stepped into his office and stood there, looking around. Many things had disappeared. None of the old pieces of furniture were there, the ones that had been there in my father's time. The English-made desk, the brown leather couch and the chairs, all were gone, replaced with a desk and a couch devoid of good taste. I could recognize nothing in the room. Nothing was left of my father's legacy but the glass light fixture that still hung from the ceiling, and the yellow brass cover on the light switch that always used to shine because old Uncle Eisa, the Sudanese janitor, cleaned it with turpentine every day. Now it was dull and dark and dirty.

I walked a while in the garden; it was neglected, everything about it changed. I went to the pool; it was empty of water, full of weeds and mud. Disappointed, I said to myself, "I wish I had kept the lovely image of the place and of my father's office intact in my mind; I wish they had remained in my memory like the last time I had left them." I remembered the lines by the famous Egyptian poet Sayed Higab: "From where does melancholy stem? From the contrast between now and then."

Coming out of the company gates, I remembered the event I used to witness once a month: the visit of the *haggana*, or mounted police. They would come in the big company gate—a line of camels, six or eight, led by Officer Muhammad in front, in extremely smart attire, all one shade of khaki: shorts, shirt, knee-high socks, and a puffy turban on their heads in a distinctive style, walking in unison to the area for visitors outside the offices, like a meeting area, with wooden benches on three sides, designed by my father.

That scene is still imprinted clearly on my memory. We knew who the *haggana* were from my father's stories about them; we always attended this meeting with my father to listen to Officer Muhammad. He was their leader: a tall, slim Sudanese man who stood tall and proud and straight. He sat with my father and told him the news of security and the main events that had happened in the villages and hamlets and every corner of the governorate, as they were responsible for keeping the peace. Incidentally, my great-uncle, General Ibrahim Fahmy, my father's paternal uncle, was the leader of the *haggana*. I don't know if it was this link that brought them to my father to make their report, or just their good relationship with him, as they, like my father, were mostly from Sudan. They talked in a distinctly Sudanese dialect that my father understood and was fond of. The visit would end when they had drunk the tea that Uncle Eisa would make for them; then they would take polite leave of my father and leave on camel-back, ambling gracefully and slowly out through the main gate of the company in a marvelous cinematic panorama I cannot forget.

The company site took up a large acreage, including a big cotton gin and vast spaces for cotton storage, living quarters for junior staff and cotton classification staff, plus a main office building with a gigantic door, which had a brass plate on it engraved with a number, and two rooms to the left and right of it to facilitate the entry and exit of cotton bales. The door was guarded by a great many armed men in their official garb of gallabiya and tarboosh, and a rifle over their shoulders. My father's office was located in the main building on the ground floor with the rest of the accountants and clerks. Above were two floors fully devoted to apartments for the company managers. The British manager—before the company was nationalized—lived on the first floor; his name was Mr. Walker, or, as we called him, Uncle Walker, and the second floor was for the deputy manager, where we lived before my father's promotion to manager.

Our House

The house was surrounded by a big garden divided into many sections. There was a swimming pool, a squash court, and a pool with brightly colored fish, and there were well-kept lawns where you could sit. Our apartment had six rooms and a big living room that held a fireplace and my father's library—shelves full of books, mostly in English. They were divided into subjects: politics, history, agriculture, geography, and so on. He received a shipment of books every month by mail from London in a wooden crate. I remember him always mentioning specific books in his library as important, such as Gibbon's *The History of the Decline and Fall of the Roman Empire*. He was also fond of literature, and read Shakespeare, Dickens, and Milton. He had been sent a copy of Pasternak's *Doctor Zhivago* before it was made into a film starring Omar Sharif. His favorite time to read was in the evenings by the fireside. Sometimes I would see him with a glass of whisky on the rocks, reading.

The garden had rooms off to the side to put up the company's guests; as I remember, Sheikh Baqouri, the minister of religious endowments, when he visited Sohag, would stay at the guest room in my father's house. Minister Ahmad Abdou al-Sharabasi was also a friend of my father's. I think he became the minister of public works after the July 1952 Revolution. At least once a year I saw him at our house.

The kitchen, too, is one of the things I remember really well. It was very large, with an attached pantry and two wooden refrigerators with lead piping

My father at the Sohag Club with close family friend Dr. Mustafa al-Mashad, 1945.

that were opened from the top and filled with ice every day to provide us with cold water. At least once or twice every month, my father would host dinner and cocktail parties. We would receive guests in the reception hall. Most of the guests were high-ranking officials in the medical directorate, foreign CEOs, and prominent judges and lawyers. The guests would arrive accompanied by their wives, not one of whom wore a headscarf; alcoholic beverages were served as a matter of course.

My father liked his exercise. He played tennis twice a week, and at the end of every year, he would take part in his company's friendly tournament for the people who worked there. He was a first-class bridge player, and he held tournaments with his friends from Asyut in that city. My mother, I remember, played an occasional game of tennis.

With the start of the hot season the swimming pool was filled with water after it had been cleared of dead leaves and the detritus of winter. Every weekend, my father's friends, with their wives and children, would come to spend the day with us and have lunch around the pool. But before all this came a very important process that we eagerly awaited every year at the start of summer: the cleaning of the adjoining gardens and clearing them of snakes, which crawled in there from the neighboring farmlands, especially after the fields became saturated with water from the annual flooding of the Nile. The clearing of the garden was one of the most exciting events for us children. The wintertime was when the snakes hibernated, hiding in their holes during the cold months. Then they emerged from their holes in the summer, having shed their skin. We used to be so happy as children to collect these light cast-off snakeskins to play with!

My father always took care to have us watch this traditional process, called "drawing out the snakes," which was done by a group who specialized in it, called the Rifa'is. There were many of them all over Upper Egypt. It was old Uncle Kittana, who was a simple man, that my father dealt with with every year. He carried a closed straw basket with a lid, and a stick, and he wore a gallabiya. He would walk through the big garden, bordered by bushes, flowers, and climbing plants, followed by a group of the employees' children—including us, of course—all wide-eyed with excitement. As he walked, he sniffed them out (they say snakes have a strong smell!) and the shed skins would reveal the snakes' hidey-holes. He also recited spells, incantations, and invocations for them to appear. Having found the snake, and seeing its head and eyes poke out of its hole, he then put his stick on its neck and pressed it into the ground—then, transferring his stick to his left hand, he would grab the snake's head with the thumb and forefinger of his right hand and squeeze its open jaws, forcing it to bite the sleeve of his gallabiya and push out its yellow venom. Often, while the snake's teeth were buried in the fabric, he would pull it to break its teeth; this process was called *tatrim*, and the verb is used by local boys

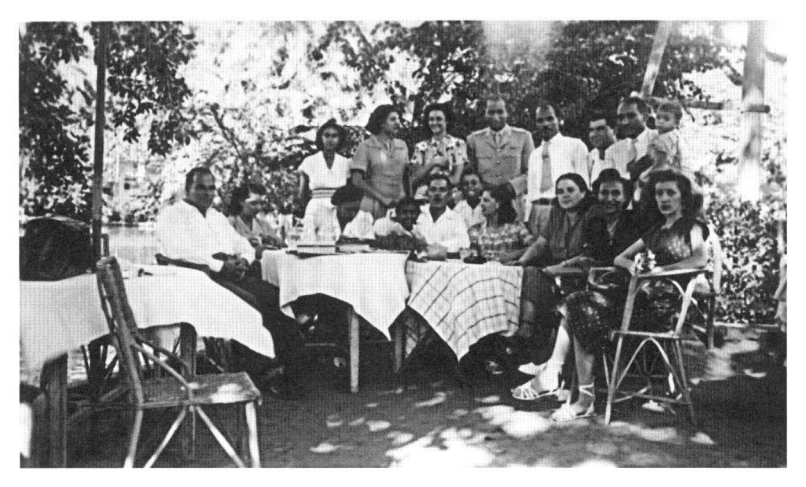

A party at our house, 1939.

My parents at a party in our house, 1946.

in fights—*taramluh sinanuh*, "knock his teeth out." After this, Uncle Kittana would put the snake into his covered basket, called a *margouna*, and close it up securely.

When we asked old Uncle Kittana about dangerous snakes, he would say, "The most dangerous is the *tureesha*, the desert horned viper. One bite is fatal. It's small and it hides in the sand; then it flies into the air and bites, while the famous Egyptian cobra lives on the banks of the Nile."

We always found it so strange: why didn't he get bitten? When we asked my father, he would say, "They are snake-charmers; as a child, his family had a snake bite him in the ear, and also he keeps the Rifa'i covenant, which allows them to catch snakes and scorpions. This covenant protects them from the sting of the scorpion and the bite of the snake." The Rifa'i covenant is: "I invoke upon you, snake, by these recitations and the fullness of their secrets, that you injure none with your poisoned breath, and come before me submissive and awestruck, or else you shall be in violation of the will of the Almighty, Lord of the Two Worlds."

My father's foreign friends always insisted that Uncle Kittana hid the snakes in his gallabiya or about his person. When the man learned this from my father, he was very upset and insisted on taking off his gallabiya and hunting the snakes only in his under-breeches with just his *margouna* and his stick, and still he produced snakes.

The occupation of the Rifa'is is one of the most dangerous; it is they who can deal with snakes and bring them out, learning the oath and passing on the profession from father to son. They collect and sell snakes in the village of Abu Rawash, for the use of their poisons in medicine.

The start of the summer season reminds me of the flooding of the Nile too. At that time, there was only basin irrigation, whereby the farmlands were divided into large basins that were filled by the floodwaters, making use of the slope of the land from south to north, and planted once a year. The lands surrounding the company were all completely flooded and the waters would come up to the walls of our compound, so that I used to hear the sound of the catfish, which was especially loud, in my bedroom at night. The basins would fill with such huge numbers of catfish that we would fish for them with fishing lines off the wall of the garden that overlooked the water.

Sohag

When I read the wonderful *Village Diary* by Dr. Esmat Seif al-Dawla about fifteen years ago, it brought back memories of the Upper Egypt I had known and experienced. He wrote about the stick dance of *tahtib*, a mock fight using staffs, which my father would take us to see, and it reminded me of this practice, organized by families in certain seasons, with its own rules. Also the game of *siga*, played with squares on the ground, which my father sometimes watched and told us of its ancient Egyptian origins; there were seven vertical lines and seven horizontal lines, making squares in which the game was played with stones, called dogs. The aim of the game was to kill your opponents' dogs (not unlike chess).

We lived mainly in Sohag, "the land of epic poems," as the Egyptian poet Salah Jaheen called it in the song "Helwa Ya Baladi" (My Beautiful Country) made famous by Dalida. Still, we became familiar with other Upper Egyptian towns such as Asyut, the capital of Upper Egypt and the jewel of that region, with its prominent Coptic and Muslim families, like the clans of Abdel Nour of Girga, Wissa Wassef, Fanous, Khashaba, and others, and its famous school, the American College.

I will never forget our visit to the Muharraq Monastery of the Blessed Virgin Mary in the Qusqam mountains near the town of Qous, and the cave where the Holy Family hid during their flight into Egypt. The Directorate of Sohag, as the area and its environs were called before the 1952 Revolution, was a poor governorate, driving its inhabitants out for lack of resources. The agricultural acreage was limited due to the proximity of the mountains. The people who lived there were smart businessmen, especially in the cotton business; the major cotton merchants in Upper Egypt hailed from Sohag. The most famous name in this field was Hajj Omar Uways, a close friend of my father's; our families were good friends, including Aunt Ni'mat, Mustafa, Hamada, and Susu. His brother, Sayed Uways, had been the manager of the Helwan Silk Company for an extended period.

The fruit trade was one of the major businesses in the region, especially in the village of Kawamel, which was famous for it; most of the wholesalers in the large markets in Cairo and Alexandria were from Kawamel. A great many businessmen who traded in fish were also from there. They are good businessmen and know the value of money. By the way, even now, when I go to buy vegetables or fish, I like to ask the store owner, "Are you from Kawamel?" Would you believe it, many times they do turn out to be from that same village! Kawamel used to be a port for all the Arab tribes emigrating from Hijaz, Yemen, and the Arabian Peninsula.

My father often went to visit friends in the town of Sahel Selim, known for its famous buildings and schools, but mainly as the town of gardens and citrus orchards, opposite Asyut. In those days, the Badari area was on our list of places to visit: it was one of the most important prehistoric sites in Egypt. Forty-five years later, I made a ring I'm very fond of, engraved with the ornamental patterns on the plates of the Badari civilization.

I experienced the best times of Upper (southern) Egypt, which, in the middle of the past century, was culturally and socially different from what it is now. The demographics were mixed, and Coptic and Muslim Egyptians and foreigners all mingled freely, as did women and men. There was good, solid education provided at Egyptian government schools. Athletic and cultural activities rounded out a middle- and upper-middle-class Upper Egypt that was both educated and broad-minded.

I would like to take this opportunity to write about the women of Upper Egypt—the women I saw and remember, whose strength I admired and whose personalities I understood fully when I grew up. The running of the house was their responsibility, from the preparation of bread to the feeding of the cattle, the ducks, and the chickens—every woman of Upper Egypt woke at dawn to knead and bake bread, prepare food, and cook: constant movement from dawn to day's end; a dynamo. She never ceased giving birth: she gave birth easily and got up to work afterward. She force-fed the geese; she checked the chickens with a finger to find out how many eggs they were going to lay; she bore the responsibility for distributing the stores of corn to the family and to the needy. She was the one who decided what was to be sold and what was to be kept, the minister of finance and the minister of trade of the family. I remember they used to feed the baby chicks boiled eggs, sometimes with their mouths. The woman was the boss of it all, and she had the final say in everything related to the family—the female pharaoh!

The Sohag of old that remains in memory is al-'Arif Billah Mosque with its twin minarets, built in the fourteenth century, and it is the minaret of the Fartoushi Mosque, built by the Mamluk Sultan al-Ghouri in the sixteenth century. The place I loved the most was the Qaysariya—a roofed market where I often went with my mother to window-shop or buy things—with its wonderful architecture.

In the streets of Sohag, I saw children collecting cigarette butts, carrying tin boxes, and always with their faces bent toward the ground. They collected them and re-rolled them for resale in a place called al-Basta. I was reminded of this in the TV soap opera *Hilmiya Nights* (written by the great Osama Anwar Okasha and directed by Ismail Abdel Hafez), in the personage of al-Khums, played by 'Ahdi Sadeq. On feast days, we saw primitive wooden swings called *zaqaziq* (singular *zaqzouqa*) set up in many corners of Sohag. Children in brand-new brightly colored clothing paid their money and took a turn. I can't tell you how I feel when I see old photographs of these traditions—my heart takes flight!

My father's position in the company and his fluency in English granted him a wide and diverse network of professional and social relations with foreigners who worked at important companies in Upper Egypt. For instance, there was the CEO of the sugar company in Kom Ombo, one of the most important and largest companies in Upper Egypt, M. Rochas, a Frenchman who, with his wife, was always visiting us at home in Sohag, usually bringing along his saluki greyhounds, a hunting breed that is slim and fast with a powerful jaw. When M. Rochas left his post and went back to France to retire, he sent us his greyhounds—Secole, a male, and Lauren, a female—as a gift to my father. They lived with us for years until their natural death, and of course my father took the opportunity to tell us all about saluki greyhounds and their ancient Egyptian origins. So as to make sure we had absorbed the information correctly, when we visited the ancient temples, he would point out to us the ancient Egyptian salukis on the temple walls.

Many years later, we had a pointer, a spotted dog called Biji, gifted to my father by Mr. Walker, the British boss, as he was leaving his post. Biji could ring the doorbell using her nose, as it was located quite low down.

Speaking of dogs, when we were living in Upper Egypt, there was a town called Armant that was famous for breeding fierce guard dogs. This was a medium-sized longhair of varying shades of gray, with a large head and powerful jaws and teeth—its bite was truly dangerous. The older families in Upper Egypt would have dog kennels, as they had stables for horses, in which they bred Armant dogs, which they called "the lion of the night." The people of Armant would take offense if you called the animal a dog—they called them "lions." They gifted them to each other, and we were always warned when we visited families from there: "Be careful! They keep Armant dogs." My father gave his mother, my grandmother, a gray Armant dog, which she kept on the roof.

My father's circle always included the irrigation engineers and managers of the governorate. They were responsible for managing the great river Nile, and taking measures to organize and monitor water usage, and had a status equaling that of the director of the entire governorate. An irrigation engineer always lived in a big house on the Nile, with a houseboat moored outside that he used to ride around and check on the affairs of the Nile and how the floodwaters were being used, as well as monitoring dams, bridges, and canals. We often visited them on the boat for tea. The social and cultural milieu where I spent happy times as a child was my father's circle of friends, in which we moved throughout the period we lived in Upper Egypt. It was varied and diverse, an immense tapestry of humanity that was part of my life since I was very young. There were relationships with every stripe and class of humanity and every culture in which my father immersed us: Christians, Muslims, villagers, intellectuals, Upper Egyptians, and Europeans.

Among the important events I often remember and whose image always leaps into my mind were the cultural excursions that my father took care to organize periodically for family and friends to important and famous historical sites. One was when I was about seven years old, accompanied by my brother Ali, two years older, and my younger brother Omar (who later became a fighter pilot and died in the war of 1973); my sister Randa hadn't been born yet. We would drive out early in the morning with a group of close friends: Dr. Mustafa al-Mashad, Aunt Souad his wife, and his daughters, Abla, Anan, and Hind (who is now a doctor, married to the famous cardiac professor Dr. Galal al-Said). We would wake up early and head west, to the Monastery of Saint Shenouda the Archimandrite, known as the White Monastery because it is built all of white stone, about twelve kilometers outside of Sohag. We would start our day by taking breakfast with the monks and priests, a special breakfast made up of the products of the monastery: marvelous, buttery stewed fava beans; pickled olives from the olive trees planted by the monks themselves next to the monastery and all around it; honey from their own hives; and, of course, Upper Egyptian molasses, which tastes like jam; milk fresh from their cows; and cream and butter with freshly baked *shamsi* bread! After the luxurious breakfast, the monks would take us on a tour of the monastery to learn about its history and importance, and to explain to us the daily life of the monks. We would spend most of the day there and set off for home when it was nearly sunset.

The fifth-century Monastery of Saint Bishay, known as the Red Monastery from its red brick construction, was four kilometers from the White Monastery and was also on the list of the trips that my father arranged for us. His friendships with the priests and monks at the two monasteries have always stayed in my memory, associated with a wonderful era that gifted me a bouquet of important cultural and historical values that I still hold onto today; they have been implanted in my psyche, causing me never to feel that there are any differences between Muslims and Christians.

One of the important images that surface from my distant memory is the Arraba Madfouna region of al-Balyana, in the district of Girga, west of the

Nile. My father always took us at least three or four times a year to visit this region. On our way there, we often passed by Girga, and after the visit, on our way home, we would always be invited to dinner with my father's friends there. Girga is famous for its pigeons—squabs, or *zaghalil*—bringing to mind the "city of *zaghalil*," as Dalida once sang. My father always told us of the importance of Girga in Islamic times. It was inhabited by the Hawwara tribes and ruled by the sheikh of the Bedouins, Hammam, whose influence reached as far as Nubia. Some of the Hawwara were friends with my father; all this leapt into my memory as I watched the TV soap opera starring Yehya al-Fakharani, *Hammam, Sheikh of the Arabs*.

Something important I want to say here is that the larger and older families in Upper Egypt used to own slaves. When we were invited to dinner or supper with them, most of the time the women would be absent (my mother never went and was not invited). We were children, so my father sometimes took us along. We always ate in the *mandara*, or the guest quarters, a large area annexed to the house for visitors to have dinner, supper, or a great feast. The food was served by slaves. Most of these had dark skin. My father explained to me the origins of slave-owning in the larger Upper Egyptian families, which passed their slaves down from generation to generation. There was a specialized group that brought the slaves in from Sudan or further afield in Africa, known as *al-gallaba*, or "the bringers." After slavery in Egypt was abolished, many slaves refused to leave the family homes where they had been born and raised.

Tahta was the birthplace of Rifa'a al-Tahtawi, the famous nineteenth-century Egyptian scholar and the icon of Egypt's Age of Enlightenment. Many of his family were friends and acquaintances of my father's. Al-Manshah was the birthplace of Sheikh Muhammad Siddiq al-Minshawi of the sweet mellifluous voice, who recited the Qur'an in the *nahawand* recitation style. When he came in from Cairo to pay his hometown a visit, my father was always on the guest list.

Families were usually named after the great-grandfather or the founder of the family, so they would be called, for example, Awlad Abu Rehab ("children of the father of Rehab"), or Awlad al-Minshawi ("children of the man from Manshah"), or Awlad Abu Steit ("children of the father of Steit").

Umm Seti

Al-Arraba al-Madfouna (Abydos) was a place that was very important to my father: first, for its historical importance to ancient Egypt, and second, because he had a British friend living there, an archaeologist and tour guide who went by the name of Umm Seti. Our father would tell us her story and explain to us why she was living in that place.

Umm Seti was an Englishwoman, Dorothy Eady, born on 16 January 1904 in London. She fell on the stairs at the age of two years and hit her head, and the doctors thought she wouldn't wake up. This incident was a turning point and the start of a new, exceptional life for Dorothy. It opened the gates of past lives of reincarnation for her. She believed fully that she had been a priestess in the temple of Seti I, where she was raised after her mother's death, and where she met Seti I (1290–1271 BC). She became his lover and ended her putative past life by killing herself when the priests objected to their love, which might bring down the wrath of the goddess Isis. Dorothy studied Egyptology at fifteen years of age with the famous Egyptologist E.A. Wallace Budge; she married an Egyptian and had a son whom she named Seti. After nineteen years of living in Cairo, separated from her husband, she moved to the town of Abydos to live closer to the temple. She worked with well-known Egyptologists, such as Selim Hassan and Ahmed

As a child (front row on the left) in the Temple of Abydos, 1952.

Fakhry, and assisted them in completing a huge excavation, the most important in the area, which was the discovery of the location of the temple garden and its details, where she had met her lover for the first time. The discovery and details accorded with what she said and described and had supposedly experienced in her past life.

I remember her simple mud house, one story with a small porch, with a simple wooden table and chairs, where she would take her breakfast and tea. She and my father would hold long conversations in English of which I understood nothing. But she took us to the temple often to explain the importance of Abydos the town, and the two temples there, of Ramesses II and his father Seti I. She was an exceptional woman, who lived believing herself to be a priestess of Seti I and one of his lovers. Our visits to this important region went on for years; my meetings with Umm Seti always stayed in my memory.

Fifty years after these visits, I happened to find myself in a seminar about the Pyramid Texts, the ancient Egyptian Book of the Dead. Abydos was mentioned in the discussions, and the importance of the temple and its significant artistic and historical treasures, and there was a conversation about it among those present. Suddenly, every image stored in my memory poured out, and I remembered Umm Seti, the breakfast, and the temple! I raised a hand and said, "You know, when I was a child, I used to go to breakfast with Umm Seti with my father." All the Egyptologists' eyes opened wide: everyone who worked in that field knew well what an important and valued figure Umm Seti was.

An odd thing in my career is that I put off creating an ancient Egyptian collection for thirty years. Some people always asked me, "How can you be Egyptian and not create pieces influenced by ancient Egypt?" To tell you the truth, I was terrified, scared. I didn't have the confidence, especially when I looked at the ancient Egyptians and their work, at everything they made and what they created: statues in temples, murals, jewelry, and woodwork—everything gave me more and more of a complex, and I told myself, "How can I ever hope to attain such a level? For shame, that I should make something that's not good enough! How could I make those great people mad at me?" So I dragged my feet until the moment came. There is a season and a time for everything, after all. I decided to understand the ancient Egyptian language. Of course, I had a large storehouse of articles, drawings, images, and also a large collection of books on ancient Egypt in addition to relationships with important Egyptologists, at home and abroad.

My lifelong friend Christine Green, whom I had met while she was working on a Saqqara dig in the mid-1960s with Geoffrey Martin, the famous British archaeologist, was someone I would always go to visit at the expedition's mud-brick house, and she would show me the most wonderful things that had been found in the burial chambers of the ancient dynasties. We remained friends even after she went home to London and became a consultant at Christie's, specializing in ancient Egyptian and Roman artifacts. She was one of the greatest supporters of this project of mine. Every time I went to London, there would be a four- to five-day visit revolving around ancient Egyptian art: a visit to the Ashmolean Museum in Oxford and to the little museum to which she introduced me and which I adored, the University of London Museum, which has the prettiest collection of ancient Egyptian figurines, collected by the prominent archaeologist William Matthew Flinders Petrie (1853–1942), and which gave me a lot of inspiration and ideas for my designs.

In Christine's office in London, I was given the opportunity to go down with her into the cellars of Christie's. She was working on a catalog to sell an important ancient Egyptian collection belonging to the Benzion family, one of Egypt's oldest and wealthiest families from before 1952, who used to own a department store. This was where I saw some original pieces laid out on the table before me for study. One of the rings caught my eye and I fell in love with its design. In my first ancient Egyptian collection, I designed a ring inspired by that marvelous piece that I had seen in the Christie's cellar, the one that Christine was working on. You know, Christie's held a dinner party in honor of Mr. Benzion and his wife, now living in Switzerland, and I was among the guests. The auction house put out Christine's catalog of the Benzion collection, which was later sold. She gave me a copy, and it remains an important reference for me to this day.

When I decided to start on an ancient Egyptian collection, Christine came to Cairo specially, and we decided to go to Luxor after we had picked apart the Egyptian Museum from top to bottom, explaining, discussing, cataloguing, and taking our own kind of inventory. In Luxor, she knew all the secrets and details of the temples. At Karnak, she led me by the hand around the back of the temple to a pile of broken pillars and stones covered with

At a hotel opposite the Temple of Hatshepsut, Luxor, 1985.

drawings. "These," she told me, "are from the time of Amenhotep III, and he had the most skilful workers." I photographed, and photographed, and photographed, all while she was explaining. We went down into an underground temple on the west bank of the Nile, where there is the loveliest depiction of the goddess Maat—Christine knew exactly where it was. She also showed me part of Karnak Temple devoted to cataloguing and categorizing the plants and flowers that Thutmose III had brought back with him from Syria, including the most important ones that had been planted in Thebes and had fruited. It was a magnificent documentation of the first botanical garden or zoo in history. I took so many pictures!

Years went by. Then I went on an organized trip with my friend the writer Ahdaf Soueif and other friends to visit Abydos and the temples there. We spent a night in Luxor, and the next day we got in our cars and drove northward to al-Balyana. The whole journey, I was overcome by a strange feeling: all the past and its images came to life once more before me. I remembered my father, Abydos, Umm Seti, and our breakfast in her simple house. It was like being ten years old again, like time had taken me back. When we got there and visited the two great temples, and I had taken lots of pictures, I asked our guide about the home of Umm Seti, which I used to visit with my father. All the tour guides there know this woman's story. "You'll find it over there, in the middle of the village," the guide told me. Unfortunately, a great many features of Abydos that I had known as a child had been erased; I couldn't find Umm Seti's house, for the town had crept in and invaded the area surrounding both temples. Before, they had been surrounded by empty space befitting the temples' worth.

The ancient Egyptians' depiction of hands and fingers, with their great variety, is hard to understand and express. I have a file chock-full of photographs of ancient Egyptian carvings and drawings of hands, feet, and fingers, a large group of which were taken from the temples of Ramesses I and Seti I in Abydos. I ask myself in wonder: "How did the ancient craftsman convey this feeling to us through murals, sunken or in relief, on mute rock?" The hand of a husband on the shoulder of his wife expresses comradeship, sympathy, and affection; the meeting of the wife's fingers with the husband's makes you feel their love. The hands of the king and the gods are where you see support and generosity.

The rendering of the offering tables, now that was something else! I have dozens of photographs of these complicated artistic compositions. The slaughtered game birds, the fruit, the *shamsi* bread—magnificent! Later, I designed a bracelet that had this type of composition. When we decided to open a small café adjacent to our showroom in Alexandria, where we offered some of my proprietary food items, such as cottage cheese with thyme and olive oil, the logo of the café was based on the ancient Egyptian offering tables.

This magnificence, this high standard, where every line and composition they drew was so carefully calculated, was always what scared me and kept me dragging my feet in designing such an important collection. My first ancient Egyptian collection, which I finally debuted in October 2012, took about eight years to create—all the while doing reading, research, visits, sketches, and discussions with experts. To be completely honest, these eight years weren't continuous. Whenever I had some free time, I would come back to ancient Egypt to study.

The ancient Egyptian artifacts in these two important temples kept their strong link, for me, with my father and the repeated expeditions he used to organize. As soon as I remembered Abydos, all the old images would burst forth from my memory; most importantly, of course, were those of my father and Umm Seti.

My School

I can't talk about my childhood without talking about school. I *must* talk about my school, Sohag Preparatory School for Girls. It was a lovely building in the English style on the Nile corniche (on the "sea," as they called the Nile in Upper Egypt); we called the corniche "Seaside Street" in Sohag city. The length of the street was planted with flame-red poinciana trees; the asphalt was clean as a whistle, as it was cleaned and sprayed with water by special carts every day, which consisted of a large metal water tank with a pipe in the rear that had holes in it, from which water sprayed like a shower; they were pulled by a mule or by horses. In the summer, the children would run after these spray carts with their clothes hiked up, taking a shower, and sometimes they ran naked! The trees were extremely well groomed—between them, there were benches for people to sit and look at the Nile.

As soon as we entered the school through the iron gates, there was a large quadrant planted with flowers and bushes. The school building surrounded it on three sides, with its staff offices and classrooms. Every morning, the headmistress would give us the morning salute from the balcony of her room, high up on the second floor. She would give a short speech with some moral lesson or a story for us to learn something from, without microphones or music. We all wore the same uniform, a beige pinafore. We took one hour of home economics per week, where we learned different ways of cooking; most of the recipes were European, such as how to make cake and *petits fours,* and one time we made Scotch eggs, which is meat stuffed with boiled eggs. I liked to go home carrying a piece of the dish I had cooked to show to my mother and father. Of course, the cook at our house made better food; but I was very proud of what I had made with my own hands, even if it wasn't all that good!

We also took a class in crafts, which was all needlework and sewing and embroidery. One of my favorite subjects was Arabic. Professor Abdel Zaher was wonderful and taught us well. Every month, he would pick out a famous book by a great writer and assign it to us to read, and then discuss it with us. Our school was an example of the best government schools of the time, which offered an excellent education in addition to paying attention to the arts, culture, and athletics.

Our headmistress was a distinguished lady from an Upper Egyptian family. She was always in a conservative skirt suit with her hair up in a bun, which made her look very respectable. At this time, you know, you could never, ever find a schoolgirl or a teacher or a headmistress wearing a headscarf. I made friends at school with the girls from Upper Egyptian families, but these friendships didn't last when we moved to Cairo after my father's death. Sometimes, though, I meet relatives or acquaintances from our time in Upper Egypt, such as the Fawwaz family, the Maraghi family, the Abu Rehab family, the Sherif family, the Uways family . . . those are just the ones whose names I remember. And, of course, life sent each of us to a different part of this wide world and set us each on a different path.

The school served us lunch every day. I have a serving spoon that I bought from a man downtown with "Ministry of Education" engraved on it. Things were well cared for; at the end of the school year, we would hold a large event with music and dancing, and put on a play. One time I took part in a play and, unfortunately, I did terribly, and got flustered on stage, and ruined everything, and cried; I never could act. The final day of school, just before the holidays, each of us would bring our own autograph book, and we would write something in each other's books for our friends to remember us by. This was very important to us. We would draw red hearts, and flowers, and arrows through the hearts: "Love Eternally from So-and-So," or "Always Remember Me," or "Until We Meet Again," or other such words expressing the power of friendship. Now I never see anyone writing in autograph books, or rather, no one in the current generation has any idea about these keepsakes. You know, I still have one of those books. It's red. I smile and have a happy chuckle at the naive memories of my green childhood whenever I open it.

At the end of the school day, we went out into the street. Outside the schoolhouse door there were carts selling lupin beans, and sprouted spiced fava beans, which they call *foul majili* in Upper Egypt, and pyramid-shaped disks of brown sugar called *sukkar gallab*. And, of course, they sold doum fruit, sycomore figs, and *habb el-aziz* (tiger nut sedge). My mother, like a lot of other mothers, disapproved of us buying street food. But sometimes I bought doum fruit.

One of the important events at school for me was the day President Gamal Abdel Nasser visited our school as part of his tour of Upper Egypt. Of course, everything was set on its ear, and we went mad with preparations! The president gave a short speech and walked around the grounds, saying hello to the headmistress, the teachers, and the students. They selected me to shake his hand. When I stood before him and looked at his face and eyes, I was dumbstruck, stunned. I couldn't open my mouth. Everything they had so meticulously drilled into me evaporated in a moment! He was a tall man with a strange look in his eyes that made you not know what to say. Now that's what they call charisma.

Life at Home

In our family, we took our big bath at the end of the week, on Thursdays. They washed our hair with olive oil soap, a square bar of the brand Nabulsi Shaheen, but the body was washed with scented soap. All this took place before bed. My mother would rub my hair with castor oil mixed with other oils, and I have passed this habit on to Fatma and Amina, my daughters, of oiling their hair before bathing. Then we would get into bed, wearing warm pajamas, and warm up well with quilts. The most important thing back then was keeping your chest warm so as not to get a cough. In addition, there was daily cleaning, which was a sponge bath with a towel dipped in soapy water, followed by another towel with just water, and if there was any visible dirt on us children, they would give us a bath. There was no gas at that time; metal pipes in the bathroom were connected to a tank at the top of the house which was heated to boiling, and supplied the bathrooms with hot water. One of the other habits was an enema, which they gave us every so often to get our insides extra clean. Each family member had their own enema with their name on it, and all the enemas were hung up on the porcelain tiles of the bathroom.

Sixty years on from these days, I learned from the Indians that cleaning out our innards is one of the most important things you can do, especially colon cleansing. They have a special technique in Ayurveda medicine of enemas with herbs and oils called Panchakarma. You know, the old Indian practitioners of medicine say, "It all begins in the gut."

Most of our medicines came from the pharmacy, compounds made up by the chemist. There were a lot of advertisements for cough syrups. You know, if we got a cold and developed a cough, before bed they would rub our chests with Vicks VapoRub and put us to bed with a newspaper between our undershirts and our bodies. Throughout the winter, we had to take a spoonful of cod-liver oil every day.

We would read *Sindbad* magazine in bed. It was the only magazine available for children and came out every Thursday, and we could barely wait for it. Its artwork was drawn by the famous Hussein Bicar, and later these magazines were sold in bound collections, which we bought.

The upholsterer who came to stuff our mattresses every two years had a bow and a beater, which he would use to beat the cotton. All the cotton was emptied out of the mattresses, then fluffed up and repacked so as not to move around inside the mattress and to be soft again. It was the same for the pillows. The quilts would be quilted in intricate geometric patterns with a sail needle, using thick thread. There was a special kind of cotton for the quilts which my mother called "hair cotton." I still like these types of cotton quilts, and they're coming back into fashion in Europe. You know, my mother would make the house staff take the sheets and pillows out into the sun every day to freshen them up; to this day, I air out my bedding as my mother used to do.

One of the things that still fills me with joy when I remember it or see it in pictures is the camera obscura, what we as children called *sunduq al-dunya*, or "the world in a box." There was always a man walking in the street carrying the box on his back, and a little bench. Once my father had me sit on the bench and look at the pictures in the box. I was so thrilled!

Summer Holidays

Once the school year in Upper Egypt was done, it was time for vacation. We always went to Alexandria to spend the three months of summer there. My father would start to move his work to the head office in that city, following up on the cotton exchange and submitting accounts and financial reports to the company. The summer season, for us, was the Season of Migration to the North—and I deliberately borrow this name from the famous novel by my friend the major Sudanese novelist Tayeb Salih. I knew him well, and he always used to chuckle, "This woman is Sudanese in origin! That's why we're friends!"

The summer holiday was an important journey in the life of our family. It required arrangements and planning under the management of my mother. Long before we left, the preparation of gifts would start: yellow peeled lentils, brown unpeeled lentils, rice, beans specially stewed, and tins of buffalo cheese whose making my mother supervised herself—annual gifts for friends and relatives, and the year's store of dry goods for us and for them; oodles of the foods for which Upper Egypt was famous, some of which would be given as gifts, and the rest for our summerhouse in Dekheila, where we spent the three summer months. We used to carry with us between twenty-five and thirty pans of *makhrouta*, a traditional Upper Egyptian dessert made of shredded dough soaked in syrup.

Umm Hashem was an Upper Egyptian lady of about fifty, from the town of Akhmim, who always had a black scarf tied tightly around her head, a gold tooth, and kohl adorning her wide eyes. (The way she tied her scarf reminds me of movie star Shadia playing an Upper Egyptian villager in the movie *An Element of Fear*.) This Umm Hashem was the most famous maker of *makhrouta* in Sohag. They say that *makhrouta* is of Coptic origin. My father would send the car specially to bring Umm Hashem to spend three days straight at our house, staying the night, just to make *makhrouta*. My brothers and I would sit by her and watch her work. First, she rolled out the dough very thin with a stick she brought with her; then she wrapped the dough around the stick and withdrew

Family holiday at our summer home. My father is in the pool and I'm seated behind him, fourth from right, 1948.

the stick very carefully. This left her with a roll of dough which she cut finely into strips with a sharp knife with a quick mechanical motion, like a machine. She turned this dough into a pile of thin strips not unlike the fine threads of *kunafa,* and after this she hand-steamed it. After the steaming, she would give us a few handfuls, sprinkled with sugar. *Shamsi* bread was also baked at home; it is of ancient Egyptian origin, and you can see it on the engravings and drawings of the offering tables in the ancient temples.

Egyptians are a strange people! Every detail of our old habits has been preserved, just as they used to be, down the ages, for thousands of years. The American University in Cairo Press published a book about ancient Egyptian words that are still in use today.

On baking day, I went up on the roof to watch the village women kneading and baking the bread, cutting up the dough, and putting it on earthenware plates, dividing it into four quarters with a reed stalk, then leaving it in the sun to dry. When the crust dried out, the dough was taken off the bread disk, leaving the loaves in their distinctive shape. I often liked to sit by the women baking, imitating them and splitting the bread. I've always been very fond of *shamsi* bread, and I've had a special relationship with it since I was a little girl. There was a special room set aside on the roof of the house for this kind of work, *makhrouta* and *shamsi* bread, which my father loved—he refused to eat any other kind of bread—and *fayesh,* which is a type of Upper Egyptian biscuit, very light and airy, and yellow because it's made with turmeric. We always dunked it in tea.

The laying in of summer provisions was a very important part of the preparations for travel, which my mother was solely responsible for. Once all the preparations were complete and this enormous mountain of supplies and gifts had been wrapped and boxed up, each box with a burlap sack bearing the name of whomever it was for, two men would take it all and set off—old Uncle Abdel Hafez, and another man whose name I can't remember—from Sohag railway station to Cairo railway station, where they'd be met by my father's brother Ahmad, who would take the Cairo portion of the gifts from Upper Egypt, namely the *makhrouta* and the tins of cheese. Then he would put the rest of the supplies on another train to Alexandria. There were other people, acquaintances of my father's, to receive the shipment there; then the provisions were stored in a warehouse in Alexandria until the family arrived.

As for the family members—that is, my three siblings and myself—our trip from Sohag to Alexandria was organized differently. The family left the house before dawn, at about 2:00 a.m., in three separate cars. The car with us in it, and my mother, was in the middle, between the two other cars. Each car was accompanied by three *haggana* soldiers, armed with rifles loaded with live ammunition. We took the eastern road by the Nile to Asyut along a very narrow road alongside the mountainous desert region. This was one of the most dangerous parts of Upper Egypt, as it was full of bandits and highwaymen, who lay in wait to ambush passing cars and rob travelers of their money and so on. We heard a lot of stories about this and about the different methods used by the robbers. For instance, they might fell a tree across the road to block the path of oncoming cars, forcing them to stop. Often, it would be a known bank van, transferring money from one branch of the bank to another, and they would stop the van and grab the money. This dangerous and scary trip, and all the stories they used to tell about it, gave me some of the most thrilling moments in my life!

During the trip, the driver's assistants told us all sorts of stories about the famous highwaymen of the time, such as al-Khutt and others like him. We always stayed awake until we arrived in Asyut, safe and sound. Then we'd start off again for Cairo, feeling safer, and from there to Helwan, where most of my father's family lived. We would spend a couple of weeks in Helwan, visiting all our relatives in Cairo according to a schedule, divided up by district! Uncle Abdel Azim, my father's brother in Maadi; my aunt Samira, my father's sister in Abbasiya; Uncles Mustafa and Mazhar and Aunt Kiki, my mother's siblings in Heliopolis, and so on. These visits were very important to my father, and he always insisted on bringing us along to keep up family ties with everyone in our clan and so that we'd get to know our uncles and aunts on both sides of the family. He was forever telling us that.

My aunt Kiki, 1939.

As we were going on these family visits from Helwan, driving along the Nile Corniche, we passed by the district of Old Cairo, including the ruins of al-Fustat, the first Islamic capital of Egypt. Here was the mosque of Amr ibn al-Aas, called simply the Ancient Mosque. This name, which my father drilled into my head, stayed with me until the name changed to Old Cairo. When we were in Cairo, we'd take the opportunity to go with my mother to buy new going-out clothes, or clothes for feast days, as well as school shoes, from the most elegant major department stores: Cicurel, Chemla, Hannaux, Sednaoui, Omar Effendi, and Orosdi-Back. These were the finest stores in Cairo, and they carried only the best and most up-to-date fashions.

These habits stayed with us on our visits to Cairo until my father died. You know, sometimes they had summer sandals specially made for us at Armenian-owned stores in Alexandria that specialized in children's sandals. Those sandals never wore out! We always wore brand-new clothes and shoes every Eid, and my mother plaited my hair into two braids tied with big bows of white satin for the occasion. Then my father would give each of us our *eidiya*, a traditional gift of money to children at the Eid, a silver twenty-piaster piece.

My mother had her dresses made in Cairo at a European seamstress's—I think she was Greek. When she came down to Cairo, she'd buy British-made winter wools and silks, and take them to the seamstress. As for our housedresses and sleeping clothes, we had them made at home in a special room at the far end of the house with a large glass window that let the light in, the sun spreading its warmth all through the room. This room had a Singer sewing machine in it, a wedding present from my father to my mother. My mother bought a type of heavy cotton fabric called *kastour*, with a thick pile on the reverse of it that made it very warm. There were large factories in Egypt that made it. Sometimes, too, we bought a type of fabric called Viyella. Atiyyat, the seamstress, and her assistant used to

Me aged five.

come to the house and spend three or four days there, making us pajamas and house clothes. My relationship with *kastour* remained robust all my life, even now, and it's always all about winter in my mind. I just love *kastour*. At the start of winter, I go out and make the rounds of all the government stores, looking for it: the al-Mahalla al-Kobra store and the Helwan Weavers' store are two places that until recently made wonderful *kastour* and Viyella. But sadly, this is all over. Whenever I find a remnant of *kastour* in a store, I buy it at once: I have a stock of it. Most fabrics are synthetic now, with the occasional cotton blend.

Can you believe it? Even now I can't get used to wearing ready-made pajamas and nightdresses, and I still keep the sleeping clothes my mother had made for me as a kind of personal heritage. I bought the *kastour* for them and decorated them with ribbon bows and flowers and rickrack braid. They've all but worn out now, but I feel like they're part of my history.

My father decided that our summer seat for the family would be Dekheila, a little village west of Alexandria. He had two houses built for us directly on the sea, twenty meters from the beach. He chose this specific location because the beach was broad there and not crowded, with only one-story cabins, mostly inhabited by the Greek community, as a great many of them worked with my father at his company. (This type of wood cabin used to be very widespread in Alexandria.) They were the ones who convinced him to buy land there and build. The second reason was that this was the location of the summerhouse of General Abdallah al-Nugoumi, a friend of my Sudanese grandfather's and the captain of the guard and commander of the Royal Guard during the reign of King Farouk. His father, a Sudanese fighter and commander, was Abdel Rahman al-Nugoumi, supreme commander of the Mahdi Revolution and commander of the Mahdi's forces, dubbed "Allah's Sharpened Sword." Abdallah al-Nugoumi's house was exceptional. It was a circular building in the shape of a chessboard rook. It had a big rock garden, built on an artificial hill rising some height above the street. You know, Dekheila used to have windmills in the nineteenth century (another piece of information I got from my father).

As we were leaving for Alexandria, our family and friends would come to say goodbye to us as if we were emigrating! I smile and laugh sometimes when I remember the scene. Now people come and go from continent to continent, from country to country, and nobody says goodbye.

Those summer months were months of abandon, splashing around in the sea, and fun family gatherings where we met all the relatives we didn't see the rest of the year because of living in Upper Egypt. The whole family used to gather at one of the two houses our father had built for us: groups of people were always coming and going, both from my father's and my mother's side, older and younger. Our house had four rooms on the second floor, and an extra, small room by the staircase. There was no corniche in front of us: the house gave directly onto a small bay on the sea. The servants went out in the morning to set up the beach umbrellas on the sand, and a little while after breakfast we went outside to play and swim on the beach, which we had more or less all to ourselves. There weren't any other beach umbrellas around us. At lunchtime, they would call down to us from the balconies to come in for lunch.

One of the people I remember most vividly from those summers is my uncle Mahmoud Idris, who was married to my father's sister Samira. He came from a rich family in the Nile Delta, always dressed nicely, and peppered his speech with French words. His father had sent him to study in Paris in the mid-1930s; he studied music and dance, and came back to inherit vast farmlands from his father, only to squander his inheritance on partying and living the high life. My late father always said, "The inheritance of the Idris family has all gone down the toilet!" Uncle Mahmoud Idris was an old pro at making kites—a clever artisan, to use the craftsmen's term. Sometimes, in the afternoons, he taught us how to make kites in different designs and colors; he showed us the different designs the Chinese used for their kites and the various tails they made for them. At sunset, all the family's children used to go outside. There were about seven or eight of us. Kites filled the sky. We fought with our kites until we brought each other's kites down. It developed into a competition—the best flyer, and the best kite, won. The judge of the contest was always Uncle Mahmoud Idris, may he rest in peace. This whole history came to mind when I watched a movie called *Kite Runner*, which was filmed in Afghanistan and starred a Scottish Egyptian actor by the name of Khalid Abdalla.

When summer ended, before the holidays were over, all the children and young people who had filled the house in the summer wrote and directed a play and put it on in front of the whole family in the big dining room. We used to push the dining table to the side and set up all the chairs like a theater. It was a dumb, silly, naive play, a lousy performance. But the important thing was the spirit of it, and that all the family's children took part in it. Some of them have grown into architects, officers, CEOs, and doctors.

The big thing for my father at these gatherings was cleanliness. He had a set of instructions on the subject, and one of the most amusing was the way he kept repeating to everyone, "Please flush the toilet when you're done!"

Marbles, too, was one of our summer games. Each of us had a jar of marbles of our own. We collected marbles of every shape and size and flaunted them and bragged about our collections. We compared them to see who had the best and prettiest collection of marbles and more colors and bigger sizes. This hobby, marbles—goodness, it was so important to us! Rich was the child who had the biggest and most flamboyant collection of marbles—at least in our eyes. Marbles were sold at the notions store—there were small stores in town with "Notions Store" on their front. I don't know what they call them now. The game of marbles was a thing for most children, and some of us, too, collected stamps.

During the summer holidays, we always paid several visits to the historic district of Manshiya, the old shopping district in the center of Alexandria. There were lots of important streets and landmarks there, and we visited them every time: the Sabaa Banat (Street of the seven girls); the Labban Police Station, where my father would always tell us that the famous pair of mass-murderer sisters, Raya and Sakina, had lived in the building right behind the station, which had an attractive façade with tall columns. All the information about the different districts of Alexandria were told to us by my father as we drove around. We visited the Greek district with its elegant buildings, and the Shallalat district, where the rich Greeks lived. In Manshiya, we always visited an area called Zan'at al-Sittat, literally "the women's crush," a market where they sell everything small that people use in their daily life. My mother used to take us there to buy all our needles and thread and hair ribbons, cheaper than at any notions store. I really enjoyed these visits. It was a long and very narrow street, filled with tiny stores all next to one another, full of different things. The street was a *zan'a*—a crush—not only in name! It was packed with people coming and going, just barely squeezing past one another.

This trip, from Dekheila to Alexandria, we used to take in the car with my father, and all along the way he would explain and tell us about everything we were seeing: Manshiya Square, with its stunning Italian-style architecture; the statues, such as the statue of Muhammad Ali Pasha astride his horse, facing the sea; the port; the Customs area; the classical buildings that are now landmarks; the Bahari and Anfushi fishing districts, with more Italian architecture; the famous fish market, Halaqat al-Samak (the fisherman's circle) at the far end of Alexandria; the marvelous mosque of al-Mursi Abu al-Abbas, and the regular folks' houses. He explained to us every district and everything we passed. He loved this place, felt that all this information was important for a historic city, and had a conviction that his children absolutely must learn all of this.

So many memories I still recall about the summer holidays! One of these is still in my mind even today; one I can't forget: it was the day King Farouk left Egypt after the 1952 Revolution. My father wouldn't let us miss such an important occasion. He stood us all up outside the house to look at the *Mahroussa*—the king's yacht—as it set sail from the palace at Ras al-Tin, bearing King Farouk with his family, leaving for Europe. The royal yacht may be one of the oldest seafaring crafts in the world. It started life in England, where it was made by the order of Khedive Ismail in 1865 to use especially for his excursions on the sea. It brought together luxury and tradition, and it was the first boat to have a wireless apparatus on board, in 1912. That day, we watched the final exit of the last of the Muhammad Ali dynasty from Egypt, for good. Of course, my dear father couldn't miss the opportunity to tell us the story of the *Mahroussa*, and its historic importance. This scene was the end of an era, and the start of a new era for Egypt. My father was a great tour guide.

At night, when it got dark, if you stood outside the house, you could see a string of pearls glittering in the sea, as if the sea was wearing the prettiest bracelets around its wrists. These were the lights of the fishing boats moving in a long unbroken line catching bluefish by lamplight. This, too, was my father's explanation.

Nice things sometimes happened as well. We used to see groups of fifteen or twenty young men and women from the Greek community living next door to us walking in the street by the sea or on the beach with a guitar, singing Greek songs. They filled the place with song and fun and laughter. I can't tell you how wonderful it was, how sweet, and how simple.

Domestic Life

My father gave my mother a cookbook that I keep to this day: *Kitab Abla Nazira* (Abla Nazira's book). Nazira Nikola (1902–92), better known as Abla Nazira, was a pioneer of cookery instruction in Egypt. She co-authored the cookbook with her colleague Bahiya Othman. The cookbook is inscribed with a dedication from my father, dated 1941. This was the most important book for Egyptian women; every woman had a copy of it. My mother used it a great deal for most recipes, especially baking. I plan to give my copy to my daughter Fatma before I'm gone so that she'll have a small part of her grandmother's life.

I laugh a lot when I remember helping my mother cook an Abla Nazira recipe—say, for a cake requiring six eggs, when we only had four eggs in the fridge. My mother would just use them and put them in, and when I burst out, "Mummy! There are still two eggs missing!" she would laugh and say "It's fine! Abla Nazira is a little too finicky!"

There was a copper whitener who would come to our house. All the red copper utensils of the house would be brought out for him to whiten the surfaces by adding a layer of tin. He would put each pot next to the wall and stand in it with both feet, then twist to polish the copper, while leaning against the wall, removing the patina that had formed on the copper. He used his feet in a half-circular motion and twisted his waist right and left like a yoga practitioner. I used to love watching him. I don't remember whether we whitened the copper once a month or more often.

I remember the water carriers who walked through the villages carrying sacks made of animal skins filled with water, which they handed out in the surrounding villages to the poorer homes that didn't have water piped in. They poured the water into a large *zir*, or earthenware pot, in the house. All the images of the copper-whitener and the water carrier, in addition to the *shadoof*—the ancient Egyptian way of bringing water up from the canal, which I used to see on the trips my father took us on through the villages of Upper Egypt—I later found at the Lehnert & Landrock stationer's and bookstore on Sherif Street in Downtown Cairo. They were all in black and white.

Lehnert & Landrock was founded by Ernst Heinrich Landrock in 1924, and specialized in art books, both old and modern, in English, French, and German. It carried rare photographs by photographer Rudolf Franz Lehnert of historical scenes from Egypt some hundred years ago. Unfortunately, the store has now been replaced by a store selling nuts and sweets and has moved to another downtown location on Abdel Khaleq Tharwat Street. I've learned that Landrock's still has another branch at the Yamama Center Mall in the neighborhood of Zamalek.

Then there were our father's frequent drives with us to places outside Sohag, and the perpetual fight between my brothers, Ali and Omar, and me: who got the window seats for the best view? Someone had to be in the middle. My father sat up front next to the driver and we were in the back. There was always an agriculture lesson to make the subject exciting when we passed by the fields. My father would ask the driver to stop, and we would get out next to a farmer's reed hut and start a conversation with him—his name, his family, how his crops were doing—and then he would take us into the field to explain to us what the farmer had planted. Most times, this hut would have a clay *zir* next to it with a metal *koz*, a kind of mug, on top of it, which all together was called the *mintal*, from which any passerby could drink—"from one mouth to another," as the Upper Egyptians say. "These are eggplants; this is okra; this is corn; this is clover." Sometimes, inside the hut, we would see a *kanoun*, a simple stove made of mud-brick where the farmer's wife would cook her food. For fuel, she used bits of wood that she collected from the fields around her.

You know, I get it from my father, this love of chatting with workmen and salespeople, finding out where they're from and how they're doing. My father insisted on having us repeat after him the kinds of vegetables; he made it into a game so that we'd learn their names. We became experts on the names and types of vegetables, and these tests would be held by my father on our way anywhere, on every journey. He would point out the window to some field and ask, "What crop is this, kids?" and we would shout out joyfully, jostling to outdo each other: "Corn, Baba!" or "Eggplant, Baba!" or "Clover!" He would be so happy and smile because he had taught us something.

Another thing I can't forget is the vast acreage devoted to sugarcane as far as the eye could see. It seemed endless. My father would stop the car and get out and buy a *libsha*, as the Upper Egyptians called a bundle. He would break it into manageable pieces and stuff it in the trunk of the car. Sugarcane was called "the pretty one's cheek" because it was rosy red. Sitting in the sunshine and chewing on sugarcane was a delight! One song with a rural rhythm that I still like to listen to, written by Abdel Rahman al-Abnoudi and set to music by Baligh Hamdi, is "Yabul-Labaysh": "Sugarcane bound in bundles / We're setting up a wedding / They bought her an anklet to fit her / She went to show it to her uncle / Well done to the groom for proposing!"

Can you imagine, these images and memories are still in my mind? I still remember them when I pass by a field and recognize the crop and repeat it in my head: this is clover, this is okra. The sight of a field, any field, reminds me of my happy childhood, and my lessons in agriculture, and the way my father gave us information through a game we all played with him. I tear up when I remember these things.

I also love willow trees. I always remember, as a girl, walking by the canal in Upper Egypt and seeing long rows of willow trees, bending over the water and touching the surface. It was a lovely sight that needed a photographer or a skilled artist to depict. Now I understand the emotion that the great poet Abdel Rahman al-Abnoudi felt, with his Upper Egyptian roots, writing his epic poem "al-Nahar" (Daylight), sung by the popular Egyptian singer Abdel Halim Hafez as "'Adda al-nahar" (Daylight is done), recorded after the 1967 war, where he says, "And our country is washing her hair by the canal." A poetic image full of melancholy, and a marvelous description of Egypt in the shape of a girl washing her hair in the canals of the countryside.

Books and Culture

My father was a voracious reader. I inherited his love of books, and likewise his distinctive, attractive, regular handwriting. Every month, he would receive a shipment of the latest English books from London: the living room of our home in Sohag was large, with a wood-burning fireplace that burned every day in winter. Around it was a library full of my father's books. I remember him always sitting by the fireside reading before he went to his bedroom.

My father also had a modest artistic side to him. Sometimes he designed some small thing for the house and had it made by the team of carpenters and blacksmiths who worked in his company. The two things I can remember and have an example of are a table in hammered copper, on four legs—this is always in my room, and I use it every day—and there was also a brass lantern that hung in our home, but I don't know where it went. He had a friend who was a famous artist of Upper Egyptian roots called Uncle Sanad Basta (1903–64). They were close. Uncle Sanad had graduated from law school and gone into the diplomatic corps, and had been appointed to the Egyptian Embassy in Washington DC. Then he left all that behind and went into art, like Mahmoud Said. My father always told us that Uncle Sanad had learned painting at the private studios of artists in Egypt, London, and Paris. He had painted a portrait of my father before he died; he also painted the poinciana tree next to the squash courts and gave the painting to my father as a gift. He started another portrait of my father at his request, but unfortunately it was never finished. I used to go visit Uncle Sanad in his home in Sohag with my father. It was a fine house with a large garden that bespoke an aristocratic family.

Sixty years on, I found myself invited to lunch at the home of the Egyptian ambassador in London. I found a great many paintings by Sanad Basta; the ambassador had devoted a great portion of his home to them. How happy it made me! All my old memories came flooding back in a moment. Uncle Sanad and my father, together in our house; the studio in his house in Sohag; me sitting for him as he painted me.

Our house was English in design: a sitting room and a fire lit every evening in wintertime for my father to read by. I remember one night like it was yesterday, when my father was sitting by the fireside. I came in, and he gestured for me to sit next to him. Then he patted his knees, a book in his hand, and he said to me, "Come here, Kazouza"—his nickname for me. "I want to give you this book. It'll be very useful to you." The book was in Arabic, titled, if I remember correctly, *Rasa'il Nehru ila Indira* (published in English as *Letters from a Father to His Daughter*). In it, Jawaharlal Nehru explains world history to his daughter, Indira Gandhi. It was translated by Ahmad Bahaa al-Din. Nehru wrote it in simplified language when he was in prison, as a gift to his daughter, who later became prime minister of India. I read the book at the age of twelve. Unfortunately, it got lost in the moves from Sohag to Helwan and from Helwan to Harraniya and to Cairo. My father wanted me to have an idea about world history and could find no better book than this to give to me. I'm going to find a copy, because it left an impression on me, and to this day, history and reading history, is one of the things I love.

My interest in a great many things, great and small, and the details of telling stories, all this I get from my father. For sure, my strong relationship with reading and books is something he planted in me from childhood. I wish he had lived longer so that I could have gotten to know him better and so that he could have been proud of me and the success I have achieved.

My Grandfather

My father was born to an Egyptian father and a Sudanese mother. His father, Muhammad Fahmy Bey, was a graduate of the Military College founded in 1811 by Muhammad Ali at the hands of Soliman Pasha al-Faransawi. My grandfather married his first wife, Fatma Ibrahim, a relative of his. Her father was the captain of the Royal Guard during the reign of King Farouk.

My grandfather's first wife Fatma, who was Egyptian, died at fifteen after giving birth to two girls and a boy, my uncle Abdel Wahab and my aunts Samira and Saniya, who died of breast cancer in the flower of her youth. My grandfather went to Sudan with General Lee Stack, sardar (equivalent to colonel) of the Egyptian army and governor-general of Anglo-Egyptian Sudan. He was assigned to Kordofan around 1901. As far as I know, my grandfather's job in the army was financial inspector; he wasn't in combat. After his tour of duty in Sudan was up, more than twenty years later, he came back to Egypt as an appointee of the Ministry of Finance with a great many certificates of appreciation and no end of medals from his bosses, both Egyptian and British. At the end of his life, he achieved the rank of deputy minister of finance in Cairo on 28 May 1954. His job at the time permitted him to move about between different governorates by boat, making his rounds and spending the night on the craft instead of in a hotel (hotels were few and far between outside the capital city at that time).

My grandfather was very careful of his health. Every day he ate boiled vegetables and chicken soup. Can you imagine? He never ate anything different! My mental image of my grandfather is of him in his room in the family home in Helwan. He had an old-fashioned high brass bed, inlaid with copper plates and mirrors. This was how the bed was in a great many Egyptian homes. He also had an *'angarib* chair in his room, made in Sudan, on which he sat to read the newspapers every day—*'angarib* is a kind of woven straw fabric out of which beds and hammocks were made for the Sudanese to sleep on in the hot summers south of Nubia (where they also use beds of *'angarib*). My grandfather had four elephant guns, which he kept hidden under the bed. They were inlaid with engravings of plants on white metal set into the wood. He used them on his trips every so often, hunting lions and other wild animals. I don't know where those magnificent weapons have gone; I think they were handed back to the state upon my grandfather's death.

We liked to creep under the bed when my grandfather wasn't there, when we were seven or eight years old, with my brother Ali, and my cousins Yehya and Nadia Fahmy, the children of my father's brother Ahmad, to look at these rifles and touch them. As far as I can remember, I think there were two great big ivory tusks next to them. My grandfather's stories about his hunting trips in Sudan fascinated us. We sat cross-legged on the floor around his bed, while he told us of hunting elephants and lions. His tales of Sudan always left us wide-eyed and open-mouthed.

My grandfather told us of the elephants that were in Sudan by the thousands. There were so many other animals, too! Hippopotamuses, crocodiles, lions, monkeys! My Aunt Farah, too, sometimes had stories to tell us. One of them was a story about someone working in their house from the Zandi tribe in the south, who have the custom of filing their teeth down to a point to make them look like wild animals' teeth, which serves to terrorize their enemies. When this man smiled, he would show his teeth that he had filed down into triangles like the jaws of a predator. My grandmother noticed that he was looking more often than he should at my Aunt Fatma, who was a plump and juicy child at the time; she got the wind up and asked my grandfather to replace him with someone else!

My Aunt Farah told us of the Dinka, Nuer, and Shalouk tribes in southern Sudan. "They're tall and go naked," she told us, and said they dyed their hair with cow urine to give it a distinctive orange color. Most of them were herders, and cows were the number-one priority in their lives. They lived in the broad savannah, where the cows have extremely long horns. "Sometimes the horns can be up to a meter long!" Bridegrooms make a gift of such cows to their brides. Their girls are tall and slim. In the 1990s, a Dinka model became very famous in London—she was 1.80 meters tall and her name was Alek Wek. It was then I remembered all the tales of Sudan told by my grandfather as he sat on his bed with us cross-legged in front of him, telling us of the magical (to us) world of southern Sudan.

The world of fantastical tales about animals and tribes, I think, left a deep impression on me, manifesting in a kind of interest in and admiration for that magical world, and has remained with me to this day. The Dark Continent, as they called it, and especially Sudan, has a special place in my heart.

During his tenure in Kordofan, my grandfather met my Sudanese grandmother, Hawa' al-Daw. He married her around 1903, in the city of Ubayyid, the capital of the province, and my grandmother gave birth to my father Abdel Moneim there. The region is so famous for its fertile lands and soil that they say, "Go there and scatter some seeds, any seeds—you'll come back to find trees!" Fruit orchards, forests really, are very widespread there, and my father used to pick up the fruit that had fallen from the trees and fermented, and put it in a big dish, and go into the forest and leave it under a tree. The monkeys then came down from the trees and drank it and got drunk! Then my father used to catch them, tie a rope around their necks, and get one of his father's soldiers to sell them in the market for his benefit!

Kordofan suffered from intertribal conflicts during the Mahdi Revolution (1881–98) against Ottoman rule, led by Muhammad Ahmad al-Mahdi (1844–85). My Aunt Farah told me that most of my grandmother's village were killed in these conflicts, and Grandma Hawa' ran away from them and sought refuge in the tent of the Egyptian officer Muhammad Fahmy—that is, my grandfather—and hid there. My grandfather didn't know what to do about this refugee from civil war, or how to act, especially that she had no one to support her, her parents having been killed in the war and leaving her to her cousin, one Amr Wadgish, for a time, but then he was killed as well. She had a brother by the name of Adam and a cousin called Halima, whom I heard of, but never knew anything about. A short while later my grandfather married her, and she stayed with him in Sudan, moving around together to different districts with his deployments with the army.

They lived together in Ubayyid, where my father Abdel Moneim and my Aunt Fatma were born. As for my Uncle Farrag, he was born in Khartoum, and Uncle Ahmad in Juba, now the capital of South Sudan, and an important port since the nineteenth century. Safiya, the youngest of my aunts, was born in Managel, near Wad Madani, a town in al-Jazira State, during my grandfather's tenure there.

A funny story I always remember was told to us by my father: when my grandfather was in Juba, my father was still a little boy, I think of three or four years old. One day he was sitting in his mother's lap at home. (The houses where they lived were all made of wire netting, to protect against the notorious tsetse fly, which caused sleeping sickness.) Then a lion happened to pass by outside the house; my father took fright and burst out crying, and jumped out of my grandmother's lap. When my grandfather returned from a hunting trip, Grandma Hawa' complained to him, "My son Abdel Moneim will turn out a coward! Go catch me a lion! I need to cook its heart for Abdel Moneim to eat, and make him brave."

And so he did. The lion caught, my grandmother cooked its heart for her son and fed it to him. I remember that my father was a brave man, but I don't know whether it was because of the lion's heart or whether it was just in his nature.

My Habbouba

My grandmother, like all the people of Sudan, believed deeply in the evil eye. Often I would see my father pin an oblong leather amulet to his undershirt, decorated with simple broad bands. When I asked him about it, he told me, "It's a protection your grandmother Hawa' made for me." A long while after my father died, I found that my mother had kept that amulet. I took it and I still have it.

The city of Fasher, the capital of North Darfur, was famous for the craft of making amulets, because it had the best sheikhs, who would write the protection texts and make them. Many Sudanese women traveled to Fasher to have amulets made for many reasons: to keep a husband, or to prevent evil, or to get back at a mother-in-law, or for any other reason. They say it's part of Sudanese tradition.

My grandfather was always telling us tales of southern Sudan and my father's childhood shenanigans, but I continuously wanted to find out more about the family and their earliest memories of Sudan. Before my Aunt Farah died (she was the oldest of my father's sisters and the one who remembered the most, in the most detail), I sat with her and she told me all about the origins of my grandmother, Hawa' al-Daw, and I wrote down all she said on a piece of paper, which I keep in my safe at home, where I keep all my most precious possessions. This paper has sat there for thirty-five years, bearing my grandmother's name and her full family name—Hawa' Muhammad al-Daw—which I learned from my aunt, along with the tribe she was from and which region of Sudan.

The dream of finding out about my Sudanese origins stayed with me all my life. Every so often I opened the safe and looked at the scrap of paper, and asked about the origins of Grandma Hawa' and the rest of the Sudanese branch of the family. Where were they now, I wondered? Was there anyone left of them? All news of the Sudanese side of the family had dried up after my grandfather's return to Cairo and his appointment to the Ministry of Finance.

My grandmother Hawa' herself I only vaguely remember. She died when I was three and a half. When I remember her, it's like a passing shadow. She really was like an angel. I remember that she was scarified with the deep scars on her cheeks that the Sudanese call *shalloukh*: this is a tribal practice meant to give beauty to the face, done at twelve years of age or the onset of puberty. The Sudanese can identify which tribe you're from by the shapes of your *shalloukh*—for instance, the Ja'li tribe have a long *shalloukh*, while the Shawalha tribes have horizontal gashes. Her lip was tattooed as well with a mark the Sudanese call the *shloufa*. She always wore the traditional *toub*, the draped garment of Sudanese women, all in white. She taught my mother how to make *weka*, that is, crushed dried okra, in the Sudanese manner. We all loved Grandma Hawa's *weka*. I still like to make that Sudanese dish, basically dried okra pounded powdery fine in the pestle and added to minced meat with tomato sauce, onions, and garlic, and garnished with fried garlic at the end, the way we garnish *mulukhiya*.

My late mother always said her mother-in-law was an angel. Grandma Hawa' used to spend most of her time on the roof of our big house in Helwan, where there was a pantry for storage of beans and lentils and ghee, and the coop where she raised pigeons alongside the chickens and ducks and geese to feed the whole family. She also had a gray Armant dog—sorry, I mean an Armant *lion*! She died of typhoid on 28 December 1947, quarantined in her room for fear of infection. Her children would look through the glass of the door to check on her. Typhoid was a killer in those days. Antibiotics weren't yet in use.

My grandfather served as an officer in Juba, in southern Sudan, in the province of Mangalla, on the Ugandan border. (In 1935, Mangalla was merged with Bahr al-Ghazal to create Equatoria Province.) When my father came of school age, it was time for him to go to school, but back in my grandfather's day, the only schools in those remote areas were missionary schools. In Khartoum, there was a famous English school called Gordon College, named after Gordon Pasha (Charles George Gordon, 1833–85, the British general who served under Khedive Ismail as governor-general of Sudan, where he did a great deal to repress rebellion and the slave-trade). My grandfather presented my father's documents to the school, which accepted him. There was no transportation from the south to the north except for Nile mail boats, so my grandfather had to hand over his six-year-old son to the captain of the mail boat, with instructions to take care of him. The boat left Juba, sailing down the White Nile, the first branch of our great river, all the way to Khartoum. The captain then handed my father over to the school authorities, and he stayed at the boarding school all the school year, coming back afterward at the end of summer to his father's post in the south. My father attended Gordon College from his elementary school years until he graduated high school, after which my grandfather sent him to Cairo, where the extended family lived in Hilmiya, to join what was at the time called the Higher School for Commerce (now the Faculty of Commerce), from which he eventually graduated.

My father's and grandfather's stories about Sudan, its places, its cities, and its rivers echoed throughout our house until we knew them by heart. Juba, Jonglei, Malakal, the Blue Nile, the White Nile. There were always connections between us and the Sudanese, and the Sudanese-Egyptians. Preserving these relationships was very important to our family. I especially remember the Sudanese friends of my aunts Farah and Safiya, many of whom lived in Maadi.

Hawa' al-Daw came to Cairo and lived in Helwan with her husband and family in peace, and died in peace as well. Her ties to Sudan were all but cut, except for a cousin who came to visit her in Cairo on a very sad day for the family—the day of my father's death. During the wake—and it was a huge wake, where the tent for condolences covered about half of Gaafar Street, I can still remember it—this smartly dressed Sudanese gentleman arrived and I saw him with my Uncle Ahmad at the entrance to my grandfather's apartment in Helwan. They spoke for a long time. He went inside and spent a long time in the sitting room, then left. "Who was the Sudanese man?" I asked afterward. "He's your father's cousin," they told me. The man left and never came back, and the ties were completely cut with the family of Hawa' al-Daw—my *habbouba* (literally "darling," but "grandma" in Sudan).

Although those ties were cut, I have kept all the memories in my head, and I have clung to every detail that linked me to my Sudanese origins. When I see a group of Sudanese people, I rush to speak to them, as if I want to show off my Sudanese side. Sudan has always been alive inside my psyche; I feel it is part of what I am. Sudan has never left me. It is always in the background, and I have never stopped thinking that one day I must go there and find my Sudanese origins and find the family of my *habbouba*, Hawa'.

It's been well over a hundred years since the Mahdi Revolution in Sudan, my grandfather's part in it, his marriage to my Sudanese grandmother, and his return to Cairo with his family. But Sudan is still in me, in my memory and in my heart. The family tree of my grandmother Hawa' is a story that has no end.

When finally I got the opportunity I had waited for all my life to visit my beloved Sudan, it was at the invitation of UNIDO, via my friend Dr. Hisham Hussein, who is a regional manager in Sudan, although he lives in Bahrain. I was invited to take a look at the manufacture of jewelry in Sudan to study the possibility of collaborating with them and developing the craft further, given my long experience in the field. They also asked me to give a talk to the Fine Arts students at Khartoum University about my experience and my story with jewelry and the importance of preserving our heritage.

I opened my safe and took out the old information that had lain there for years. I went in search of my Sudanese *habbouba*. I arrived in Khartoum and was introduced to a great many important families. I gave every important Sudanese person I met a photocopy of the information I had in my safe. They all concurred that the al-Daw family was an important family in the Kordofan region.

I went to the university and met the university president. The main building of the university used to house Gordon College, where my father had studied ninety years before. It's a big building, part of which is old, and part new, added to the original building after expansion. Of course, the difference is immediately clear between the old English architecture and the new, modern section.

Imagine how I felt, giving a lecture in the same place where my father had studied more than ninety years ago! I kept asking myself, "I wonder what the school was like when my father was studying here? Where were the dormitories? Where did my father sleep?" It's such a hard feeling to describe. It gives you chills, and you feel nostalgic and melancholy and sorrowful all at once. All my life, my Sudanese origins had been of great importance to me. Everything related to Sudan drew me toward the roots of my father and the Sudanese blood that runs in my veins. I really love Sudanese people, and I always take an interest in what is happening in Sudan, politically and socially.

Back to the story of my *habbouba*, Hawa' Muhammad al-Daw, whom my grandfather married in about 1903, in Ubayyid, the capital of Kordofan, and whose tribe had lived through the upheavals of the Mahdi Revolution. This is exactly what I heard from the Sudanese people I met on my visit to Khartoum with UNIDO. I found out from them that my grandmother's origins were from the Habab tribes in Yemen (that is, Qahtanites), who moved to eastern Sudan from the Arabian Peninsula centuries ago to make a living. The descendants of this tribe in Sudan are called the Hababi people. I remembered that my Aunt Farah had told me indeed before she died that she was from the tribe of Habayna (a slightly different pronunciation), a branch of the Habab, and the al-Daw were also a branch of the Habab.

During my visit to Sudan to see the state of their crafts, part of our program was a visit to Omdurman, the old capital of Sudan before Khartoum, and where most of the goldsmiths and craftsmen are. I went with a group of important goldsmiths from Khartoum, headed by the famous goldsmith Bulbul. He was the most prominent jeweler in Khartoum, from a family all based in the gold market. I walked with him and we saw the workshops specializing in preparing raw materials and the ones where designs were made up, and I wrote down my observations on the state of the crafts there. Bulbul always asked the workmen there for information: "The professor is looking for her *habbouba*." Whereupon I'd pull out my little paper and show it to them. They would look at it and ask me a few questions. Imagine the great surprise, about which every goldsmith in Omdurman agreed: the al-Daw family were a family of goldsmiths and silversmiths! The twenty-four most important goldsmiths and silversmiths in Kordofan were all from the al-Daw clan!

I can't tell you. I swear, my hair stood on end with surprise and shock. It's not a new thing—it's in the blood, then! And it's been in there for ages! How can inherited traits come down like that through the generations? Truly . . . it's amazing.

My Mother

My maternal grandmother was named Aisha Hanem Hafez (Hanem is a Turkish aristocratic title). She was a Turkish-Egyptian from the upper echelons of society. Her grandfather, Muhammad Pasha Hafez, was an architect who had studied at the palace of Muhammad Ali Pasha and married Fatma Mazhar. Aisha Hanem, my aristocratic grandmother, fell in love with my grandfather Mahmoud Ezzat, a lowly clerk, who was as handsome as a movie star, and she married him against the family's wishes. She had three sisters: Dawlat, or Doudou, married to an ophthalmologist, Dr. Abdel Hamid al-Kurdi; Zeinab, or Zouzou, who married Abdel Megid Pasha Ibrahim, the minister of transport; and Malak, who married Othman Pasha Muharram, the minister of public works. Her brothers were Mazhar Pasha Hafez, married to Aziza al-Manasterly; Ismail Pasha Hafez; and Hussein Pasha Hafez, who had socialist leanings, gave away everything he owned to the poor and needy, and never married. My grandmother's cousin was the actress Bahiga Hafez, who broke with the family and went to work in the movies, the black sheep of the family.

The people in that family were all stunningly attractive: my uncles were like Hollywood stars, and my aunts were gorgeous, like Princesses Fawziya and Faiqa—so much so that my younger uncle Samir was once chosen to act in a movie with the famous actor Anwar Wagdi—he had a two-minute cameo as a police officer, but after that there was no more of it. God rest his soul, he was the Don Juan of his age.

Back to the aristocratic family: their daughter marrying a humble clerk was beyond the pale. But she put her foot down, and the marriage went ahead. There was another catastrophe in store when Aisha had seven children: Abdel Hamid, Zeinab, Mazhar, Mustafa, Samir, Kiki, and Zubeida. That was when Mahmoud Ezzat died, leaving her a widow with this heavy burden. The Ezzat family lived in the west of Helwan, and the Fahmy family lived in the east, near the Japanese Garden.

My maternal grandmother, Aisha Hanem, with my mother, in the streets of Cairo, 1938.

After my grandfather died, the extended family didn't help my grandmother financially—I never did find out why. On her own, she bore the weighty responsibility, and suffered from want all her life. I believe that my mother's speedy acceptance of my father's marriage proposal was because she felt bad for her own mother's financial plight and her many responsibilities. My mother, Zubeida, was nicknamed Zebda, which means "butter." That is a symbol of beauty for Egyptians, as it indicates fair skin. She was a very pretty woman, like the American movie stars, especially Rita Hayworth. My father's early upbringing and his work with the British had given him a deep admiration for Europeans and their open-minded nature. He married my mother after he saw her on the Helwan train with her mother, reading a French magazine. It was a traditional marriage, which took place in 1940. My mother left for Sohag to join my father in Upper Egypt, where he worked. My siblings and I were all born in Sohag: Ali, my elder brother; me; Omar, our middle brother; and Randa, the youngest.

My mother lived in luxury in Upper Egypt with a husband in an important job, surrounded by friends in high positions. The house was always receiving visitors—ministers, deputy ministers, CEOs of foreign companies—for dinner and supper. These were soirees in which men and women mingled freely, a sign of the open nature of Upper Egyptian society at the time. My mother played tennis at the Sohag Club with no restrictions, wearing a short white skirt.

I never remember seeing my mother cooking. She only supervised the cook and told him what to do. I remember our house had a huge kitchen, with black cast-iron British-made ovens. The glazed tiles, too, were from England, oblong and white. They still sell them today! They call them subway tiles. Can you imagine, seventy years on, I had my kitchen tiled with the same tiles I saw in my childhood (probably foolish nostalgia, as they call it!).

One unforgettable day for me was when we said, "We don't like zucchini," when Muhammad, the Sudanese servingman, was giving my father his food. My father issued an immediate order that we were to be served zucchini seven days running. After that we never opened our mouths again, or ever objected to a dish, or said that we liked this or didn't like that. We shut up and ate what was put in front of us.

One time, my mother took it into her head to start an enterprise from home. My father bought her six water buffalo. They were kept in a barn by the Nile, next to the sycomore fig tree and the waterwheel. My mother went to visit the barn once a week; the servants brought the milk daily for us to use in the household, and with what was left over, she taught the women how to make cheese. I never had such delicious cheese—perfect and unadulterated. She always made gifts of it to friends and family. There was a thick layer of ghee lying on top of the cheese when you opened the tin! Now that was luxury buffalo cheese! And she also had *Usta* (master craftsman) Abdel Hamid make us buffalo yogurt at home.

Our house had a fleet of servants, and one of their responsibilities was buying things from market: vegetables, fruit, meat, and so on. I remember two of them, Abdel Hafez and Nifa. The first was short and thin, the second

My mother in her wedding dress, 1940.

tall and thin! They were always together, like Laurel and Hardy. There was a set of iron scales in the kitchen with a pair of bright brass pans that always shone. Things were measured back then in pounds and ounces. Now, when I see the prices of things back then, it makes me smile.

We also had a servingman and a cook, and there was always a young country boy and a group of company chauffeurs. I remember very well old Uncle Eisa, an awe-inspiring Sudanese, the head of the janitors—my father was very fond of him. He had an imposing air about him, a man of about fifty. He wore a pristine white gallabiya, positively glowing with cleanliness, and a big white turban on his head. He was held in great respect by all the workers. We children were scared of him, especially if we did something wrong, such as bouncing on top of the cotton bales or hiding between them, and he always kept us away from them for fear we'd get hurt.

Now I remember an incident that I'd like to note. In the late 1980s, we opened a store selling high-quality craft products, called Al-Ain Gallery. A smartly dressed man in his mid-sixties came in to buy something, I can't remember exactly what at the moment. After a few minutes of chatting, he asked me, "Are you Zubeida's daughter?" I said yes. "We used to be neighbors," he said, "Our houses were next to each other. And I should have married your mother. She was a very beautiful woman." He was clearly besotted. "But your father beat me to it!"

I went home and told Mummy what had happened. The man was from the Nuqrashi family, and I'll never forget how she blushed and hid her face! "Zuzza," she giggled shyly, "Now you're reminding me of my checkered past!"

We were the cream of society. The club, the car, the dinner parties. As a child, I lived in luxury and good fortune, with no worries or anything to darken my days. But everything was upended for our family after the sad evening that changed the course of our lives. My father burst a blood vessel in his brain and died. He had high blood pressure. The day he died will remain the longest day in my life, a painful memory imprinted in me down to the last little detail for ever.

I remember it like it was yesterday. It was nearly dawn. I woke up to an unusual sense of urgency, people I didn't know were moving around the house, running to and fro in the passageway outside my father's big room. My mother was frantic, running to the phone and calling doctor friends. Uncle Eisa and Uncle Muhammad, the janitors, and someone else were being given instructions by my mother. They were going in and out of my father's room; he was screaming that he had a headache and clutching his head, a trail of blood trickling from his nose. Dr. Mustafa al-Mashad, my father's friend, arrived, with two other doctors whose names I can't remember. They disappeared into the room with him for a long time.

With the dawn of 1 January 1959, my father had left for another place, another world. He was in his early fifties.

Our life of luxury ended with my father's sudden death, and a different stage began, a new life, commanded by my mother with admirable courage, now a widow, in her late thirties—still young. "We still love those who have been snatched away / They live on in our hearts, here every day." These words by Abdel Rahman al-Abnoudi make my eyes tear up whenever I hear them.

Helwan

My father was one of the first Egyptian employees to be appointed to a high position in the British company where he worked. The company was nationalized—that is, confiscated by the Egyptian government—a year before his death. During that year, the company's legal situation and its relationship with the Egyptian government remained unstable, and upon my father's death, absolutely no compensation was given against the time he had worked with the company, although he had been with them his whole life, nor was a pension paid out to his family. We found ourselves in a sea of troubles that there was no solution for—we were truly, at that time, in the hands of God.

After my parents' life in Sohag, and with all their children born there, we had to leave Upper Egypt and move to Cairo, to the district of the Helwan baths, to live with the Fahmy family, who had moved there after a period of living in Hilmiya and Abbasiya upon their return from Sudan. Helwan at that time was the cleanest place in Greater Cairo, with the purest air, the best weather, and bright sunlight. For this reason, it was a popular winter resort, not just for Egypt but for the world.

My dear Upper Egypt will always have a special corner of my heart. I miss the Upper Egyptian dialect, which I understand and love to listen to, with their pronunciation of the "g" as a "d." The Upper Egyptian people are straightforward, strong, and brave, and I am always happy and my heart leaps when I'm traveling to the place where I spent the early years of my life. For a long time after we made our home in Cairo, it stuck in my mind that eggs were *kuhreit*, as they call them in Upper Egypt, and a turkey was *dik Malti*, rather than *Roumi*.

My elder brother Ali was sixteen at the time. Omar was eleven, and Randa was seven or eight. I was thirteen.

At the start, we lived in a large apartment building for about five years; I don't remember exactly how long. Then we got the chance to move into an apartment next to my grandfather's house in East Helwan, in a distinctive building with a wonderful location, right next to the Helwan light railway, which we called the Metro station, on a corner by the Glanz Hotel on Riad Pasha Street, with a big back garden. At the bottom of the garden were rooms that were rented out to expatriate students from Arab countries. The building was in the Art Deco style, three stories high, with middle-class families living in it. The owner was an Armenian lady called Madame Angele.

After we settled in Helwan, I started attending the Helwan Secondary School for Girls. The school building was spectacular. It had been a hotel built by Khedive Ismail, facing the medicinal sulfur springs of Helwan, accommodating visitors to the springs. I remember that at the side entrance there was a place to park bicycles. A lot of girls cycled to school. We also had a big play yard, and another yard with tennis, volleyball, and basketball courts, as well as a big gym on the ground floor. The top floor of the building was a boarding school for the girls who came from other African countries, most of them from Somalia and Eritrea. I remember that they were very beautiful, with lovely figures. Their features were tiny and delicate, and most of them were tall. There were also some girls from Arabian Gulf countries, but not many.

Many princes from the Arabian Gulf went to school at Helwan Secondary at the time, and attended the boarding school. I remember a client from Bahrain from the Khalifa Family, Sheikha Mariam bint Ibrahim. Her husband, Sheikh Eisa, had completed his secondary education at Helwan Secondary, and lived at the boarding school until he graduated. Whenever I met him, he would speak to me about the pleasant days he had spent at the Helwan Secondary School for Boys.

The Helwan boarding schools were full of aristocrats' children: royal families and the children of heads of state. It was the same throughout Egypt, not just in Helwan. The schools and universities of Egypt were a draw for students from all over the Arab world. Victoria College in Alexandria is where the late King Hussein of Jordan graduated, as well as Zaid Ibn Shaker, the former prime minister of Jordan.

Our move from Upper Egypt to Cairo after my father's death was a sea change in the routine of our lives. After a life of luxury, we were forced to keep to a budget, as our resources were limited, and all my mother had was a small income from some modest investments my father had made before he died. My mother, who had been living the high life, had to shrink her needs and expectations to the bare minimum: any trips, any movies, all these had to be pared down for us to survive. She drastically reduced her outings, except for some visits to family and telephone calls to her lifelong friends in Sohag.

My mother's social life, formerly so open and lavish, was transformed to focus on the household, the family, and her children, and trying to provide for them and give them a good life with her modest means. The land my father had bought—forty feddans in al-Abqa'in, near Hosh Eisa—hardly brought in any income to speak of. Its revenues were all small sums, but they helped, in addition to the income from renting out the villas in Alexandria. She was a wise and frugal mother. Everything was calculated. She had to rent out the two villas that my father had built by the sea, keeping only one ground-floor flat in one of them for us to spend our summers. When a tenant would arrive, my dear mother would get on a bus at the crack of dawn bound for Alexandria—we had no car. She never complained to me of how hard it was for her or how she suffered, or said anything at all. She did it all with good grace, without a word. She began to do everything for herself, cooking, having learned the basics from Usta Abdel Hamid, her cook in Sohag—how well I remember him working in our big kitchen there! He was short and wore an apron and a tall hat.

My mother scrimped on what she could. She hired someone to clean the house once a week from top to bottom, and the produce for the house was brought in by the cleaning lady from a distant market, where food was a bit cheaper. When yellow dates, red carrots, and citrus fruit were in season, she made jam, and sometimes she made cheese for us at home. There is a part of the sheep's stomach that we call the *manfaha*, the source of rennet. She would get the butcher to keep it aside for her, and we had a jar of it in the house from which she would make cheese in a straw basket with two handles that was hung up until the cheese drained. After the cheese hardened, it was cut up and put in the strainer where she'd sprinkle it with salt and cover it up until it was put away into jars.

My mother always kept making white cheese, and I still have her old cheesecloth. It hangs on the kitchen wall in my house. That is to say nothing of jellies, pickles, and cakes! We never wanted for anything, only it was all homemade. Take the marmalade rolls that she made and rolled in *santarafish* sugar (that's what we used to call granulated sugar, a corruption of the English "centrifuge" that was used to make it) and served to guests instead of store-bought sweets; to this day, in season, I always make my mother's marmalade and give away some of it as gifts. It's a tradition of mine now, part of my mother's heritage that I always want to keep alive and use in our household. My daughters call it "Grandma's jam."

The time to make tomato sauce was when the price of tomatoes dropped. Garlic and onions were also bought and stored when the price was low. I liked to help her make jam, especially date jam and marmalade. And we would peel dates and stuff them with almonds and cloves. I also helped her make red carrot jam, and she taught me how to wrap cloves in a piece of muslin to make the jam smell nice.

So many things I learned from my mother! So much that our household never buys store-bought jam. We make it all at home, and I give some of it to the girls for their own households, with their supply of onions and garlic and ghee and butter. There were the dry goods we laid in as provisions for the house—lentils, beans, bulgur, and Upper Egyptian *kishk* (which my mother used to make with a fried onion after soaking it in broth and adding a spoonful of yogurt). You know, this Egyptian cuisine is part of our heritage, which we must preserve. All this is a gift from our Upper Egyptian friends. To this day, the habit of laying in provisions is still in my blood: white cheese comes in from Mallawi in Upper Egypt; they make the best white cheese. Every January, we buy ghee and melt it down; my brother Ali sends us fava beans and rice, which he plants on the land we inherited from my father.

My mother would go to market every day to buy some of what we needed: vegetables, fruit, meat, chicken. Summer and winter clothes? Well, she learned to sew, and made summer dresses for me and Randa. As for winter clothing, we bought ours from medium-end stores. Everything, whether it was food or clothing, we bought on a budget.

I spent our days off school and Fridays with my mother in the kitchen, observing all the little things she did and helping her whenever I could. I think the experience she transferred to me through my constant watching gave me a PhD in home economics! She used to call me Zuzza; this is why I like my granddaughter, Thuraya Moussa, to call me Zuzza. Later, I taught her the nickname "Zuzza Kazouza" so she could bring together both my parents in one nickname.

I still remember all the little details my mother implanted in me about cooking that make a dish better or worse, and I still keep them up now when I'm advanced in years. Especially with stuffed peppers, which have to be small, and they all have to be the same size or they won't look nice on the plate! And you have to add a spoonful of vinegar to the stuffing. She always liked to give me the little details that make all the difference to a dish. Also, home management: from organizing closets, the fridge, and the cooker, to the general cleanliness of the house, and budgeting. My mother was an amazing woman.

I never cooked as a student, but my continual watching of my mother, and the quality and flavor of the food she produced, gave me a deep love for the kitchen. I felt it was a wonderful world of creativity, just like goldsmithing or silversmithing. I always said that the kitchen was my second option: if I hadn't been a silversmith, I would have liked to become a chef.

When my daughters Fatma and Amina talk about me in interviews with the press or on TV, they say, "We really don't know where our mother finds all this time! She makes everything homemade!" Another thing my dear mother taught me was darning socks. When my father was alive, my mother had a sewing box and she'd sew on my father's shirt buttons if they fell off. There was a wooden egg in it, as big as a mango, which she put inside the socks and then darned them if they had holes. The sewing box had a lovely design: a piece of furniture in a room of our house devoted to sewing. It had lots of drawers, with threads of different colors and thicknesses. (Of course, nobody darns socks nowadays. Everything gets thrown away and we buy new ones.)

My mother also learned dressmaking at this time. She bought a German magazine that was well known to all the women of that era, called *Burda*, founded in 1950. It had patterns inside. She used it to make my clothes, always choosing simple designs and Egyptian cotton in tasteful colors. A nice design was something I would like to have over and over in different colors.

I believe that my mother's experience came to me through keeping her company and watching her every day. This is why Helwan, I think, is associated in my mind with my mother, because the time we spent there was the time I was closest to her, listening to her lessons, and learning so much, whether directly or through observation. There are some things I saw her doing that I didn't register at the time, but years later I might find myself in a situation that made me remember my mother and understand why she did what she did. Oftentimes I do the same as she did, and I say the same things she said.

My image of my mother, to the end of her life, was that of a brilliant, impeccable housewife, protecting and sheltering her children like a lioness. She was supremely concerned with her household: everything clean and organized and a time and a place for everything. I remember when the poor dear collapsed at the end of her life with a stroke, and we took her to hospital where they took care of her. She had to spend a few days under observation. As we left the room that evening, my siblings and I, she tried to say something and gestured in agitation with her hands, saying something incomprehensible. About half an hour later, we realized she was telling us that she'd left the apricot jam out and we had to put it in the fridge or the ants would get at it. It was apricot season, so of course she had made jam.

I also learned something else important from her: not to allow my mood to interfere with my plans and not to let anything affect my workday. I'm blessed that I love my work, and I won't let anything stand in its way, it's true. We have a saying in the family that the girls and I get from our mother: when she was sick and got up to take medications to get better and start working, she would say, "Kids, I don't have time to get sick!" It's been passed down to my daughters, and they say it at the start of every winter, when they start taking Vitamin C and immunity boosters, "because we don't have time to get sick!" Then we all laugh and remember my late mother. Truly, as they say, "those who have children never die."

Never in my life have I seen a woman who suffered such a total transformation of her life without ever complaining as my mother. She shouldered the burden wonderfully, with courage and fortitude. She had a huge responsibility on her shoulders; she was aware that the reality could not be changed, and took on the task of organizing our new life according to the new situation, raising four children by herself. She did what she could with what she had, as the sudden death of her husband was something she had no choice about, but she accepted it without bitterness or complaint. I think the greatness of my mother lies in this. God rest her soul.

The image I have of my mother in my memory now is her at the end of her life, with her white hair plaited into two thin braids; sometimes my sister Randa and I would braid it into one, so she stopped cutting it. She always had a scarf tied around her head. Often on my way out the door, she would ask me, "What do you want for lunch?" She would put her hands together in prayer and bless me and wish me success.

Often, when I came home exhausted after all day rushing around, I used to go into my room and close the door and collapse on the bed fully clothed, trying to stem the flow of thoughts in my mind—as the Indians say, "the monkey jumping about inside my head"—I would hear the door gently opening and soft footfalls in the room, a hand patting my own and a gentle voice. "Zuzza, I made you a dish of *kishk*; I know you like it." I would open my eyes to see my mother, smiling, with a dish of *kishk* in her hand. She made it with lime and chicken pieces, with a quarter-loaf of pita bread and some salad next to it, which I'm fond of. I remember this story often. Would you believe it, to this day, lying in bed between sleeping and waking, especially at dawn, sometimes I hear the same soft footfalls in the room? Do souls really come back to the places where there are people they love? I remember two days after she died, I went to sleep on the bed she slept in when she came to visit. I missed her terribly. I awoke with a start at dawn: my mother was in front of me, smiling, but she was young, in her forties. So beautiful. She was wearing a lovely skirt suit; I loved the way it looked on her. Her hair was in its short cut. "Are you okay?" she asked me. I was shocked. I couldn't understand.

One time, the Lebanese journalist and poet and TV presenter Zahi Wahbi was hosting me as a guest on his famous program *Khallik bil-bayt*. When we were done recording, he made me a gift of his poetry collection and said to me, "I'd like it if you used one of the poems from it in your work." I read the book and selected a poem that captivated me: "My Mother, the Pinnacle of Women." He depicted his mother and described her calling down blessings upon him as he left the house. This was exactly the same as I remember with my own mother, and I ended up making a necklace bearing the poem. It's still in high demand and always a good seller. I'm very fond of it, and I always wear it and remember my darling mother.

> My mother who bid me goodbye in the morning
> With a modest braid and hands uplifted in prayer
> Accompanied me to the door. "Come home soon," she said.
> The windmill of laughter, my mother;
> The fountain; the first spring;
> The pinnacle of women.

Unfortunately, I discovered my love for my father and mother too late. I never understood what made them tick, their experiences that they had shared with me, until I was older. That was when I appreciated the value of all this in my life, and the traces they left in me. Sadly, we only seem to appreciate this when we're older.

Now, whenever I feel a heavy weight on my chest or a discomfort in any situation, I sigh, "Oh, Father; oh, Mother." One of the ways in which I feel I've become like my mother is in the deferred dreams: clothes, expensive shoes, bags—all these are dreams I erased from my life for long years. But now I bring them back and try to buy what I want—within reason, of course.

You know, after I got a government job, I sometimes darned nylon stockings. And there was a cobbler in Bab al-Louq, next to the stairs of the station, who fixed the heels of shoes when they wore out. At day's end, after college, I took my shoes to him to fix. I would wait by his side on a stool until he had repaired the heels. I had a limited budget, which allowed for, among other things, two pairs of nylons a month. We had to darn them. And there were little shops that darned socks at that time, like the shops that repair clothing now. Truth be told, I don't know what's become of them.

Our apartment had three bedrooms, a hall, a big kitchen, and three balconies giving onto Riad Pasha Street in eastern Helwan. The house was close to the Japanese Garden, which was called Kushk al-Hayah (the kiosk of life). It was a public garden designed and built in 1917 by Egyptian architect Dhul Fiqar Pasha, and one of the famous places to visit in Helwan. We were only one street away from my grandfather's house on Gaafar Street, which led up to the hills and was surrounded by empty land, with the Helwan Observatory and the Behman Psychiatric Hospital at the end of it. The latter was built in the English style in red brick with a sloping roof, surrounded by lots of gardens and trees. Often, on Fridays, we would get together with the girls in the family and their friends and, in a big group, get on our bikes and ride up to the Helwan Observatory on the hilltop.

My grandfather's home was a big apartment on the second floor, with five rooms, part of a large square of stone-built buildings with a courtyard in the middle, in the colonial style. This block was called the Aqairib Mansions, after the wealthy Jewish owner; I heard that his daughter Lucy had married a French Jewish diamond dealer and left with him for Paris.

I loved that apartment, and the neighbors, who were very close with my mother, just like family. Auntie Hekmat and Auntie Ragaa used to watch out for each other. The neighbors on the floor below my grandfather's apartment were Jewish, Madame Faber and her son Willy. I remember we used to play with them. They had to emigrate to France after things changed for the Jews in Egypt after the Tripartite Aggression of 1956. Many of them had to leave Egypt. About fifteen years later, Willy came back to pay the house a visit and take photos for his mother, because she missed the house she had lived in. We found out that they had later moved on to Israel from France.

Two more of my grandfather's neighbors were Madame Mary and Madame Sasha, from White Russia. They had the most wonderful crocheted curtains with angels, flowers, and deer worked into them, which they had made themselves. They emigrated as well—I don't know where to—and sold their furniture. I wished I could have bought those crocheted curtains, but unfortunately I couldn't afford them. Sometimes my Aunt Safiya used to take me and my cousin Nadia to the house of Madame Mary and Madame Sasha for tea. They made very good biscuits and cakes, and their house was in such good taste, so charming and intimate. They reminded me of the ladies in the Russian films adapted from Chekhov and Tolstoy. Our friends and acquaintances also included the Azzams, the family of Abdulrahman Pasha Azzam, who wrote the Arab League Charter.

Helwan Society was family-oriented and close-knit. All the families knew one another. There were many large social clubs: the Cement Workers' Club, the Silk Company Club, and so on. The clubs weren't just exclusive to the company workers. There was a social network of families that provided company and a wonderful life for the people who lived in this pretty and peaceful suburb. My latest visit to Helwan was at the funeral of the last of my aunts, my Aunt Safiya. My heart broke for the town and its cherished memories in my life. How did it come down to this? What a shame.

It's well known that Helwan flourished when it was turned into an international winter resort, starting in the reign of Khedive Tewfik (1879–92). He built a beautiful palace there where he used to live on occasion; and he had royal holdings there, where the ministers would meet. The palace was named Tewfik's Hotel, and it was later converted into a vocational school.

Helwan was full of large and medium-sized hotels. The Glanz Hotel directly faced our house, taking up half a block; there was also the Evergreen Hotel and the Hotel des Princes, and the large and medium-sized families of Cairo would come to spend part of the winter in Helwan to bathe in the healing sulfur springs.

The Glanz used to hold grand balls in its large colonial-style garden. It would be all lit up, and the strains of classical music played by an ensemble wafted up to us, never overpoweringly loud or annoying. I would sit on our square balcony that my mother had designated as her garden, full of roses and jasmine—at night there was a gentle breeze bearing the scents of all these flowers—and listen to music and look at the elegantly dressed men and women getting out of their cars on their way to one ball or another.

At that time, the ladies of Helwan used to agree on a day to get together at someone's house for tea, where they would listen to someone playing the piano. Or they would go down to Cairo—the downtown area now—and sit at Groppi's, or organize any other social activity. They were always dressed to the nines. My oldest aunt, Farah, was always going out with her lady friends, smart as could be: a fur coat, nice jewelry, and hair styled in the fashion of the 1950s and 1960s. There was Auntie Aida Shaker—a great beauty—who had a son, Muqbel Shaker, the head of the Court of Cassation and the Supreme Judicial Council. There were Auntie Rabi'a and Camilla Zein al-Abidin, who used to attend the famous Umm Kulthum concerts and have reserved seats in the front row, right in front of The Lady herself. These were the monthly activities of the ladies of Helwan. Oftentimes, too, when they couldn't attend the concert in person, they would get together at one of their homes on Thursday nights, when Umm Kulthum sang, to listen to it on the radio, with dinner and peanuts and pumpkin seeds and all sorts of things. Winter in Helwan was something else.

In eastern Helwan, one of the people who wintered there was the famous writer Tawfiq al-Hakim. His son Ismail, who died young, used to rehearse with his band The Black Coats in a house not far from ours. You could hear them at a distance, music that was different from the music we were familiar with at the time. The poet Bayram al-Tunsi also moved to Helwan at the end of his life, and it is said that Hafez Ibrahim, the so-called "Poet of the Nile," spent his early childhood in Helwan.

Among the houses I can't forget, which are stuck in my memory, was the house of "Barsouma the Bonesetter," which housed Dr. Rushdy Barsoum, the orthopedist, and Dr. Abdou Barsoum, the dentist. It was a big house with a wooden staircase. They lived there, but their clinic was in Faggala. We were always told that the family had a magical compound, a poultice that they put on injuries. I remember once that I fell and dislocated my elbow; they brought in someone from Dr. Barsoum's clinic, who put it back in place and put the poultice on it and bandaged it up. Just putting the elbow back into place made me pass out.

The Barsoums were a Christian family with another big house in Maasara, next to a monastery where there was a *moulid*—that is, a saint's birthday celebration—every year. It was called Moulid al-Erian, and they slaughtered sheep and cattle and gave the meat to poor families, both Muslim and Christian. On the fringe of the *moulid*, there was a circus. We loved to go there every year. I remember every detail: a gigantic tent, a shooting gallery with pellet guns that we'd aim at little explosive packets set up on the wall, and the iron weight that ran on twin tracks for the young guys with muscles to run along the tracks and try to ring the bell. This reminds me of the wonderful work *al-Leila al-Kibira* (The big night, referring to the Prophet's birthday celebrations) by Salah Jahin and Sayed Mikkawi, with puppets by Nagi Shaker, which was put on at the Puppet Theater, and especially the song "I'm the movie hero with the handlebar mustache!" Our favorite thing was the guy who rode a motorcycle around a huge vertical ring! Delightful childhood memories. Nobody in those days said, "This person is a Christian, and this one is a Muslim; and who gave the Christians the right to hold a celebration and give out meat to the poor?"

Another house I can't forget was the house of Abu Gabal, which was opposite our house, to the left, on the side facing Hotel Glanz. This was a big house too, also taking up half a block. It had a high wall that hid it from view; the only way you could see inside was through a big iron gate worked with beautiful ornamentation. As I passed, I could see through the wrought-iron gate that there was a beautiful garden around the house. I still remember that all the plants were cacti, a range of them in all sorts of shapes and sizes. It was a rare cactus garden, said to be one of the largest collections of cacti in Egypt after the Muhammad Ali Palace in Manial. (Of course, I don't know whether this was true.) They said, too, that Abu Gabal had a coffee tree and a cocoa tree in there as well. I never saw anyone go in or out of the house. It was abandoned, but the garden was always well tended and clean. The cacti were arranged in marvelous patterns, manicured like the hands of a well-groomed lady. This house, in my mind, was the Mystery House—that's what I used to call it. Something out of a Hitchcock movie.

My lifelong friend, Ibtisam al-Ansari (the daughter of Safiya al-Ansari, representative of the district of Maadi at the State Council) lived at the other end of Gaafar Street. Ibtisam told me a very touching story about the Abu Gabal house. She said that every morning on her way to school with her classmates, when she passed the Abu Gabal house, they would meet an old man, light-skinned and plump, standing outside the house, holding a bouquet of flowers. He would approach the sidewalk where they passed, select a flower from the bunch, and hand it to her. Sometimes he would give her a bunch of pansies he had picked from the garden. She never found out who he was, or who tended this great big garden so carefully, or who lived in this opulent house, built in the style Helwan had become famous for. The story always reminds me of an Italian neorealist black-and-white movie. Later, I heard that the Abu Gabal house had been sold, and I never did find out what happened to the magnificent collection of cacti.

My friend Magda al-Gindi, the prominent reporter at *al-Ahram*, and wife of the great writer Gamal al-Ghitani, lived in Helwan. She told me the same story about the old man who stood there giving out flowers to little girls. Helwan used to be cosmopolitan, bringing together different cultures and classes and nationalities. Egyptians, both Muslim and Christian; families from White Russia and Yugoslavia; Armenians, Greeks, and Jews; we all spoke one language, Egyptian Arabic, and we all went to the same schools.

There were foreign schools in Helwan as well, such as the Sainte Famille School, run by nuns, with a convent in front of it. My friends who went to that school told me that it had its own church for the Christian students to pray in, and a special place for ablutions and prayer for the Muslim students, with wooden closets next to them stocked with necessities such as prayer rugs and other items. There was a boarding school as part of it; a close friend tells me that as a child, she had chest allergies and asthma, and Dr. Nabawi Muhandes advised her mother to spend the entire winter in Helwan, but since the family didn't live in Helwan, the mother sent her four-year-old daughter to boarding school there, which was a paragon of cleanliness and care. It's interesting that the children's bathroom and its cleanliness were overseen by the nuns themselves, but the girls would keep their undershorts on while they showered!

The convent facing it had a dispensary for treating eye and skin infections under the nuns' supervision. Many low-income folks took their children there to be treated for conjunctivitis, which was widespread, and something called prickly heat, which people got in the hot season and the flooding of the Nile, and showed up as little red spots on the neck and chest. When we got prickly heat, my mother would put talcum powder on it. Most low-income people in Helwan were Muslims, but they went to the convent for treatment.

There's a well-known story that the older residents of Helwan always exchanged about Mounir Lesha, the son of Lesha, a Jewish man, and brother to Esther and Farida, the latter named Farida by her father after the queen of Egypt at that time. Mounir was educated at the Helwan schools and was raised with the children of Helwan. He made many friends there. However, toward the end of the 1950s, when the Jews left Egypt for Europe, he emigrated to Israel, not being rich enough to go, as other Jewish families had done, to Europe or Los Angeles.

Then came the 1967 war with Israel. In a cruel drama, the young Mounir Lesha, now a reserve officer in the Israeli army, came face-to-face on the battlefield with his professor Fayeq al-Mughazi, the physical education teacher at Salah Salem Secondary School for Boys, from which he had been called up as a reserve officer in the Egyptian army. The wonderful thing is that Mounir Lesha was overcome by his love for the country where he had been born and raised; he did a touching thing that became a byword for the folk of Helwan afterward, namely, he led Mr. Fayeq and his group to a safe passage back to the towns on the Suez Canal.

Helwan was a big family; everyone knew everyone else. Girls and boys would walk to school together without discrimination; the clubs of the major companies welcomed not just the families of those who worked there, but all the families of Helwan, to play sports and games without any restrictions—no one said "But she's a girl!" or "But he's a boy!" It was a society without sectarianism. We all went out biking with Auntie Safiya, the youngest of my aunts, to the Helwan Spring at night, especially on moonlit nights, with empty bottles to fill up with the sulfurous waters of the spring. And we would drink the water there too, which smelled awful (though they said it was very good for you!). It was a pleasant ride down Ain Helwan Street to the spring. It wasn't busy, the breeze was pleasant, and there were no crowds. It was a long street, lit only by the moonlight. Many times we would burst into song and raise our voices, singing all together.

What I learned about Helwan from the book *Helwan: Its Nature, History and Landmarks* (by Ahmad Fayzallah Othman, 2019) is that the sulfurous springs were an ancient discovery, used back when the plague was spreading in al-Fustat, after the Arabs came to Egypt in the time of Amr ibn al-Aas, as a place for healing. And later, Khedive Abbas Hilmi I rediscovered the sulfurous springs, which helped cure his solders of an outbreak of scabies, which had become widespread in the army.

There were two summer cinemas in Helwan: Cinema Faten and Cinema al-Casino. We used to go when something good was playing, and eat soft pretzels called *simit*, *duqqa* (a mixture of salt, pepper, thyme, and cumin), and Turkish cheese. The famous wax museum was also in Helwan; it was the first wax museum in Egypt.

Helwan was mostly one-story houses with high walls: the architecture was distinctive, the houses all one color, a creamy white, with small gardens. The privet trees gave off a delightful perfume in spring and summer. Guava trees were also planted in a lot of homes.

Helwan was divided into west and east. The streets were always named after historical figures and the important men and families who'd lived there. Take Mansour Street, the main thoroughfare: it was named after Mansour Pasha, the husband of Princess Tawhida, Khedive Ismail's eldest daughter. The street parallel to Mansour was named for Haidar Pasha Yakan, Muhammad Ali's eldest nephew. Mustafa Pasha Fahmy Street was named after Safiya Zaghloul's father, who was prime minister in the era of Khedive Tawfik. Sheikh Baqouri also lived in Helwan; he was the minister of religious endowments during the Nasser era. The families of Sheikh Deraz and Sheikh Maraghi were in the western side of Helwan, next to my grandmother Aisha Hanem's house.

Sheikh Sanhouri, the famous Qur'an reciter with the mellifluous voice, used to winter in Helwan with his family; Yakan Pasha's family, as well, lived behind my grandfather's house. Our house overlooked some of their balconies. Shushu Yakan and Angie Yakan were the nieces of Adli Yakan (1864–1933), who served three times as prime minister of Egypt. He was a true leader and patriotic politician of Albanian Turkish origin, who took part in signing what was called the National Charter. Directly opposite us on the left lived Prime Minister Ibrahim Abdel Hadi Pasha and his daughter. A while later, he moved downtown, but his daughter lived in Helwan until the end of her life, and she remained a friend of the family.

My grandmother, Aisha Hanem Hafez, always told us that Khedive Ismail paid all the attention he could to Helwan, especially the sulfurous waters, encouraged people to move there, and gave out plots of land as gifts to Muhammad Ali's family, the high-ranking classes, foreigners, and regular folk, on condition that they develop them. He issued a decree in 1870 founding the Helwan Railway to connect the suburb of Helwan with Cairo, and it was officially opened in 1877 (this was later developed into the Helwan Metro). Among the people Khedive Ismail gave lands to in the Helwan area was his mother, Khushyar Hanem (also known as al-Walda Basha). She was behind the idea of founding the Rifa'i Mosque, facing the Sultan Hassan Mosque below the Citadel, as a burial ground for Muhammad Ali's family. Ismail gave her an entire estate, which he called The Mother's Estate. We always passed by it driving to Helwan; there was a shortcut from the Nile Corniche to Helwan that passed by the estate.

We scheduled everything by the famous Helwan Metro. Our daily question was, "Are you taking the 8:15 or the 8:30?" The Metro was dead on time, super punctual. It was the lifeline of the people of Helwan. They structured their lives around it. And the last train from Cairo on Thursday night, from Bab al-Louq to Helwan, left at precisely 12:20 after midnight, and on it you'd find the smartest-dressed folk from Helwan and Maadi in their three-piece suits and their evening gowns on their way back from the last concert or showing in the opera and cinemas.

At home, we used to watch the television that our mother bought us on instalment. We were the first family in our building to buy a television. It was extremely bulky, surrounded by a big wooden sideboard.

The television programs at the end of the 1960s were very exciting. The announcers—like Leila Rustum, Amani Nashed, and Salwa Higazi—were highly educated. There wasn't anything flashy or over the top. Everything was

The Bab al-Louq train, Helwan, 1953.

unfussy and their make-up was subtle. Leila Rustum interviewed superstars of literature and culture such as Taha Hussein, Abdel Rahman al-Sharqawi, Abbas al-Aqqad, and the Brothers Rahbani and Fairuz. The conversations were sober, intimate, and eye-opening for me on a lot of subjects.

There was also announcer and poet Farouk Shousha, and there were programs on poetry and literature. There was Hamdy Qandil, who hosted a nature program called *Animal World;* Mahmoud Sultan; Dr. Hamed Gohar's *Sea World.* I remember all of this now when I see the new channel devoted to golden oldies, Maspero Zaman, which fills me with nostalgia for that era.

The Faculty of Fine Arts

I was never the super-smart girl. I was always average. I hated math and algebra and had zero understanding of anything to do with numbers. Up until I was forty, I used to have nightmares of being in an algebra exam, and I'd wake up in a cold sweat. I finished my secondary school certificate with a middling score and applied to the Faculty of Fine Arts because my uncle Mustafa Fahmy, my father's cousin, was a graduate and convinced me to join. I had never had any outstanding artistic talent; I was an average draftswoman, with, again, middling performance in art class. I took classes to improve my skills, which come before the aptitude test for the college; then I passed the exam and was accepted. At first, I went into the preparatory year, which everyone takes before choosing a field of specialization.

The first day I set off for the college, I had found out who was with me from Helwan and who from Maadi—they had been with me in the entrance and aptitude exams—and we had agreed on a time to meet, and all took the Metro. We got out at Bab al-Louq, and took the trolley-bus (a big bus with an electric connection that was an important means of transportation in the 1960s) from Falaki Square, hoping to get to Zamalek, but then it stopped at the end of the line, and we found ourselves in Ataba. We got out and suddenly I was overcome by a fit of crying. I was terrified. "We're lost!" I sobbed to the girls. "We're lost!"

"Azza," the others calmed me down. "Is it even possible to be lost in the middle of Ataba Square?"

The girls took action, asking around about another means of transportation, and we got on another bus to Zamalek, where the Faculty is situated. I always associate my first day of classes with getting lost in Ataba.

Long years later, I remembered this silly story on a trip to Nepal, where I had traveled alone to see the state of jewelry making in the region north of India. How had I changed so much from a naive girl with no experience in anything to a person who goes all the way around the world after the vocation her heart has chosen, to enrich her thinking and her cultural and technical storehouse with the different adornments worn by the peoples of the world?

In the Faculty of Fine Arts, I chose the Department of Design. Back then it was called the Department of Furniture and Interior Decoration. My professors were all great artists: the well-known sculptors Gamal al-Sigini, Salah Abdel Karim, Abdel Salam al-Sherif, and Hanna Simayka, who taught us art history. All of them were illustrious professors with prestigious names, who had left their imprint on the world of art and art history. Gamal al-Sigini, the great sculptor, cycled to the Faculty from his home. The world was simpler then. Dr. Shehab, the dean of the Architecture Department at the Faculty, also cycled to work. I was the hardworking girl who did all that was asked of her, but no exceptional artistic aptitude jumped out of me during my college years. I graduated in 1965 with a general grade of Very Good; truth be told, I don't even remember what my graduation project was.

At that time, all college graduates were employed by the government via the Workforce Office. I was appointed to the General Information Authority, a branch of the Ministry of Information, with offices downtown. My job was to design the political pamphlets that the Ministry put out. This was a very important period in Egypt politically, and the director of the Authority was Dr. Muhammad Hassan al-Zayyat, who asked us to create pamphlets explaining Egypt's situation vis-à-vis Israel. I remember the pamphlets were

Me (far left), with my friends at the Faculty of Fine Arts, Zamalek, Cairo, 1962.

of a gigantic Egyptian soldier crushing a tiny, feeble Israeli soldier underfoot. We prepared other pamphlets about education and health, and about the Revolution's new plans to bring about progress in the country.

I believe I was always hardworking and responsible as an employee, doing what was required of me down to the last detail, and carrying out what was requested with all the skill I had. I like to think I was one of the hardworking employees that they felt they could rely on. But—and what a but!—did Azza Fahmy like her job? I always felt that there was something missing in my relationship with my work, something I couldn't put my finger on. I did my work well, and I took responsibility for everything they had me do; but this gave my heart no joy. This wasn't what I loved; it wasn't what I wanted to spend the rest of my life doing. Somehow, somewhere in the world, I knew there must be something else. Perhaps it was waiting for me, out there; and for sure it would suit me better than what I was doing then. I decided to look for it.

"Don't accept a life where you feel there is none"
—Shams al-Tabrizi

2
AMONG THE CRAFTSMEN

The Beginning

You know, the craft I chose to follow didn't just fall onto my head out of the sky. I set out looking for it, and it took a long while of serious searching until I found it. Two years passed as I tried to find out what I would really like to spend the rest of my life doing. I thought I'd try out things I felt I cared about and see if I liked them and how invested I was in them once I started doing them. This is what my simple thinking told me to do. I'd like to tell you how the story started.

All my attempts to change my profession over those two years never worked out. I tried different things: first it was designing children's books, because I liked children and I thought that was enough to make me a successful children's book designer. Maybe it was naive of me, but I took it seriously back then. My dear friend, the late great Ihab Shaker, used to illustrate children's books with his wife—the dear friend and skilled writer Samira Shafiq—which became famous throughout the Arab world, and especially in Egypt. One day I was sitting with them, discussing my difficulty finding something I liked. Ihab and Samira, enthused, convinced me to take a course that was being held by the Ministry of Culture back then about writing for children, to make me more aware of child psychology. Ihab thought we might be able to work together on children's book collections. "Take the course," he said, "and then try out drawing and illustrating books, and I'll give you something to try."

I took it very seriously for a month and a half. I finished the course, and Ihab gave me a short children's story to try out my skills. With zest, I worked on it, and came back to him a while later with my concept.

Honestly, I still blush when I remember Ihab's face upon seeing the result. It was some kind of sub-zero result. Of course, I understood, without him having to tell me, that this job wasn't meant for me. He set the papers aside without a word. As for me, I threw all I'd worked on into the trash.

I closed this page forever and turned over a new leaf with my friend Evelyne Porret, a Swiss ceramicist who had come to live in Egypt and fallen in love with it. She married a famous Egyptian poet, Sayed Higab, and when they separated, she decided not to return to Europe, and became one of the major ceramic artists in Egypt. She lived in the village of Tunis in Fayoum, chose a plot of land on which to build a house, and decided to spend the rest of her life in this village and this country that she had fallen in love with. She opened a pottery school there, and taught a great many people from the village, and Tunis is now an important destination for anyone wanting to view the state of ceramic arts in Egypt. It is a village with a special artistic nature, where a great many writers, artists, journalists, and intellectuals have chosen to have homes built in beautiful traditional forms. Some of them live there permanently, while others vacation there. This village developed into what it is now all because of Evelyne. Evelyne's experience in Fayoum could be a role model and an opportunity for a wonderful study on how to develop a craft and preserve it at the same time.

But back to me and Evelyne. To find out if this was what I wanted to do, I decided to try it out. When I decided to work in ceramics, I started with a few simple lessons with Evelyne; but after just a bit, I decided to close that door for good. Unfortunately, I got bored easily, and I wasn't fond of what I was doing. This issue of getting bored was the litmus test by which I knew if something was for me.

I kept trying—some of this, some of that. I was still working at the Ministry of Information, in the era of President Nasser. The big art books available, and references on art in general, were very scarce. The state at that time concentrated on importing only "essential goods" for the people. That type of book was considered a luxury.

Still, I must mention here, with admiration and pride, the role of the culture, translation, literature, and publishing movement at that time, because it was a great and very good effort. In different fields, it played a part in shaping the personality of an entire generation. The *Alf Kitab* (Thousand Books) series, for instance, which we bought for one pound each, I recall, and the *Iqra'* (Read) series; also, there was a focus on theater, music, reference books, and translation. There was a great leap forward, an effective one, during the time of the enlightened army officer Tharwat Okasha, the minister of culture. The big art books and references that required high-quality color printing were unavailable on the market; what was available could only be bought from the Sharq Bookstore downtown, which specialized in subsidized books from the Soviet Union, which were very cheap.

That bookstore, with the subsidized Soviet books, played a huge role in cultivating an entire generation. I read Dostoyevsky, Chekov, Tolstoy, Gorky, and Gogol, the greats of Russian literature forming an important part of my education and the culture of an entire generation at the time. I remember at that time that my love for ballet led me to buy a book about the Bolshoi Ballet, with its famous school: it contained incredible photographs of ballerinas like Galina Ulanova and Maya Plisetskaya, the stars of the Bolshoi production of *Swan Lake*. Unbelievable—like butterflies on the wing. Can you imagine that I saw the legendary Galina Ulanova *in the flesh* dancing at the old Khedival Opera House downtown before it burned down? I watched *Swan Lake* from the highest perch in the balcony for 25 piasters.

Then the fatal moment came. It really was life-changing, because it was a watershed in my life. The First International Cairo Book Fair was announced. The year was 1969. The fair was held at the International Exhibition Grounds, which at the time were located where the new Cairo Opera House is now. It was a huge cultural event for all of us. We were going to see art books imported from abroad!

I and a group of friends from work were keen to look at the books on display by foreign publishers. What I cared about were the art books from Europe, England, and America. I went to the exhibition with my friends Fatma Barrada and the late Soheir Eisa, of the Translation Department. The German stand was one of the places showing foreign art books. I can still remember the tiniest details of the moment that made my life do a 180-degree transformation.

I was looking for art books, not literature. I came to a shelf with large books on it in the German Pavilion. Imagine, to this day, I remember how the pavilion looked and how the books were displayed there. There was this shelf I went to without a second thought. I reached for a particular book and pulled it out. I swear, I don't know why that book exactly and not any other. Was it the one I was meant to find? I pulled it out and read the title, which I couldn't understand as it was in German. I opened the book and my eyes fell on a piece of jewelry: a pair of earrings made in silver, shaped like an animal, a donkey. It was created with a granulation technique. I leafed through the book—not, of course, able to read a word—which was full of photographs of silver jewelry of the Middle Ages.

I can't describe to you what I felt at that moment. The top of my head became prickly all over with pins and needles, like the blood was rushing to my head. A light came on in my brain and my heart beat faster. I said to myself at once, "This is what I want. This is what I've been looking for." I think this is the moment that they call insight because the heart, too, can see.

Jewelry, ornaments—how had I never thought of them before? How had it never occurred to me that what I was looking for was jewelry making and design? How had this happened all of a sudden? I really don't know. I think there may be moments in the life of every human being when one is in a place that has no connection to the earth we walk on, moments with a divine calling, a spiritual condition. Moments when it isn't your mind that thinks, but when the decision comes from the heart. The heart sees its desire, the thing that owns it from then on. I had to answer the call. I was overcome by an overpowering feeling coming from my heart, telling me, "This is the way." The siren had summoned me.

I want to add something important here: these turning points in life are something we need to be alert to. We need to be aware of what's happening to us. When the strong and clear call comes, leap up high. Grab onto it and hang on tight. This is your chance in life. Don't ever let it slip away. These are times that don't happen often in people's lives, and only the lucky ever get that chance.

Don't ever think the little things we do, the little decisions we take, are insignificant. Sometimes a decision that seems small to others can change a person's life. Take my decision to buy that book. Who could have said that this book would change my life? And not just my own life, but the lives of my daughters and their future? For it was the casement through which the light burst in, my guiding light. It opened up so many doors of light for us as a family, filled with joy and the enthusiasm for a vocation that we all fell in love with—through our work, we accepted great challenges to develop a traditional Egyptian craft that was all but extinct.

Back then, I had family obligations. I was helping my mother with the monthly expenses. By nature, I'm a planner. I budget everything, especially daily and monthly expenditures, and even more so back then, because I didn't have much. But buying that book—ah, that was the exception. Back then, that book cost seventeen Egyptian pounds, and my entire salary was nineteen pounds and seventy-five piasters. The decision to buy it was rash, impulsive in the extreme. It had nothing to do with any logical calculations. But it was a clear decision to make, without a second's hesitation: I am buying this book. I had a strong and sure conviction that this was what would bring me together with what I wanted.

A bold and rash decision! But my feelings and my mind said that it was the right thing to do. I was confident and sure, and I bought the book—the book I found by pure chance—although I have a deep conviction now that there is no such thing as coincidence. Everything happens for a reason, and there are signs. The more time passes, the more I believe in this, especially after taking up and reading about spirituality and meditation. I was able to interpret what happened in this providential moment: God helped me and lit up my path. I was seriously and faithfully looking for the thing I wanted to do with love. I was in a continuous process of searching and seeking until God sent me a sign to guide me. I felt an intuitive flash when my eyes fell on the book, and I now believe that I didn't see that book by chance, but that it was cast into my path by Fate to map out a path in life that I was fated to tread. As the Prophet Muhammad—peace be upon Him—says, "Each of us finds ease in what they are made for."

That book is the dearest book to me in my whole life, the most important book in my library. It's always in front of me, and I take great care of it. It's a constant reminder of the moment that turned my life around. From that moment on, I took my first steps on my journey, and started a love affair, an affair of understanding, a relationship that has never ended since. I pray to God that I can keep giving and growing and working until my last breath.

Jewelry making was a profession that fell on me from the sky in a providential moment, which I think was calculated for maximum benefit to me by a higher power. I consider myself a very lucky person to work in a job I adore. Maybe "adore" isn't a strong enough word to express how I feel. But there isn't a word for this love and this relationship. It is love, it is adoration, and it is like the love between a man and a woman but in another form—an addiction that you can't understand. I don't think a day has passed in my life that I haven't done something for my work: considering an idea, reading poetry or proverbs, designing, finding inspirations as I'm walking, conceiving of a new project. Now, after all the years of accumulated experience, this profession has taken on a new and broader curve, which is development, training, and education.

My relationship with my profession is passionate. I looked seriously for it for a long time until I found it, practiced it, worked at it, and helped develop it. At every stage, there were difficulties and mistakes, and lessons learned on every level. It's a perfect love affair. It occupies the center of my life, right after my daughters Fatma and Amina. I feel that the profession of goldsmith, with its every detail, runs in my veins. If you cut my veins open, rings and bracelets would probably come pouring out! It's something greater than anything in this world, a real vocation for me, a serious one. How can a little piece of metal, whether gold, silver, or brass, something you wear in your ears or on your fingers, or wrap around your neck—a product that's unimportant or inconsequential to most people, or a luxury at best—how did it come to turn my life around this way? How did it change me so much? I always feel, after I've finished a good collection or a beautiful piece, that I did something patriotic for my country!

I'm a strange personality. I'm a traditional person—a Helwanite, as my friends call me. I'm very sober and reserved in my social activities, because of my upbringing. But when it comes to my job, I'm the complete opposite. Sometimes I have moments approaching madness, or at least foolhardiness, when I break with tradition. I feel an idea come to me that's powerful and rebellious; after thinking and becoming convinced of it, I go in search of what will fulfil my feeling and make my idea a reality. Nothing can keep me from it, not if the world turns upside-down. And my love for my profession and the identity I have created over all these years is a boundary for me that no one can violate. I will defend it with everything I have, and nobody in the world can destroy it. It may be just a piece of metal, but the love and attention you pour into it as you make it lifts this piece to another dimension—the more devotion you give it, the more beauty and art it gives back; it returns your devotion. I want to admit right now that every piece I have made in my life is one whose idea I completely believe in, and which I made with great love, even my old pieces that I sometimes feel are a bit green or primitive from the artistic point of view of design and execution—truly, I see something in them even now that I don't know what to call, but it's something that gives them a special kind of beauty.

The truth is, my overwhelming interest in this profession has had an effect on my personality. It has reflected on my life's journey in general, lifting me up onto another plane, and developing me over time to achieve bigger and bigger things, things that aren't mine alone, but belong to a whole country, because my relationship with jewelry and my understanding of it and learning the skills of everything to do with it have expanded my sense of responsibility toward the artisanal tradition of my country as a whole. The long career I've engaged in with love and patience, careful to keep learning and understanding and developing, has changed me as a person and driven me to see my profession in new ways; part of this is protectiveness and unhappiness over my national heritage, which is being lost without being recorded or developed, and another part of this is my ability to contribute to developing this heritage and transforming it into something artistically new, now that I actually do understand these matters of heritage and craftsmanship and training to a great extent. By the way, I never attended any formal schools or institutions to learn the craft; I taught myself.

Later on, after twenty years of collecting material, this drove me to record everything I had seen and experienced in an important book on Egypt's stunning jewelry. This book is currently the only reference on Egyptian jewelry in the past hundred years, most of which has slipped through our fingers, sadly, as we stood watching.

That reminds me of my friend, the artist Helmi al-Touni. When he attended the opening of an important exhibition of mine—I think it was the ancient Egyptian collection—he wrote me a letter I still keep. In it, he wrote things that made me understand, and interpret the feeling behind an Azza

86　AMONG THE CRAFTSMEN

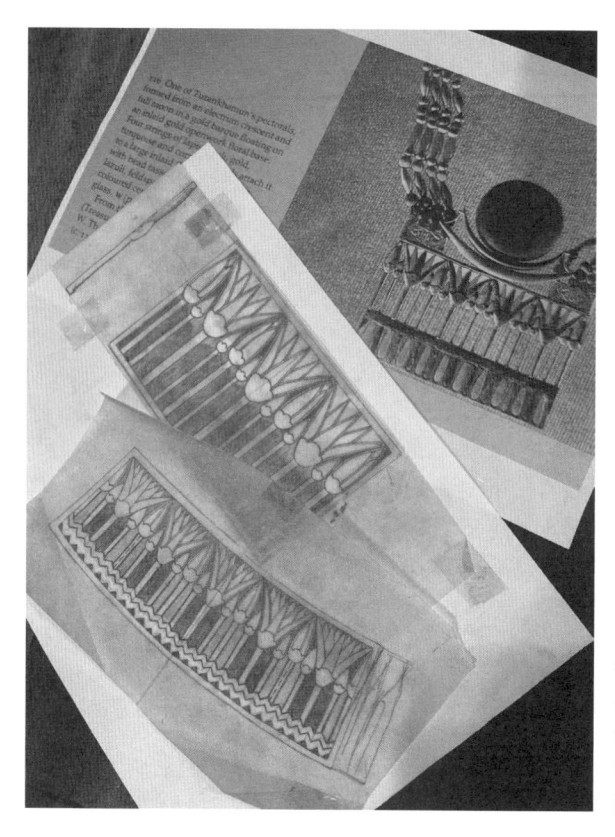

The inspiration and sketch for the lotus flower incorporated in one of my recent pieces.

Fahmy piece, and what people get out of it when they see it. It was about a meeting and discussion that he had had with the great Palestinian poet Mahmoud Darwish about social commitment in the lives of intellectuals or artists. Darwish believed that a true intellectual—an unpretentious intellectual—will manifest this in their work naturally. He believed that a person's true love for their country comes out in their work, even if it's just a doodle of a bird. The bird, he said, indicates one's country—a patriotic bird! According to Darwish, this is because it reflects the soul of the person who drew it. And this is where the value of an Azza Fahmy piece lies—art to wear with a patriotic spirit. Each piece carries all the love that lies within her psyche for her homeland.

　　This little piece of metal, which everyone wears, I now know how to make well. I can conceive of it, fill it with content, design it, and execute it technically. A large part of myself goes into it: my heart, my knowledge, and all my experience; my readings; my culture; and my pride and love for my country.

I'll tell you how I figured it in my head: I'd been to an art college where I spent five years learning how to design and draw, and yet I could see from the first moment that what I was missing was the know-how of the craft. I wanted to make jewelry myself. I knew how to design it, but I needed to be able to execute the designs I drew. I wanted to work with my own hands. At the time, middle-class and upper-middle-class families who wanted to get a piece of jewelry made, or who had a gemstone or cabochon they wanted made into a piece, would go to the family jeweler and ask them to make the design they desired. But I wanted to draw and design *and* make what I designed. There's a great difference. An artist's feel for their raw material and how to deal with it and understand its possibilities is completely different from getting someone else to carry out their design.

I decided to pay a visit to the Department of Jewelry and Metallurgy at the College of Applied Arts. I had the option to enroll in the college and

The Sagha, or silversmiths' and goldsmiths' district, in the 1950s.

study for another four years to learn jewelry making, winding up with a BA in metallurgy. But when I visited the college, I decided against it. Instead, I had an idea, a simple solution in which I was guided by my practical thinking. I was already an artist by training. I had studied design and draftsmanship for five years at the Faculty of Fine Arts. All that was missing was practice at the craft, learning how to deal with the raw material, and familiarizing myself with the technique. I thought about it and said to myself: "If you want to be a carpenter, you go become a carpenter's apprentice. If you want to be a blacksmith, you go learn the trade from a blacksmith. Simple! I'll be a silversmith's apprentice! I'll go to learn the craft at the Sagha—the goldsmiths' and silversmiths' center—in Khan al-Khalili, the famous artisanal district in Historic Cairo, where almost all the jewelry makers are headquartered." And then one time, chatting with my friend Sara al-Mougi about not knowing how to find a workshop to learn the basics of goldsmithing—since I wasn't familiar enough with that district—she responded at once, "I know a silversmith there. I'll ask him if he would agree to teach you the trade."

A short while later, she told me he'd said yes, he was okay to have me in his workshop and teach me the trade. His name was Usta Ramadan and he had a small silversmith's shop. I decided to start.

My first day at Khan al-Khalili, following the directions Sara had given me to get to Rab' al-Suramatiya (Cobblers' square) in Suramatiya Street in the Khan, parallel to Sagha Street, I arrived at Usta Ramadan's little workshop. Up a narrow, tall flight of stairs I went to the second floor of the Rab', which was filled with miniscule workshops set in a row, accessed by a long corridor. I kept asking for directions until I got to Ramadan's.

The workshop was about three by four meters square, with a big window overlooking Sagha Street, an extension of al-Mu'izz Street, and with a *tazga*, a wooden workbench, in the middle. Ramadan was sitting in front, surrounded by his apprentices, all boys.

Usta Ramadan welcomed me and had me take a seat at the window looking onto the street. "This is the deluxe position. Finest spot in the workshop." The workshop had four craftsmen; I still remember my place in the workshop and the window overlooking the most beautiful collection of Mamluk architecture you ever could see—the Complex of al-Mansour Qalawun, with its gorgeous dome ornamented with calligraphy all around it. I was so fond of it. Can you believe it, fifty years on from my time at Usta Ramadan's workshop, every time I'm in that area I keep looking up to stare at the calligraphy on the dome of Qalawun? My admiration for the fabulous calligraphy hasn't diminished a whit since I first laid eyes on it when I sat down in Usta Ramadan's workshop half a century ago. This is what they call the eternal art that the Mamluks left us.

I think the jewelry I design now, into which I incorporate the marvelous art of Arabic calligraphy, and the idea of using Arabic calligraphy in the jewelry I make, was originally inspired by looking at the dome of al-Mansour Qalawun, sitting there by the window. These moments of contemplation gave rise to a long relationship between me and the heritage of this great nation. I always said to myself, "If those geniuses managed to incorporate Arabic calligraphy into their buildings, why shouldn't I do the same—but in my own way?"

That day, Usta Ramadan asked me to draw a design I would like to execute on a piece of paper. I remember selecting a simple ring, with a crescent moon and a star on it—the Egyptian flag back then—the first piece of jewelry I ever made. Usta Ramadan gave me the silver for it from his storage in the workshop, and some tools to make it. I sat there hammering away at the piece of silver, following the instructions he gave me exactly.

I remember that day like it was yesterday. After I'd finished work at the ministry downtown, I had taken the bus to al-Azhar and gone into Ramadan's workshop. It was 3:30 in the afternoon. Then, I started making the piece of jewelry without once looking up. I didn't feel the time pass. Suddenly, it was 9:30. Six hours had flown by while I worked and I hadn't even felt it pass. And what's more, I hadn't become bored once. I knew my wish had come true. That was when I felt that this was what I wanted to do for a living for the rest of my life. At last! Hallelujah! I can't tell you how it felt to reach that point.

I left the Khan at about 10 o'clock, after all the shops in the district had closed, and the narrow streets were dark and the lights had all been put out. I was floating. I really can't remember how I got to the Bab al-Louq station to take the Helwan Metro to my mother's house, I was so ecstatic with joy. I was walking as if I had sprouted wings. Light, so light! Happy, so happy! I got home and found my mother very worried about me, because I had never stayed out so late. I had the conviction that day—without any doubt—and my certainty only increased later—that this was the vocation I had been seeking for a long time. At long last, I had found what I was looking for.

My training at Usta Ramadan's lasted for about two months. I would finish work at the Ministry of Information and then go to Khan al-Khalili by bus. I got on the bus and paid, if I remember correctly, two piasters from downtown to Port Said Street, and from there to al-Azhar Street. I got off at Wikalat al-Ghouri and crossed the main road into the street where the Khidr al-Attar spice store is. Then I would cross Muski Street to the Sagha, and from there to Khan al-Khalili.

I paid Ramadan a sum of money at the end of every week for his time teaching me, and I bought my first lot of silver for about LE3.50. The weight of precious metals at that time—whether gold or silver—was calculated in dirhams—a dirham was about 3 grams.

This was the first capital with which I started my professional venture—three pounds and fifty piasters. I made about five rings with this amount. They were simple, primitive even: just a square with a crescent and a star on them. They were naive and simple, but there was something different about them.

My mother didn't really get what was going on. What was this all about—a university graduate, supposed to be an interior designer, going to work as an apprentice in Khan al-Khalili? Well, it *was* strange to her, something she couldn't understand, especially as I'd also started to get some extra commissions designing interiors, which brought in a little extra income.

Now I realize that taking pivotal life decisions is no easy task. Don't ever imagine that there's no fear involved in making a change in one's life, personal or professional. On the contrary—a lot of times I was absolutely sick with worry and fear. But the support of the friends around you makes a difference to the process of taking decisions and following through with them. It makes you stronger and braver.

As for the first five rings I made with my own hands, my friend Nehad Salem helped me sell them in the first boutique that opened in Zamalek, owned by Zeinab Selim, the wife of the soccer star of Egypt at the time, "King" Saleh Selim. It was called Vita Mia, and it was one of the most upscale businesses in Egypt at the time. It was at the top of Hassan Sabry Street, right after the Post Office. After a while, Zeinab called me and said, "I sold your five rings!" And she gave me forty-five pounds. I couldn't believe it. To me, this sum was true, genuine riches. When I go down memory lane to think of the start of my career and think of the sum of money with which I started out, I smile happily. I remember—years after I got into the business—being in Hurghada, and passing by a hotel run by a friend, the actor Hisham Selim. His mother and father, Zeinab and Saleh Selim, happened to be there, and they invited me to take tea with them. Sitting there, drinking tea, I said, "I believe, Zeinab, that it was because of you that I had good fortune: you contributed the first real capital I made in my life."

She laughed and pointed at herself. "Me?" But it's true.

Usta Ramadan gave me the first push to understand the simplest basics of jewelry making, and with the money I made, I bought silver to make more pieces. In my breaks from training, I was curious to look in on other workshops and get to know their work. They were, as I said, tiny rooms set all in a row on a narrow corridor, the craftsmen all clustered together, their specializations complementing one another. There was the mounting workshop, where precious and semiprecious stones were mounted; the polisher, who polished jewelry pieces; the carver, who shaped semiprecious stones such as turquoise and coral; and the plating workshop, which plated jewelry with gold and silver—an entire production line in which each profession complemented the other, an interconnected world of which I was now a part.

"Ask, and it shall be given you; seek, and ye shall find; knock, and it shall be opened unto you." Matthew 7:7. This verse is inscribed in Arabic on the doorway of the Hanging Church in Old Cairo.

Khan al-Khalili

From that moment in the early 1970s, I started my life in Khan al-Khalili, and it went on for about twenty years straight. Just as my father and mother had played an essential part in forming my personality from childhood to early youth, Khan al-Khalili—the whole district—formed a large and important part of my identity and my close connection with Egypt's heritage. I experienced what Naguib Mahfouz had written about the district in a realistic and practical manner: the streets, the alleys, the *wikalas*, the *rab*'s and the craftsmen centered there, who worked and traded, and sometimes lived in those buildings.

UPSTAIRS PLEASE
SELEHDAR COMPOUND
A BIG MARKET FOR MANUFACURE
AND SILLING
KHAN EL KHALILI PRODUCTION

ورش السلحدار لتصنيع منتجات خان الخليلي
م ربع السلحدار - خان الخليلي

5 RABEH·EL SELEHDAR

The second workshop in Khan al-Khalili where I trained as a jeweler, 1971.

There was the royal quarter, where Caliph al-Hakim bi-Amr Allah had lived with his retinue, his knights and his commanders, starting at the Northern Wall where al-Hakim Mosque is, with its fabulous Fatimid architecture, and the calligraphy on the building, which is the loveliest my eyes have seen, adjoined by the city walls and gate of Bab al-Futouh, out of which armies marched. On the other side is the gate of Bab al-Nasr, where triumphant armies, returning after victories, were received, leading down to the southern gate, Bab Zuwayla, or, as it is also commonly called, Bab al-Metwalli, along the long backbone of this city where so many magnificent monuments stand. All this made me richer culturally, artisanally, and professionally. It was the first real-life lesson in understanding the heritage of my beloved Egypt.

Al-Mu'izz Street, with all its architectural treasures delights me still: the Aqmar Mosque (on your left as you're coming from Bab al-Futouh), whose famous roundel on the façade always called to me to incorporate its design into a beautiful piece of jewelry; the Complex of Sultan Qalawun (and his son al-Nasir Muhammad, as well as Sultan Barquq) with its abundance of ornamentation and geometrical patterns in marble, astonishingly modern in design, inside the main hall, which I incorporated into bracelets. How did the craftsmen of olden times manage to manipulate architectural lines and create such contemporary-looking forms?

The Mamluk era was when Egypt became the main crossroads for east–west trade, which explains the wealth the Mamluks enjoyed and the buildings and palaces they built as well as their incredible craftsmanship,

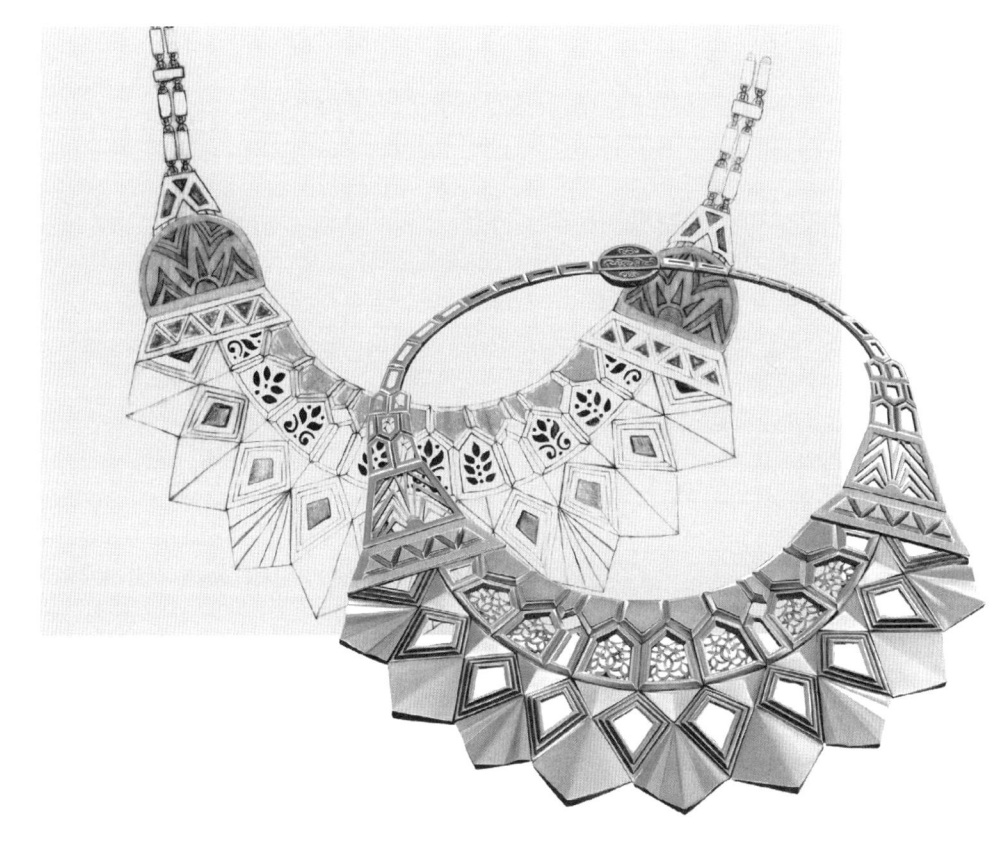

I call this a Muqarnas Necklace because I was inspired by the *muqarnas* (an ornamental arrangement of multi-tiered niches) of the Mamluk-era Palace of Amir Qawsun to design it.

which may well be considered the Renaissance of Islamic art. There's also the famous hospital—the Bimaristan—of the Qalawun Complex, and its fountain whose shape, half a century after I started, was the inspiration for a necklace in my most recent Mamluk collection.That collection was produced as part of my company's celebration of its fifty-year anniversary. We decided to design a collection for the occasion that had an important cultural element, and we chose the Mamluk period. All the collection's elements were based on Mamluk architectural ornamentation. The Qalawun Complex on al-Mu'izz Street, the Sultan Hassan Mosque on Rumayla Square below the Cairo Citadel, and the Mosque of Mu'ayyad Sheikh next to Bab Zuwayla, enjoyed the lion's share of our research; experts consider them the most important examples of Mamluk architecture remaining in Cairo.

Naguib Mahfouz's masterpiece *Palace Walk* (*Bayn al-qasrayn*)—now I know what it was named after. It literally means "between the two palaces," and it refers to the area between the Eastern Palace, built by the Fatimid caliph al-Mu'izz li-Din Allah, and the Western Palace, built by his son al-Aziz bi-Allah. And then there was Burguwan Alley and the Khurunfish district, and the café on the street corner that used to have an incredible Islamic-style wooden bench: I always used to stop and stare at the intricately carved and inlaid woodwork.

I would walk on, and before I came to the intersection with al-Azhar Street, I would find myself at the great Khidr al-Attar spice store, in front of the Hamzawi district, the oldest spice market. This is a neighborhood of spice stores, all next to each other on the main street and in the alleys to the right and left as well. You'll find yourself walking among huge sacks stuffed with spices from all over in the world. The smell of spices is everywhere, filling the air. On the corner of Hamzawi, there's the Ashrafiya School, built by Sultan Barsbay; one of the pieces in my Mamluk collection is a pair of earrings on which all the inspiration for the design is taken from the inlaid pulpit of the mosque in his *khanqah* in the Mamluk cemetery. Then, farther on, is the Hamzawi district, and the Sanadiqiya (the box makers), where boxes of all shapes and sizes used to be made to hold the different goods manufactured in that neighborhood where wonderful architecture is mixed in among the people and their daily lives.

There's also Midaq Alley, which Naguib Mahfouz immortalized in his novel of the same name: despite its small size, it's a microcosm of the world. This whole neighborhood is a masterpiece of skilled urban planning—each *wikala* or *rabʻ* had a practical part to play in the production line of craftsmanship—and it was my playground for twenty years. It lives in me to this day. I wanted to get to know more about the district and its history, and the people who built these amazing structures that formed Egypt's personality at the time. I took to reading and researching, but didn't really go very deep in my readings. Still, I did manage to gain a reasonable amount of information about these places and the great people who built them and their history.

In the end, everything I saw in this neighborhood blended together: the architecture; the brilliant urban planning; the building façades and their amazing proportions; the harmony of colors; the other elements utilized in the buildings, such as iron, brass, gates, wooden doors, pulpits, marble floors; all of this went into my storehouse of memory and mental archives. I must have absorbed it well, because it comes out when necessary, whenever I need it.

Now, in my artistic maturity, I can't give the designers or artisans behind these great works enough credit. Their grammar of harmony is clear in all their architectural forms: the square, the rectangle, the circle, the triangle. They applied the golden ratio to their works. It is truly astonishing. All this I see through the lens of my own eyes, with my own understanding. And when I look at the work of Western designers now, making designs inspired by our East, I understand what Edward Said says in *Orientalism* about the way the West sees and understands us.

During breaks from my work, I often crossed to the other size of al-Azhar Street to walk to Cairo's southern wall and Bab Zuwayla. I would start with the stunning entrance to the Ghouriya Complex with its soaring wooden roofed-in street, and the amazing *ablaq* work on the walls and dome of the mosque, giving it power and beauty. I would walk through the great market, which used to be one of Cairo's major ancient marketplaces, the Silk Market, where luxury Persian carpets, silks, and fabulous fabrics from the east were sold. We can see many depictions of this market in the drawings of the early Orientalists, with the traders in their imposing turbans and traditional garments, standing there selling their grand carpets hanging on the walls and spread out on the ground.

Hosh Qadam

I would walk on, along the Tarbi'a—the long, narrow passageway that leads to the Ghouri Wikala, with tiny stores right and left, clinging to the wall of the great mosque. On the right, it takes you out onto the mosque wall—everything is precisely calculated, with exemplary proportions and relations. At the entrance to the Wikala was a tiny store selling the traditional *milaya laff* at the entrance to the Tarbi'a. I used to stand in front of the little store, watching the owner showing the women how to wrap the *milaya* elegantly and femininely around themselves. I remember the wonderful belly dancer Tahiya Karioka wearing it so flirtatiously in the movie *Li'bat al-Sitt* (The women's game—and her name in the movie was Li'ba, which means "game" or "toy"), opposite the marvelous actor Naguib al-Rihani. I was sad the last time I went into the Ghouri neighborhood to see the beautiful mosque of Sultan Qunsuwa al-Ghouri—such an important historical monument—with its façade covered in cheap lingerie, for sale in all shapes and colors!

Walking on my way, I would pass by the alley called Khashqadam—they pronounce it Hosh Qadam—or Lucky Footstep in Turkish. This is where the famous duo of colloquial Arabic poet Ahmad Fouad Nigm and musician Sheikh Imam lived. A lot of young people used to go there to listen to their political songs, which were so famous at the time. There was an innate sculptor there, too, by the name of Mahmoud al-Labban: he couldn't read or write, but he made marvelous sculptures. In this area too was the home of the head of the Traders' Guild, Gamal al-Din al-Dhahabi. They say he was called al-Dhahabi (which means "the golden one"), because he had so many gold coins. There was also the Fakahani Mosque, with its beautiful door. I used to stand there and wonder, "What can I do with all this beauty in my collections? How can I draw inspiration from these beautiful wooden inlays in my designs?"

Then I would arrive at Bab Zuwayla, the largest of Cairo's gates, set into the southern wall of Historic Cairo. It's a gigantic gate, with the two minarets of the Mu'ayyad Sheikh Mosque on top of it. Bab Zuwayla was so called because it was the gate out of which the trade caravans exited on their way to the city of Zuwayla, deep in the Libyan desert. It is also known by Egyptians as the Metwalli Gate. By the way, the original door of the Sultan Hassan Mosque is currently installed as the door of the Mu'ayyad Sheikh Mosque.

In front of the mosque is Sukkariya Alley, which Naguib Mahfouz used as the title of one part of his *Cairo Trilogy*—*Sugar Street*. There was a sugar and sweet factory here long ago, where sweets were fashioned into the shapes of animals, people, and plants. Their great popularity with buyers made the artisans of this craft supremely creative. Bumper crops of sugar cane back then made this trade widespread; confectionery was very popular, and the sweets took different forms: horses, dolls, and flowers; and it's said that the popular *Arousat al-Moulid*, the traditional sugar doll made on the Prophet Muhammad's birthday, is a product of this craft of old.

The Fatimid era witnessed a flourishing of this industry. There is a story which I'm not sure is true: that the Fatimid caliph al-Mustansir bi-Allah promised his troops, upon their return from battle, an *arousa* (which means "bride" and also "doll") for each of them to marry—and he did, giving them a wife each out of his slave girls. In the next battle, it was the anniversary of the Prophet Muhammad's birthday, so once again he gave them an *arousa*: the confectioners' market owned by the caliph made beautiful dolls out of sugar to give to the triumphant commanders.

Walking out of the Metwalli Gate, I would find on my left the most beautiful wooden screen—of the type we know as *mashrabiya*—but set on the ground, not hanging on a wall, at the entrance of al-Salih Tala'i' Mosque, the last of the Fatimid mosques. Would you believe it, every time I passed by that woodwork, I would spend at least ten minutes contemplating the artisan's craft and the ornamentation he had created: the proportions and thicknesses of the wooden pieces, the pieces' relation to each other—something to teach in art books! (Wherever I go, I do the same thing.)

After that, I used to go into the Khayyamiya (also known as the Qasaba, or market, of Radwan Bey), which was the second-largest Mamluk market after the Qasaba of Cairo in al-Mu'izz Street and the surrounding areas. They say it used to house twelve thousand stores. Ever since Mamluk times, this place has been devoted to making tents and marquees for Mamluks, sultans, and princes, for use in seasons of celebrations and festivals. Horse-drawn carts called *sawares* used to come down from the Citadel to that street to buy and trade. Dozens of craftsmen sit in small stalls, making colorful artistic pieces out of scraps and remnants of fabric, with great skill and speed, with needle and scissors. It's a craft that has made its way into our genetic map and become built into every craftsman.

After that, I would go to the Surugiya, or saddle market; this is where the saddles for horses and donkeys were made out of leather and decorated with folk patterns and ornaments in brass in the shape of crescents, stars, and hands. Folk artisans made an art out of ornamenting horses and carriages, decorating them and making them flashy and glittery with all these little details. I had a great admiration for them, and they gave me ideas for ornaments that I would like to design and develop. They added something to my mind's cultural storehouse. How I loved the shapes and forms of those ornaments! Jewelry for animals.

The Geographical Society Museum in Tahrir Square, also known as the Ethnographic Museum, which I'm very fond of, has a glass case devoted to ornaments for animals. How I enjoyed my repeated visits to that place, founded originally by Khedive Ismail! I pretty much had everything in it memorized. I learned so much from that museum from my frequent visits. In the mid-1990s, I designed a necklace I was very fond of, inspired by a horse's bridle and the necklace with which rich people used to decorate their horses' necks, made out of silver, and occasionally gold.

The Surugiya is where saddles were sold. At times, it was also known as Souq al-Mahamiz (Spurs market) or Souq al-Laggamin (Bridlemakers' market)—this is what I heard from the oldest tradesmen in the neighborhood. *Mahamiz*, of course, refers to the spurs with which you spur a horse on to move faster, and *laggamin* is named for bridles. For kings and military leaders, the spurs used to be made of gold and silver.

This part of Cairo was, and still is, my favorite. I used to love walking there, and every time I found inspirations and new ideas for jewelry pieces to design and to manifest our wonderful history for women to wear. Can you imagine, no matter how long I spend away from it, whenever I go back to walk there, my eyes find something new to look at and photograph, and I return filled with joy at my discoveries. I always feel that I have lived through these times in a previous life.

Hagg Sayed's Workshop

A while after my training started with Usta Ramadan, I felt I had absorbed all I could of the basic rudiments of knowledge. I had the skills I needed to make a simple piece. This period lasted about two months, during which, after my work in the government office, I would go to Khan al-Khalili and train for about six hours. I took Fridays off.

I wanted to expand my skills in jewelry making, so I said to myself, "Girl, why don't you go train with somebody new? Get some experience with someone else." At the time, Hagg Sayed—or Sayed al-Hagg, as they called him—was the doyen of pharaonic and Coptic rings in the Khan, which were well known at the time, and very popular with tourists. Truth be told, I don't know why they call them that; from my study of Islamic and Coptic jewelry, I never saw anything like them in the history books, or even remotely resembling them. Anyway, Hagg Sayed's workshop was in Rab' al-Silihdar. Suzanne al-Masri, the Egyptian jewelry artist, had trained with Hagg Sayed for a while before leaving for America with her former husband, the writer Nabil Naoum. Suzy introduced me to Hagg Sayed, so I went to work with him after leaving Ramadan's workshop. Hagg Sayed's workshop was bigger, with about eight craftsmen.

Word spread that there was a university graduate working as an apprentice (in Egyptian, "apprentice" is *sabi*, literally meaning "boy") at a workshop in Rab' al-Silihdar. I climbed up to the workshop by a staircase starting in Sikkat al-Badistan to the courtyard open to the sky on the first floor, surrounded on all four sides by tiny, diverse workshops. The workshop owned by Hagg Sayed was in the front, facing outward. I noticed as I sat working that the door would open and people would come in to take a look at me and smile at me. I felt that I'd become a spectacle for the people in the Khan to gawk at!

I helped the workshop meet its quotas for the so-called Coptic rings, which I never liked. After a while, I progressed to the pharaonic rings to learn a new technique. I didn't like the so-called pharaonic rings either, but I had to learn how to make them. Sayed insisted that I learn the craft the same way his ancestors had learned it—that is, dating back to about 1900. The "scissors" that I learned on, I had in fact seen in museums. Who were the first people to invent the scissors? Anyway, he trained me to weld metal with a *masraga* (spirit lamp), a method I had actually seen on the walls of ancient Egyptian temples. This involves blowing into a twisted copper tube in front of a flame coming out of a brass spirit lamp, guiding the flame with a strong blast of air to melt the metal. I huffed and puffed until I was out of breath for two months, after which the Hagg had mercy on me and moved me up to something more modern, a hand-held welding torch and a bellows with a foot pump that you worked continuously up and down to provide a current of air. I became an expert at using the bellows. I used them for fifteen years running until I moved on in the craft and took to working with a blowtorch hooked up to a butane gas canister—a technological breakthrough at the time!

I worked at Hagg Sayed's for about a year and a half, with breaks, as I remember. I would finish work at the government office and take the bus to the Khan, then keep working until nightfall. Many times, in addition to helping them meet their quotas, I took some silver from them to practice on my own designs. At week's end, I paid for what silver I had taken, in addition to three pounds a week for my use of the place. My concentration was all focused on learning every stage of the craft. I attempted to familiarize myself with every stage of silversmithing (cutting, welding, filing, finishing, and polishing) and learned all the jargon of the trade and used it in conversation—*zard, sanabek, duqmaq, qistag, al-sok, al-falaq, qatra, bizra, shaft, basta*. I was very happy to learn later that *zard* was a Mamluk word, meaning the tiny metal rings that link the parts of a piece of jewelry together. It was used in Mamluk chainmail to make it pliable like fabric, and the place where this chainmail was made was called the *zardkhana*.

Sitting at a *tazga* for long years and watching craftsmen work so I could learn was such an important thing for me. Each one had an open drawer in front of him into which he swept the filings of the gold or silver he worked; on the *tazga* in front of him was a container with *ghallaya*—literally 'boiler,' but it wasn't a boiler, it was their name for a mixture of water and nitric acid. It was always there in front of the craftsman, to drop a just-welded piece into it to remove all traces of the welding and the materials that aided the welding from the metal. I always found the craftsmen taking the jewelry out of this solution with their bare hands, but I used the back of an old toothbrush to get it out. They laughed at me. Hagg Sayed told me to dunk my hand in the *ghallaya*, saying, "Toughen up!" Later, of course, I found out the scientific name for the *ghallaya* and the sulfuric acid. I was afraid of getting sick from constant contact with the acids, so I stopped and got a pair of plastic tweezers to pull the work out, and I didn't care about their mockery any more.

Fifteen years running, long years of using files, sandpaper, and acids, have made my own hands rough as sandpaper. Of course, forget that I even had fingernails in the first place! Often, I found the area around my fingernails blackened with shavings and filings. When I got home, I had to wash my hands vigorously, scrubbing back and forth with a brush around my nails to get the discoloration out.

One funny thing is that forty years later, I was having my fingerprint taken and I found that my right hand had practically no fingerprints left, from the acids and the sandpaper. From then on, whenever I was asked to give my fingerprint for something important, I had to bring along a report from a specialist saying "Congenital Condition—No Clear Fingerprint." In all truth and honesty, I'll tell you this: my roughened hand is a great prize to me. It represents the value of work for a human being. Now I think of the movie *al-Aydi al-na'ima* (Soft hands, 1963), where a pampered aristocrat is pushed by circumstance to work, and takes off his protective garden gloves to acquire "a pair of gloves forged by sunshine and hard work" in the form of rough hands.

My lifelong relationship with crafts and craftsmen and tired, working hands, sometimes with a different skin texture by dint of the nature of their profession, has given me a deep respect, admiration, and love for them. My hat is off to the old master craftsmen, given the titles *Ma'allim* or *Usta*, with whom I lived for twenty years, and their meticulous craft, and their great ancestors, the unknown craftsmen who left this world unknown, leaving marvels on which they put not so much as their name.

I was on a very tight budget in those days. Each day I went to Khan al-Khalili, I had a limited amount to spend, especially if it was the end of the week and payment to Hagg Sayed was due. On that day, I had to save the two piasters I usually spent on the bus ticket. I would buy a small sandwich of round white flatbread filled with spiced stewed fava beans with a boiled egg inside from an Armenian restaurant downtown. I loved that sandwich! Then I would walk to Khan al-Khalili, eating the sandwich with great appetite and gusto. From Soliman Pasha Square to Abdin, then through Hassan al-Akbar Street, where it is said the great architect Sir K.A.C. Creswell lived and recorded most of our Islamic monuments in a great archive. From there to Port Said Street to al-Azhar Street. Frequently, I would take a detour through Abdin to look at the beautiful royal palace and the spacious gardens in front of it, to say nothing of the buildings there, constructed at the start of the last century, which used to be inhabited by the palace staff, mostly Nubians.

Finally, I would arrive in al-Azhar Street, and from there into Khan al-Khalili from any of the entrances on al-Azhar Square. I knew all the stores there by heart and their owners by name. They had come to know me, too, and greeted me on my way in. They called me "the university craftswoman who works with Sayed al-Hagg."

Mentioning the sandwich makes me think of something unrelated, but I want to say it. I remember the first time I went to London to exhibit my work. I was very scared, and I had very little money. On the flight, I made a sandwich out of the meal they served, because I wanted to save up and not buy dinner when I arrived. This occurred to me when I had made a name for myself in the region, many years later, and was selected to judge a jewelry competition. I was flying first class on Emirates Airlines. When they served me the meal, I looked at it with a calm, content smile, remembering my beginnings and the distant past, which I can truly call a happy past. I enjoyed every moment of my experience, and I learned so much. I never felt I was sacrificing anything or living a hard life, or any of those things that people talk about.

My relationship with Hagg Sayed and his workshop left its mark on me. I developed a strong friendship with the guys working there over my time among them, which was hardly short. I listened to their stories about their families, and often ate with them the meals that the wives brought to the workshop for their husbands, especially the stuffed cabbage leaves made by Egyptian women in a wonderful, spicy recipe. Sometimes I would drink the tea made on the spirit stove—strong black tea full of sugar in very small glasses. This was their dessert. Sometimes a man would come into our workshop carrying a skin full of buttermilk on his back, selling it among the workshops. I loved it.

Hagg Hassan Yaqout was Hagg Sayed's neighbor; his workshop was next door. He was the most famous filigree maker in the entire neighborhood. He had a brother by the name of Fayrouz—Hakkak Fayrouz Sinawi, which means 'Fayrouz the Carver from Sinai'—and he was given this name because of his profession. Two other filigree craftsmen were Eid Shiha and Gamal al-Sunna. This marvelous, intricate craft of filigree making is almost extinct now, although it became famous in the Islamic era. It is a technique that was first introduced into the Ottoman Empire from Central Asia and the Byzantine civilization. Some of the most important jewelry pieces in the Ayyubid, Fatimid, and Mamluk eras were filigree. Filigree makers were always scarce; now the only one in the Khan is Hani Yaqout, the student of Hassan Yaqout and his son by adoption and profession. You know, the Egyptian word for filigree, *shiftishi*, comes from the word for lacy and transparent fabrics, and I think the verb *shaff*—that is, to be transparent—is somehow related! They say that clothing is *shiftishi*, that is, delicate and feminine and flirty, and filigree, as a technique in jewelry, is created with very fine wire in lacy geometric patterns that are see-through.

This was all a lovely time that lasted for about two years running. I came to understand a little bit about the mindset of the craftsmen I worked with, and our relationship grew easier, perhaps a little more equal, now that we were not so far apart after all. I might be a university graduate, but I was working under them and learning from them. This may have helped erase their sense of a class divide, especially since most of them couldn't read or

The workshop of Hassan Yaqout, 1973.

write. They felt that they deserved a great deal of credit for teaching this university-educated woman the craft and the secrets of the trade and raising her up professionally. They were my teachers in a very real sense for a long time.

Another thing I can't forget is that, in the afternoons, Hagg Sayed always came into the workshop late, and I could tell that he wasn't himself, irritable and short-tempered. Sometimes he would scream and shout in the workshop and start throwing the hammers and awls around. One time a big hammer flew right over my head and almost cracked my skull, and luckily I dodged it before it split my head open. After Hagg Sayed went this far, Saad would come in—Saad was the big boss of the workshop—with a cup of tea to which he added four spoonfuls of sugar, then take out a folded piece of silver paper from of his pocket and unwrap it. He would take a small brown pellet of something like chewing-gum and dissolve it in the tea. Hagg Sayed would drink the tea, we'd leave him alone for a bit until his nerves had calmed, and then he was a changed man, calm and smiling. In short, he was a different person entirely. Since this was repeated every day, I asked them, "What's with that thing you dissolve in tea every day?"

They told me, "It's opium."

I had never heard of opium dissolved in tea before! When I asked where they bought it, they told me, "From al-Batniya, a neighborhood next to al-Azhar. Would you like to go? They sell it right out in the street, like sweets."

Well, my eyes bulged right out of my head! I couldn't believe it. One day I decided to visit al-Batniya to see this bizarre scene. I went with Saad from the workshop and we went into the famous street next to al-Azhar Mosque—famous, that is, for selling hashish and opium—but that day there was nothing being sold in the neighborhood.

The Malatili Bathhouse

One day, the workmen said, "Would you like to go to a traditional bathhouse?" Delighted, I said yes, of course. It was something new that I had never seen before. The foreman of the workshop, Saad, spoke with his wife and they agreed that she should take me. That day, I left the workshop early because the bathhouse was open for women from nine to five, after which it was the men's turn. I had to bring my own towel and bar of soap, and a black bag of rough wool that they bought for me. Saad's wife had brought a cooking pot full of stuffed vegetables and some soup in a bottle, and I brought fruit—oranges and bananas.

I remember that we walked down al-Mu'izz Street to get to the bathhouse. It was called Hammam al-Malatili, on Margoush Street. It had a small door. We went through a passageway into a courtyard on the right, where a very big lady was sitting to guard the bathhouse from would-be intruders. I went into the bathhouse to find myself face-to-face with something out of a book of Orientalist painting done by the Europeans who depicted these places in the eighteenth century. Naked bodies of different shapes and sizes: large women and thin women, big, small, curvy, short, tall, brown, white, and olive-skinned. We sat in a large, circular marble hall with a large platform of white marble in the center. On it sat women chatting, women laughing, women walking, women wrapped in bath towels, while other women leaned, relaxing, on the walls. What chatter, what laughter, what socializing and storytelling!

Set all around the hall were small, open rooms. Each room had a marble platform in it and was filled with steam that came out of an opening in the floor. I went inside and sat in the steam for about half an hour. You can't see anything for the steam. Then a great big woman, full-figured and strong, came in. She was what they called the *ballana*, the woman who bathes you. She took the rough wool bag and scrubbed and scrubbed my body with it, producing vermicelli-like twills of black stuff that came off with all the scrubbing, even though I bathe every day! I really don't know where all this dirt came from. My skin was two shades lighter! When we were done, I washed myself with my bar of soap, took my wool bag, and got up. I sat to one side for a bit, drank some soup and ate some of the vegetables Saad's wife had brought, and then we left. I will never forget the experience of the traditional bathhouse, nor the steam room where I bathed in the early 1970s. Then, in 1973, the famous director Salah Abu Seif made his classic movie *The Malatili Bathhouse*. That was the same bathhouse where I went to bathe once, Saad's wife and I.

I came to know and experience new worlds quite different from my own, which came in very useful when I expanded my business and started to need skilled workmen. Circumstance was what had brought me into contact with that world, and in a very natural and spontaneous way I'd shared, at least in part, how they lived. This was what helped me understand these people and the ins and outs of dealing with them: their language, their practices, their mental habits, their ways of speaking, and so on. You know, this all happened spontaneously, without any intention on my part. I really do have a powerful curiosity to find out everything. I was very happy to chat as they shared stories of their lives, and to eat spicy stuffed vegetables with them. I'm thrilled to have gone to the traditional bathhouse and to have had a glimpse into this life and worlds that I would never have had access to on my own if not for the time I spent in that world.

On my lunch break, I would go out for an hour and look around the Khan. There was a *wikala* there called the Cotton Wikala, on your left on your way to the Hussein Mosque. It is said that the Cotton Wikala was used to store cotton that came from different regions in preparation for its sale, and the farmers who brought in the cotton stayed at Rab' al-Silsila, which used to be four stories high, with very tiny rooms. Inside the *wikala* was an antiques trader who sold doors and wooden screens and bookcases in the Islamic style, called Hagg Abdou Saber. Everyone with an interest in this kind of thing shopped there. The most amazing Islamic door cost two hundred pounds at the time. Then, when you went deeper into the *wikala*, there was the workshop owned by Hagg Ibrahim al-Sunni, the largest and finest workshop making mother-of-pearl inlay for boxes and tables in Khan al-Khalili. After that, deeper in, there was a collection of workshops that also produced mother-of-pearl inlay.

Rab' al-Silsila, next to the Cotton Wikala, had a high stone archway over the entrance with chains dangling from it. The archway surrounded a door called Bab al-Ghouri. This area was home to an old market, and the chains were fastened to the archway to prevent the entrance of beasts of burden. You climbed up to the *rab'* by a single long staircase, all one straight flight, about twenty-four steps high, to find yourself in a small courtyard that gave off onto a large group of small rooms, now occupied by small-scale silversmiths, jewelry makers, gem workers, and gem setters. It's said that this *rab'* used to be a hostelry for the people who came to Cairo from the provinces bringing their crop of cotton to be sold at the Cotton Wikala. It's also said to have more than four hundred rooms. Often, I would visit my dear Armenian friend, Edward Advestian, the most famous gem setter in Khan al-Khalili, and his knowledgeable mentor, Avedis Severian. I sat next to him to watch him set big diamonds (the craftsman's name for the center stone in a ring is *qurta*)—and secure it with meticulous craftsmanship. There was also Hagg Farouk Abdel Khaliq in the *rab'*, a well-known diamond merchant. He always set aside the old Turkish diamonds to show me and explain where they came from and why they looked different. He knew I had a great passion for them. Sometimes, years later, when I had money, I would buy an Istanbul gem from him to add to my collection for study and research.

On my way up, on the right-hand side of the staircase, was the store of George Aziz, a friend who always had old things I liked. To the left of Rab' al-Silsila there used to be an amber-carver sitting on the ground with his wares around him, with a primitive wooden lathe in front of him that he used for turning the amber. This is really stuff straight out of the eighteenth-century paintings you used to see! I would stand and watch him: how could he carve amber with such skill? He turned it just like they carve the wood for the *mashrabiya* wooden screens.

Old Beads

The old beads that used to be sold in Khan al-Khalili began to occupy a great deal of my attention. They were sold in little shops next to one another in a passageway next to the old arch at the mouth of Rab' al-Silsila. There's a sign on the wall here: Sikkat al-Badistan, to the left of the *rab'* on your way in from the Hussein Mosque. These are the only shops that specialize in the sale of old beads, the ones that were worn by villagers, Bedouins, and Nubians. Al-Mansouri and his sons Muhammad, Ali, and Hussein were the best known of these dealers. They were the biggest dealers in old gold and silver beads from Nubia, the countryside, and the desert. Oh, how often I bought from him! He also had new, imitation pharaonic beads made in Luxor, which they called "mummy beads." Next to the Mansouri store was the shop owned by Khawaga William, who specialized in the sale of amber and agate. He was always smiling and laughing, and he'd invite me in for tea and we'd sit and talk.

It was in this area that I met a person who left her mark on me: Anna Ghali, a descendant of the old, prestigious Armenian families that used to rule Egypt. She was related to Noubar Pasha, three times prime minister of Egypt, during the reign of Khedive Ismail (1878–79), Khedive Tawfik (1884–88), and finally Abbas Hilmi II (1894–95). Born in Istanbul in 1885,

With George Aziz, Khan al-Khalili, late 1990s.

she was married in Cairo in 1907 to Naguib Ghali Pasha, the eldest son of Boutros Ghali Pasha, who became prime minister of Egypt in 1910. It started out this way: almost every week, I would see a petite woman who looked European walking in Khan al-Khalili with a young man (probably her chauffeur) behind her holding a parasol to shade her in the summer. Most of the time, she could be found sitting with the dealers of old beads. When I asked Mansouri who she was, he said, "That's Madame Ghali." She mostly sat, picking out old and ancient beads and pieces and coins in silver, gold, and bronze, and so on. It was clear that she was well versed in the history and origins of these products. I paid her a visit at her home in Giza—upon her request—when they introduced me to her as "the university graduate here to learn silversmithing." I greatly enjoyed my visit with her and our fascinating conversation on the history of old beads. This lady kept making necklaces by hand until she was ninety-nine years of age—an example that astonished me and drove me to pray to God that I could keep doing the work I loved until I was ninety-nine! Madame Anna Ghali was foremost among the philanthropic ladies who did charity work. She founded a charity, which she ran, that funded forty schools, and held sales and bazaars at her home to fund her charity. This magnificent, strong woman died in 1984.

Among the things I liked and used a lot in my work was agate with the edges sanded down, used extensively in Bedouin and countryside jewelry. I had never found out its origins, or where it was from, until I happened to find a book in London on the history of beads, and bought it at once, hoping to find out the origins of this important product that had played so large a role in decorating the village and Bedouin women of Egypt. At last, I found out where it came from: it was sourced in India and came in great quantities from the east coast of India via the Red Sea. It first arrived at the port of Quseir by boat and was then conveyed to Cairo by caravans of camels, while some went to the Arabian Peninsula for sale during the Hajj season of pilgrimage to Mecca. In Napoleon's *Description de l'Egypte*, it is written that the duties on it were paid in Spanish Maria Theresas, which were widespread and used abundantly in Bedouin jewelry. The Silk Road across Asia, which went all the way down to the African continent, bore a great many Bedouin cultures and crafts to other great civilizations far away, which in turn came to us and enriched our artisanal culture.

I was extremely eager to find out the history behind manufactured glass beads since they were incorporated as such an important supporting element in many types of jewelry all over Egypt. After much research and study, I found out that the city of Jablonec nad Nisou, in the Czech Republic, was the leading manufacturer of glass beads in the world. It was located in the Bohemia region, famous for its glass and crystal. I paid a visit to this important manufacturing and craft center fifteen years ago to watch this unique process, and explore the relationship between manufacturing, education, and art, and learned a great deal from what I saw.

At the gate of the Cotton Wikala sat old Uncle Mustafa the Engraver—the best-known brass engraver in Khan al-Khalili. I liked him very much, and he was a great craftsman in addition to being a charming old man. His face was all wrinkles, and he was always smiling. In front of him was a small table on which he put his work. I would stand there, looking and learning and marveling at how he divided up the surface of a plate with a metal compass. It was the only tool he used, together with the steel pencil that he used to engrave the brass. He worked with astonishing speed to draw the pattern on the tray, without a picture for reference or any design in front of him. How astonishing this craftsman was! In the archive of his mind, he had memorized and stored every Islamic motif and ornamental pattern: leafy patterns, geometric patterns, and calligraphic text. He also knew every animal and human form, engraving them with a skill, ease, and speed of which I've never seen the like. He had practiced it since his childhood, and it became part of his mental archive.

"Crafts confer a mind upon those who excel in them"
—the *Muqaddima* of Ibn Khaldun.

Shafiqa and Metwalli

I had divided Khan al-Khalili into districts that I wanted to visit and get to know better, to get to know what crafts their craftsmen practiced and what each of them specialized in. If I saw District X one day, then I would see District Y another time, and so on.

Rabʿ al-Makwi was opposite Rabʿ al-Silihdar. There I met Muhammad Samaka, the maker of brass filigree. He made countryside-style *kerdan*s, which are large, heavy crescent-shaped necklaces, all worked with fish of different shapes and sizes. This is why they called him Samaka (the fish).

Samaka helped me execute the pieces I designed for the movie *Shafiqa and Metwalli*, based on an old folktale and directed by Ali Badrakhan. This opportunity came to me after I had started working in Khan al-Khalili. My great teacher Nagi Shaker, the puppet maker, was doing all the sets and costumes for the movie. The first part of the film was directed by Sayed Eisa, just back from studying in the USSR. Nagi believed that I could make the jewelry for this movie with him, giving me this wonderful opportunity, from

With my friend and teacher at the Faculty of Fine Arts, the great puppet maker Nagi Shaker, 2013.

which I learned a lot. The total contract for all the jewelry in the movie came to two hundred Egyptian pounds—though after that there was a disagreement with the director and he walked out, and I didn't even get the two hundred pounds. I had everything made at Muhammad Samaka's because back then I had no experience working with brass. Brass requires a much hotter and more powerful flame for welding than silver and gold. My movie experience was very useful to me, and working with Nagi Shaker enriched my knowledge a great deal.

In the Khan al-Khalili district, I also remember Hasib Yazdi. His store, in Suramatiya Street, was just a little stall. Hasib was a gem dealer of Iranian origin. He was one of the biggest gem dealers in the area. I learned a lot from him before turning to India and Bangkok for my gem purchases. I used to see Bedouins from Sinai in his store, carrying small sacks containing sand and turquoise. They showed him the contents of these bags, the pale turquoise color mixed in with the sand. Hasib introduced me to Class A turquoise and milky turquoise, and how to tell them apart.

Most of these Bedouins, I noticed, had missing fingers, a thing they all had in common. When I asked Hasib, he said this was a result of the primitive method the Bedouins used, which involved crawling inside the caves where the veins of turquoise could be found and placing dynamite in the mountain and detonating it so they could get the turquoise out. When Sinai was invaded, the Israelis used the most modern techniques to extract this wonderful stone, which is the most important and best known turquoise in the world—Sinai turquoise. They say that the Israelis took over all the mines of Sinai and mined them out.

Khan al-Khalili Street starts from Hussein Square and goes down to the Sagha, passing by the Qaitbay Gate, next to Qattan's—the prominent Iranian trader in luxury carpets and old Persian silver, which was converted into the Naguib Mahfouz Café in 1989, the year after the great writer earned his Nobel prize (he had a special seat reserved for him in the café). A little way on is the store of the Agha Zada family, one of the best respected clans in this historic market. To the fourth generation, they have kept bright the name of its founder, Amir Agha Zada. Amir Agha Zada emigrated here from Iran in 1919 to start his trade in gemstones. After him, his son, Ali Agha Zada, took over the business in 1930, continuing what his father had started, and refining their diamond trade considerably. I was introduced to Ali Bey—he was given this honorific by all the traders in the Khan, and he was very worthy of it—and later on, in 1967, Amir, his son, also went into the family business. I will never forget the day I went into this store to complain that he had wares in the window that were replicas of my designs, the decorated Fatimid water-jar filters. He reacted by immediately having someone working in his store gather up the whole collection they had in stock to get it melted down. I will always remember the upright manner in which this young man behaved. Now, the fourth generation is Karim and Walid, the sons of Amir Agha, following in their father's footsteps.

Also, there's the Qadi family, who specialize in original amber rosaries. Their stores used to be in the center of Khan al-Khalili, and I always liked to stand and look at what they had on display, often going inside for a chat with them, trying to understand this craft and learn more about the world of real and manufactured amber, and how to tell them apart: the types, the countries that produced it, and what made one rosary better and more expensive than another. I always asked, "Where do all these things come from?" I also found out about black coral, or as they call it, *al-yosr*—how they collect it in great quantities in the Gulf of Suez and then inlay it with silver—tiny dots on these little beads that I had not known about before. This black coral formed an important part of the world of rosaries. Khorassani's, the famous store for these, was opposite Ali Bey's store.

So many worlds, so many human stories I experienced over the twenty years that I lived intimately with this neighborhood! Like the girl in her twenties whom I always saw around: she knew everyone, she was young and pretty, and I never knew where she fitted into that society. I would see her at the stores of all the big traders and craftsmen. Sometimes, when she saw me at one of those stores, she'd get up and bring me tea. She was always very nice to me. One day I was walking in an alley of the Khan, and I saw a leading merchant—an older man, too—saying to her, "Meet me at my car." Of course, I got it. She was in love with a prominent craftsman in Khan al-Khalili and wanted him to marry her. Unfortunately, he refused. Most of her time she spent by his side—providing tea, and coffee, and food, and so on—and after a time, I heard that she had committed suicide. I was so sorry for that girl.

The Brass Workers

During my little lunch-hour tours, one of the things I enjoyed was to go to al-Nahhasin, the copper and brass district, off al-Mu'izz Street, a large and important area in front of the al-Mansour Qalawun complex. Al-Nahhasin Street ends in Midan Beit al-Qadi, also known as the Seat of Prince Mamay, which ends with the Hallmark, Weights, and Measures Authority. The street was so named because all the copper and brass manufacturers and traders gathered and set up shop there. You could see sheets of copper and brass and wire, and hear the din of hammers and mallets shaping vessels and other things. Long ago, the blacksmiths' market used to be next to it, called Souq al-Haddadin.

Al-Nahhasin used to be very important in olden times; all the cooking pots, trays, washing tubs, and braziers were made there. Copper workers used to be called the *qazangi*, in reference to the old name for a large copper pot, the *qazan*. I used to walk along this wonderful, historic street where there were stalls all next to each other, selling old copperware and brassware, which they sometimes called antiques (*antikat* in Egyptian, or *'adiyat* in Classical Arabic). From stall to stall I went, sitting with the owners and chatting. Every shape and form of brass and copper could be found in these stalls. Old copper trays, brass braziers, the brass mugs used in the bathroom (I bought a collection of these), old oil lamps with a wick, and so on and so forth—things that took me back to my grandmother's era. What made me sad was when I saw the old street signs with their distinctive blue enameling for sale there: thieves pulled them off the streets and alleyways and sold them.

I made friends with all the copper and brass merchants in the twenty years I spent there. It became my habit to go take tea with them often, and they always showed me this piece and that, telling me their stories. There were things that I didn't know the use of. Over the twenty years, I bought quantities of copper and brass, which I put in my house. From copper trays with matching cups, to old oil lamps, to the long-spouted ewers and bowls that were used for washing hands after eating (the ones we see in old movies) before there were taps and sinks, and so many other things that I bought from the merchants, who you could call antique dealers of a type. I'm fond of the brass and copper I bought, and I have a history with every piece. My mother always laughed when I came back carrying a piece I'd bought that I was proud of. "My dear girl, what on earth is this junk you keep collecting? At your grandmother's house we sold them to the rag-and-bone man when they went out of fashion!" Most of "this junk" now lives in my home. It means a lot to me.

I would sometimes see tiny cooking pots at a copper and brass dealer's, and was told, "When a bride comes to us for the copper and brass part of her trousseau, that is, the cooking utensils, the whole family comes along with her—her mother and her little sisters. These little pots were gifts we'd make for the little girls to play with—and so they'd remember our store when they got married and get their kitchenware from us!" A marketing ploy in a simple form! I bought a collection of the toy pots, which I loved to use as ashtrays in my home—most of them have now been stolen. When you walk around the copper district now, you'll find that all these things are no more. Aluminum has taken over the market and all the stores.

The process of shaping metal utensils always caught my attention. How could a flat sheet of copper be transformed into an attractive shape—a ewer, a cauldron, or a Turkish coffeepot? How can this flat sheet, in the hands of a skilled craftsman, become a concave or circular utensil for eating or drinking? This is a significant professional achievement requiring great skill, training, and intelligence. Unfortunately, this is all over now. The craftsmen to whom these skills were handed down from their mentors or fathers are no longer around. Using only steel tools, they would shape the outside through hammering. I remember that there were copper makers sitting at the mouth of the Salihiya Alley, and I always went to watch them as they worked in the street, with the school of al-Salih Nigm al-Din Ayyub behind them. You know, the dome of the school was the first dome to be built in a historic school in Cairo. This was the place where new Mamluks pledged their allegiance to the sultan, built by Sultana Shagarat al-Durr in place of the royal school in her husband's building.

The sight of craftsmen all hammering copper and brass to form Turkish coffeepots, the Salihiya school behind them, and above them a minaret with a dome on top called a *mabkhara* ("incense burner," because it resembles a type of covered incense burner), was, to me, a scene out of the history books and nineteenth-century paintings.

Khan al-Khalili and the silversmiths' district were a good place for me to start my journey of learning the trade, a journey I needed to take with these master craftsmen and teachers—there was simply no other choice. They gave generously, never withholding any piece of information from me. They shared all their experience, and never concealed any trade secret. They never saw it as competition of any sort—rather, they were proud that a university graduate was coming to learn from them. But—and there was always a "but" after a while in my life—while these technical skills of the time were sufficient for my simple beginnings, which I consider a type of innocent and spontaneous design, after a time my ideas and designs outstripped the level of my technical awareness and abilities—my mind, as they say, was running ahead of my hands.

Here I would like to explain an important point: the difference between a skilled craftsman and the artisanal artist—my observations, of course, being limited to the craft of jewelry making. The first is what we call in the profession an *usta* or a *ma'allim*; this is a person with a great awareness of the tricks of the trade, extremely good at what he does, very efficient and skilled, having acquired all he knows from other *ma'allim*s. The higher level of training that he achieves with pride after a while leads people to call him *sayegh katalog*, or a "magazine silversmith." The Armenian silversmiths are the best example of this: they have the ability to copy any piece of jewelry from a photograph or catalog or magazine. Most of them always owned copies of the most up-to-date and most fashionable magazines or catalogs of European jewelry and gems made by international fashion houses such as Cartier's. These came out annually in internationally acclaimed publications in addition to new designs and concepts for setting gems such as diamonds, rubies, sapphires, and emeralds.

The second, though, the one we call an artisanal artist—it's all in his head. He is the thinker, the composer: he conceives of the piece and executes it. Anything that comes into his head and stirs his emotions—whether it's a real image from nature that he designs and executes in his own way, with his own vision, or an original image that is surrealist, or cubist, or modern—he uses to create original pieces with a fresh conception and a contemporary view or vision. This type of jewelry requires a high level of artistic education. The professors of this world of design specialize in this approach. They explain the logic to you as they train you and help you develop your thinking and creativity into a piece of art that could be exhibited in art galleries or museums. After a while, it became my dream and my goal to study and learn this type of approach.

The Sagha

The Sagha, the goldsmiths' district, is the main community where all the processes, preparations, and fabrication of most of Egypt's gold are carried out. It is the neighborhood facing Khan al-Khalili, separated by a street that is an extension of al-Mu'izz Street, now known as Sagha Street, but which used to be called long ago—in the eighteenth century—Khurdagiya (scrap metal merchants) Street because it was full of stores selling scrap metal. Later it came to be known as Gawahirgiya (jewelers) Street, because a number of jewelry makers were based there. Toward the end of the 1960s, throughout the 1970s, and up to the early 1980s, Egypt was at the forefront of the production and working of gold in the Arab world. It is said that the industry produced from 300 to 350 tons of gold per annum, and the workshops in the district numbered nearly five thousand, covering the needs of

Silversmith in the Sagha, or silversmiths' and goldsmiths' district, 1973.

both Egypt and the wider Arab world. Now this number has dwindled to only a few for a number of political and economic reasons.

There are four entrances to this important quadrant: Bab al-Sirr (the gate of secrets—I don't know why it's called that), al-Bab al-Awal (the first gate), al-Bab al-Wustani (the central gate), and al-Bab al-Talit (the third gate). They are not exactly gates as we know them; they are merely entrances to extremely narrow alleys, from a meter and a half to two meters in width. Walking into this area is like walking into a maze: alleyways so tiny you wouldn't believe it, all leading into each other. Tiny stores set next to each other, their windows filled with gold, mostly 21-karat. A great quantity of this gold was looted after the 25 January Revolution in 2011, when the police abandoned their posts; this is why thick iron doors were installed, locked at night for security, to protect Egypt's gold treasure.

In this district is centered all the buying, selling, preparation and production of gold and silver. Goldsmithing, silversmithing, and creating jewelry; plating in gold, silver, and platinum; everything that this craft requires can be found in this quadrant known as the Sagha.

Gamal Gold Plate

In the early 1960s, the main person controlling the trade in raw and scrap gold in the Sagha was a Jewish man by the name of Yousef al-Afrang. His brother, Banou, was his business partner. In 1968, al-Afrang sold his business to one Bibawi Tawfiq; after Bibawi died, the al-Tazi and al-Shubukshi families appeared and began trading in gold. When their stores opened each morning, they displayed the prices of the precious metal on the international stock exchanges. Very frequently, the prices would change two or three times in a day, according to the international rate. It was a 100 percent male-dominated society. Women had zero presence here unless it was to buy and sell: a woman coming to sell her gold because money was tight, or a woman coming to buy new jewelry. The exception was a very few workshops where you could find young girls laying out the pieces to be welded on the bench, or *takhta*, consisting of a large rectangular piece of asbestos, onto which metal to be welded was placed (asbestos is now banned worldwide as carcinogenic). These included the workshop of Khawaga Fawzi Mikhail, who had girls helping him lay out the small links for chains. The food vendors in the area, selling macaroni, *kushari*, falafel, and fruit, were all men. I was the only girl with dealings in this craftsmen's district, otherwise entirely male at that time. I was one of the first university-educated women to break into this world to learn and understand the craft, the nature of things, the realities of this neighborhood, and the relationships in this society. I could see a goal before me very clearly, and this was the only way for me to achieve it at the time.

On my way to the Coppermakers' Street, in Sagha Street on the right-hand side, there was a store bearing an imposing sign that read, "al-Gamal [the Camel] Company for Gold Plate." The windows of the store were full of wares on display, bright and glittery. At the top of the window, the famous emblem of the company was displayed, a golden camel on a green background. This was the official store of the most important company in Egypt for gold plate, specializing in selling all sorts of countryside-style jewelry made from copper and plated with 21-karat gold. The buyer received a five-year guarantee against fading or pitting of the plate. This company had about seventy branches all over the country, and it licensed other companies to sell its products. I knew two outlets in the area: the Gammaliya branch, and the Ghouriya branch. These branches were distributors of the products of the factory owned by Lito Murad and his cousin Murad Murad, both Karaite Jews. They were probably residents of Maadi, as I heard in the Sagha. They had established this industry at the start of the century, founding their factory in 1912 in Khan Abu Taqiya. It was built in the old English style, four stories high, and it fulfilled all of Egypt's needs for gold plate. It is said that it employed around a hundred people at the time. The same factory had another branch, selling the same products but made in solid 21-karat gold, in a store next to al-Maqasis Mosque.

The descendants of Lito and Murad, Hafez and Aziz, also cousins, ran the factory until the late 1950s or the early 1960s. After that, their factory was confiscated to be "nationalized" and placed under government oversight—owned by the government, really. It was taken over by the Segal company. They say Lito emigrated to Australia and died in 1968.

Toward the end of the 1930s, Sadeq al-Kabir was licensed to distribute the al-Gamal products, and Said Sadeq inherited the profession of selling gold plate from his father. Every so often, I used to pay a visit to Said to familiarize myself with Gamal Gold Plate products and their varieties. I would sit and chat with him and he would show me the different designs and the names of each of them. The *Hilalat Fallahi* necklace, with crescent pieces in the countryside style, was the major piece of jewelry for the village women of Egypt. Other types of necklace included the *Cleopatra*, with a centerpiece meant to represent the famous Egyptian queen—but Heaven protect us all from the way Cleopatra looked, and how she was drawn, and how it was executed!

As for the earrings, well, the less said the better—at least on the design side of things. There were the *makhrata* (mincing knife) earrings, shaped like a crescent moon, with a little bird on them, and sometimes two birds; there were the *saqya*, or waterwheel, earrings, which were circular; there was the Seal of Solomon style, resembling a Star of David; the *tabaq al-qishta* (dish of cream); the *qurs marwaha* (round fan); the *shibbak al-nabi* (the Prophet's window, or sometimes *shibbak al-Hussein*, Hussein's window); and there were the *khangar* (dagger) earrings—shaped like a dagger, these were worn by the desert Arabs and the Bedouins who lived around Cairo. Dozens of styles were worn by Egyptian women!

I want to clarify an important thing the reader must understand: in large part, the traditional countryside designs that may have been made of gold-plated brass at the end of the nineteenth and the beginning of the twentieth century, were very finely crafted, both in design and execution. I'm speaking of examples that were truly museum quality. We all have seen these fine examples in the old Egyptian movies, like the Hilalat necklace and marvelous earrings worn by most of our famous belly dancers, such as Nabawiya Mustafa, Tahiya Karioka, Samia Gamal, and Naima Akef; they

An example of *tabaq al-qishta* (dish of cream) earring design.

An example of *shibbak al-nabi* (the Prophet's window) earring design.

became emblematic of the village style. Probably all the jewelry worn in the movies was plated, but well made.

One of the most attractive solid village pieces, as well as the heaviest, I saw about eight years into my practice of the craft, in a small town in Sharqiya Governorate called Gezirat Sa'ud, on the edge of the Sinai Peninsula, inhabited by the Tahawi Family, who were of Arab and rural stock. They raise horses and catch birds of prey, and train the famous peregrine falcon, which commands a very high price in the Arabian Gulf. It was an important experience where I saw a solid, well-made gold piece, made as it should be, owned by the Tahawi family.

Over time, the designs were developed and new elements added to many of them to create variety of forms and boost sales. Unfortunately, this "development" and these additions were done by amateur craftsmen and draftsmen, with limited knowledge of the rules and basics of good design—in addition, of course, to the shift from meticulous handcrafted pieces to pouring metals into steel molds to speed up production, and the tendency to simplify designs to save time and money, resulting in poorer quality workmanship. Sadly, a great deal of meticulous craftsmanship has been lost; our production for the masses has become poor and shaky compared to what it was in the last century and inferior compared to the original standard.

At this stage, I bought large quantities of Gamal gold plate of all shapes and sizes. I used them as a reference when studying village designs. I had most of the rural heritage of our country at my fingertips. I thank God for placing me in that neighborhood at that precise time, so that I could collect, with love and understanding and a thirst for knowledge, the great heritage of our country, which I later documented in my book, *The Traditional Jewelry of Egypt*, which is now the only reference book available on the subject.

What's odd is that the same models we used to see at the First Gate, the Second Gate, and the Central Gate, at the shops making village-style pieces in solid 21-karat gold, were mostly so well copied at the gold-plate stores that an average buyer couldn't tell the difference between the real piece and the replica. How many times I heard stories about ordinary women and gold plate! Frequent among these were tales of a woman short on money taking the necklace her husband had given her at their wedding or some other occasion and pawning it to get some cash, while buying an identical one in Gamal gold plate, until she could get the original gold one back when her situation improved—so that her husband would never notice it was missing! And the husband never knew the difference.

Here's another piece of information: the Gamal Company pledged to buy back their old pieces from customers who wanted to sell them, whether because they were short on money or because they wanted to change the style they wore. It was permitted to exchange styles and for 25 percent of the original price to be returned to the customer. That is, the company subtracted 75 percent of the price of the piece, and delivered the old pieces to the manufacturer to be melted down and the 21-karat portion salvaged.

There was another company that produced gold plate, called al-Samaka (the fish). Its output couldn't compare to al-Gamal, and after a while they quit the market, driven out by the powerful competition.

Said Sadeq's relationship with the Gamal Company ended in the early 1990s. He went into a different business, selling scrap gold to be reworked, and died a while later; currently, his son is running the scrap gold business.

I always visited the Segal factory. Often, I had my silver pieces gold-plated there. I dealt with that company exclusively to get my jewelry plated for fifteen years. Their plating is of very high quality and guaranteed. The jeweler Ahmad al-Desouqi, head of the plating department at the Segal factory, had forty years' experience in the field, and I dealt with him for long years. He was a solid craftsman. After that, the company no longer had the capacity to produce the traditional Egyptian pieces they used to; their work became confined to selling trays and ashtrays and plating others' products with gold.

I visited Segal—formerly Lito and Murad's—about ten years ago. It was for sale, and they asked me to help them find a buyer and find a good use for the molds and the machines devoted to Egypt's history of village jewelry that remained in the factory. When you walk through the factory door, to your left is a monstrously huge metal press, British-made: a gigantic sculpture. On the upper floors are British-made machines all in a row for making chains, and a group of smaller presses. There are rooms filled with molds for necklaces and earrings of all shapes and sizes. The antique British machines were pieces of art in my eyes, things that really ought to be in a museum. Unfortunately I couldn't afford to buy those marvelous machines, which represent an important part of jewelry making in Egypt. Now is the time to give credit where it's due, to Lito Murad and Murad Murad and their factory in Khan Abu Taqiya. And the company that sold their products, al-Gamal, played a large role, and deserves the greatest and most significant credit over four or five decades, in producing and marketing the great majority of the traditional jewelry that the Egyptian people wear.

Egypt's Gold and Traditional Jewelry

The Sagha district shone and bustled in the season of the cotton harvest. If a farmer had had a good harvest and had a bit of money he wanted to save up, these savings would be worn as bracelets on his wife's wrists or a necklace on her chest, and the little girls had their share of gold earrings. The windows of the Sagha were full at the time of the harvest sales, flashy and glittery and bursting with 21-karat gold of all shapes and sizes. The First Gate and the Central Gate had a bunch of small stores that specialized in this type of jewelry, like Shafiq Ghali's, Amin Nour al-Sirgani's, Taha al-Sirgani's, and Abbasi's. I used to find the narrow alleyways packed with people in from the provinces. It's important to note that the villagers of Upper Egypt were the main customers for 21-karat gold in that area—the *a la franca*, or "foreign style" people, as they called them, wore 18-karat gold.

One of the oldest goldsmithing families was the Sirgani family, in business since 1776. After that came the Ghali family, in business since 1800, and the Khurasani family who started in 1918. My friend Engineer Rafiq Abbasi tells me of his great-grandfather Abbasi, who started his jewelry making in 1888 at the Sagha and handed it down later to his sons Ahmad and Muhammad, whose names I see over the doors of their stores at the end of al-Sagha Street. He told me that his father had told him that in the first half of the twentieth century, he would open his shop at 6 a.m., timed to match the arrival of the train from Upper Egypt at 6 a.m., bringing the cotton merchants and farmers who'd sold their crops to buy gold jewelry for their families.

Gold bracelets were arranged on a stand called *al-mishkak*. Every type and form of bracelet was placed on a separate *mishkak*. The wealthiest of the cotton merchants would sometimes request two, three, or even four bracelets from each *mishkak*, to hand out to the family. In the end, such a merchant would buy two or three kilograms of gold to distribute among his womenfolk. The Abbasi family had a guesthouse above their store to provide breakfast and lunch for these important clients from Upper Egypt.

A landowning farmer would calculate how much he had made on his crop, and if it had sold for a good price, he would buy gold for his wife or daughter: a necklace, earrings, or bracelets. This was his bank, if he ever found himself in need. Farmers and traditional folk had no truck with banks. They bought gold for their womenfolk and sold it when cash was needed. The bank, to them, was their woman's bracelets and her necklace, or their little girls' earrings.

As for the marriage gift, called the *shabka*, families came to this neighborhood with the decision already made of how many grams of 21-karat gold to spend on it—"We want a thirty-gram/fifty-gram/hundred-gram *shabka*"— according to the family's social status. The goldsmith would start showing them the available pieces of that weight. The price of gold was stable to some extent at that time. Now a customer will come with a predetermined budget and say to the goldsmith: "I want a *shabka* for six/nine/twelve thousand pounds." The goldsmith always gave the buyer an invoice with the number of grams, the fineness of the gold, the price of labor per gram, and the type of jewelry bought. The family kept this important invoice to use when it was time to sell. In most cases, the buyer would return the piece he wanted to sell to the same merchant he bought it from.

A sight I saw often at the goldsmith's will illustrate the theory of the bank carried on the arms of village women or in the little girls' ears. If a father bought something for his daughter after the cotton harvest, he only bought earrings. The odd thing was that after the family picked out the earrings, the goldsmith would get out a pair of handheld pincers called a *qassag*, put the earrings into the girl's piercings, and use the tool to twist the gold wire at the back into a spiral behind her ears, making it impossible for anyone to take the earrings off her, as they were fixed into her earlobes. When she wanted to exchange or sell them, she would have to go to a goldsmith's to have them cut off with pliers. Putting earrings on this way was insurance against theft. Of course, this business confused me to no end design-wise when I was looking at the earrings at the Geographical Society Museum and acquiring examples of them during my research and study on what the vast majority of Egyptians—that is, villagers—wear for jewelry. I said to myself, "Why is the piercing segment of the earring that fits through the ear so very long, out of proportion with the rest of the earring?" Later, I understood that in many of these earrings, the goldsmith deliberately makes the part that enters the ear long, to permit him to close it up and wind the gold wire around the girl's ear, thus insuring her against the earrings being snatched out of her ears.

I have three or four village-style gold earrings in my collection: I bought them from an antique dealer in Khan al-Khalili by the name of al-Mansouri. The most attractive pair, with the best design and execution, is the *saqya* pair, which I consider to be one of the best village-style earrings in their design and execution in general: they were made up of over a hundred separate pieces.

Al-Mansouri's store was visited by a group of Upper Egyptians who sold old things, "house castoffs," as they called them. Their work was truly wonderful, very different from the gold of the Central Nile Delta—Tanta, Beheira, and Daqahliya. When I asked him, he told me, "These are from Upper Egypt, from Qous." Qous is an important city in Islamic history, located in Qena Governorate, through which people used to pass on their way to the Arabian Peninsula for the pilgrimage to Mecca. I remember once going with my father to Qous to visit a friend. There was a covered market there called a *qaysariya*, an old district where the street was covered with a wooden roof, like the Khayamiya (tentmakers') district in Cairo. There were *qaysariya*s in most of the regions of Upper Egypt. The most attractive pieces in my collection are worked by the famous *qaysariya*s of Upper Egypt, in Qift and Qous—designs that bring together meticulous craftsmanship, gorgeous design, and quality execution. When I went back to my old books on Islamic crafts, I found that Qous was a town that used to be famous for jewelry making in early times and, what's more, it used to house a mint during the Fatimid Caliphate.

Sheikh of the Silver Merchants

Hagg Muhammad al-Mikkawi was born in Cairo in 1902. He was the sheikh, or big man, of the silver dealers in Egypt. His father Ibrahim al-Mikkawi, said to have been his mentor, came here from Mecca in the early nineteenth century, when he started this trade. He was ambitious and hardworking: he was the first to bring steam and electricity into the rolling mills that form the plates and sheets of valuable metals, the process known as *galkh*, which used to be done by hand, the rollers pulled with ropes by a worker. In addition, this important manufacturer was a creator of original designs, especially in the field of Bedouin silver bracelets, *damaleg* in the language of the Bedouin and desert Arabs. He became so famous that Sheikh Lamin, the supreme silversmith of Sudan, visited him in 1920, and drew inspiration from some of his ideas for Sudanese jewelry. He stamped all the bracelets with a hallmark bearing his name written a calligraphic monogram known as a *tughra*.

Al-Mikkawi controlled the market, producing silver for all the Bedouin of Beheira Governorate and the Western Desert all the way to Matrouh and Siwa. On my visit to Libya, I found *damaleg* at antique stores hallmarked with the Mikkawi name. It is said that the Beja people and the Ababda tribes, all the way down to Sudan, were among the circle of his customers. His factory, or his main workshop, was at the top of al-Maqasis Street in #6 Wikala. His production is said to have been on such a large scale that the Hallmark, Weights, and Measures Authority in Beit al-Qadi, Gammaliya, received the large quantities he produced by the cartload.

Ibrahim al-Mikkawi, the father, went bankrupt at the height of his glory, and there are conflicting stories as to the reason, one being seemingly that the Jewish traders and silversmiths came together to plot and speculate against him until he had lost all his money. Muhammad al-Mikkawi then inherited the craft from his father, and opened his own store in the Sagha, becoming one of the biggest traders in scrap silver in the profession. The bracelets with the Mikkawi name on them are among the major historic pieces of that time. One of the stories Hagg Muhammad al-Mikkawi told me about his mentor Ibrahim is that the Bedouin of the desert used to come to him trotting in on camelback! They would spend the night in the little khans around the neighborhood, then take his silver products and leave, crossing the deserts until they reached their towns in the oases and towns of North Africa, carrying a part of their silver heritage, designed and executed in the workshop of this venerable old master.

Al-Mikkawi was the first modern Egyptian silversmith to put his name on the silver pieces he made, like his great forefathers, the master craftsmen who had put their names on the marvelous pieces they made, which I had witnessed at the start of my life in the profession on examples in the Islamic Museum and admired very much. I have a few brass and copper pieces in my collection, especially trays, bearing the name of their makers.

Some of my happiest moments were spent sitting with Hagg Mikkawi. He served me tea with mint, and we had endless conversations about the profession. What history, what stories! Trade secrets, and the people who worked the silver! He talked, and I wrote it all down. I remember him sitting in his little workshop against a backdrop of many large British-made safes and sacks overflowing with silver. He was the biggest dealer in scrap silver in Egypt and the main supplier of all the Sagha and Khan al-Khalili shops that worked in silver. I used to sit on a padded leather bench opposite him. First, he would order tea with mint for me, and tell me, "Look at this, lady." Then he would show me the pieces he had bought that day: earrings from the oases, an anklet from Fayoum, a ring from Upper Egypt, a silver cigarette case from someone's house, and so on. All these pieces were sold for scrap, that is, to be melted down and reused.

The recycling of raw materials, especially silver and gold, is central to this industry; they call it *tigarat al-kasr*—scrap dealership—in the trade. Most silver in Egypt is recycled, and most gold as well. Very often, I used to buy intact pieces, and also broken pieces. I have various batches and pieces of broken jewelry in my collection, which I keep for study purposes to see how the craftsmen connected the parts together with such skill—indeed genius—or sometimes to preserve an important ornamental pattern, or part of one, or an important technique included in a rare example of the craft. I keep dozens of broken pieces! They have been invaluable to me in the process of execution and design. (I found out later that museums around the world also keep incomplete pieces for research and study.) I bought them at scrap prices, that is, the value of the weight of the precious metal in them. Sometimes I couldn't afford them, in which case Hagg Mikkawi would let me pay later or in instalments.

This man was an important and wonderful archive of the history of jewelry making. I truly learned a great deal from him. He knew all the makers of silver and gold all over Egypt, as he was the most solid source of raw material. He had some idea about all the workshops in Cairo and the provinces, as he had dealings with them all, and he was the final depository for traders and individuals who came from all over to sell silver when money was tight.

The sacks and safes in Muhammad al-Mikkawi's store contained treasures of Egyptian silver jewelry the like of which I had never seen. I bought the pieces I needed to study from him and also to preserve this heritage, which would have ended up in the smelter's vat, and eventually recycled. (Most of the pieces in my book are Egypt's heritage that I saved from the smelter.)

An example of a *kirdan libba* (seed pendant). A *kirdan* (pendant) typically contains several hanging pieces, chains, or different motifs.

Hagg Muhammad liked to tell me stories about everything to do with this profession and its craftsmen. I took down all the stories in a small notebook I kept with me, and made notes about each piece he had, whether I bought it or sketched it if I couldn't afford it. When I got home, I put them on index cards with the sketches I had drawn, along with the notes I had made about the piece such as where it was made, the maker, which village or tribe used to wear it, and the relation the piece bore to any piece I had seen in a book or museum.

Hagg Mikkawi introduced me to the master artisans of the craft. Each piece was made up of several parts, and there was a workshop that specialized in producing each part. He would take me by the hand and introduce me to them. Hagg Farag al-Aqra' was the most prominent maker of thick

Fayoum bracelets. You went up to his workshop above the Sagha by means of a long, narrow staircase. Naguib Aziz and his father Aziz Rizq, by the First Gate, specialized in making the so-called "doll" that held up the face veil of the burqa. William al-Afarizi made jewelry for the *zar* spirit-appeasement ritual, and his shop was also by the First Gate. I very much enjoyed looking at his special *zar* jewelry. The silversmith Muhammad Fadda (*fadda* means "silver"), who had a shop in al-Suramatiya, made amulets out of silver and recited Qur'an over them; his customers were all women. Ma'allim Atiya Baqi specialized in making a circular bead they called the "olive" out of 21-karat village-quality gold. The great majority of Egypt's village women wore necklaces out of these beads. Kamel Uweida made the *libba* necklace, which had many strands: one, or two, or three, depending on his customer's budget. There was also Khawaga Yousef Matatia, who made gold beads of different sizes for threading. His shop was on the corner. A customer bought as many beads as she needed depending on how much money she had—for a short or long necklace—and did the threading herself. As for the *makhrata* (mincing knife) earrings, they were the specialty of Ma'allim Yaqoub Salib. There were also goldsmiths and silversmiths who specialized in making jewelry for Bedouin customers who lived on the outskirts of Cairo, in Hawamdiya and al-Saff, and wore burqas that incorporated a piece of gold known as the *basma*. I mourned that I had not photographed these master craftsmen in their place of work and added them to my archive. I did not own a camera, and mobile phones hadn't been invented yet.

I need to say something important that the reader may not know: the vast majority of Egypt's jewelry, whether in the Delta or in Upper Egypt, was produced in Cairo by workshops specializing in serving these regions. Each workshop made a single model: for example, 21-karat gold Seal of Solomon earrings, 21-karat gold dish of cream earrings, 21-karat Prophet's window earrings. A long history of designs, pieces, and names derived from folk heritage. Anklets and necklaces, too, each had someone who specialized in them.

For twenty years running, I came and went to this unique community. I lived there and became familiar with its crafts and *ma'allim*s and *usta*s, as well as the designs and types and history of these pieces which formed part of our identity. The goldsmiths, silversmiths, and workshops in Egypt's provinces and rural areas at the time provided only a small proportion of jewelry manufacturing; most of what went on there was the sale of pieces made in Cairo, or repairs of broken pieces for clients.

The distribution system involved the person called the *aboneih*, who was the main, indeed the only, distributor of the work made in Cairo in each of the cities, towns, and villages of the Delta and Upper Egypt. These were individuals with a good reputation. Their job was distributing the jewelry produced by the Sagha for the provinces and the villages and hamlets in the Nile Delta and the Nile Valley to the gold dealers in these places so remote from the capital, for an agreed-upon fee. I always saw them walking about the Sagha carrying seven or eight kilograms of Egypt's heritage to distribute among the provinces.

There was so much valuable information about Egypt's heritage and craftsmen, I can hardly describe or recount it all. Hagg Mikkawi was a treasure trove for me, and I loved nothing more than to sit by him for hours, enjoying listening to him and making notes of everything he said about jewelry, raw materials, silversmiths, and goldsmiths, and the history of this profession and these pieces. I could never in my life have dreamed to stumble on such a mine of information. I felt the weighty responsibility of these words from a trustworthy source—the sheikh of the silversmiths, who had met every craftsman working in this profession, as well as the traders and manufacturers of the provinces, the deserts, and all the teeming villages and towns of Egypt. All of them had passed by him at some point, and he knew everyone. He was a walking encyclopedia!

This information that I received drew me in and expanded the circle of my interests. I developed an interest in learning people's history—the villages and those who inhabited the Nile Valley, the deserts, and oases. At that time, I needed to read about the origins and homelands of different tribes, how these tribes were interrelated, and interacted with their neighbors, how they migrated from one region to another, their intermarriages with other tribes, and why there were similarities between the jewelry of different regions. Some of this research was effectively anthropological study, and I deeply enjoyed it.

I visited Hagg Mikkawi regularly during my training period, and continued to visited him often after I opened up a small workshop, to buy silver from him, melting it down, flattening it into sheets, and pulling out the wires for fabrication. I spent useful and enjoyable times with him: he enriched me with information about my life's vocation. He introduced me to all the tradesmen and silversmiths of the Sagha, and I think he was pleased to make my acquaintance—I was something new and strange that he hadn't seen before, a girl from university learning silversmithing as an apprentice in Khan al-Khalili, and also extremely interested in Egypt's jewelry heritage, its history and origins, and here he was, a dealer who knew all of that world's secrets.

I spent enjoyable hours and days with this expert, who gave me all the information about this profession. Quite often he would take me on tours of the Sagha and the famous Harat al-Yahoud (Jews' alley), which was a complete neighborhood unto itself. I bought a lot of things from there, especially when I was making the jewelry for movies or theater productions, which required jewelry made of brass. There were Jews, Muslims, and Christians living in Harat al-Yahoud, and until now you can see traces of the Jewish community that used to live there, such as Stars of David on the wrought-iron doors. On one occasion during my tours with Hagg Mikkawi through the mews and alleyways of the Sagha, barely wide enough for two people walking abreast, I met a child of about nine years old coming out of the place where gold bars are made, carrying about four kilos of 21-karat gold. In his hands, he carried about seven or eight long gold bars, and was walking around quite at ease, even carefree! This was something I could not understand and was stunned to see: this child was carrying a fortune in his hands, walking down the alley to deliver it to his employer. When I asked Hagg Mikkawi about this phenomenon, he laughed. "Lady, things here are secure! He's the apprentice of Usta Erfan! No one can touch him. If someone did, the whole world would be in an uproar and rush to defend him. This kid is employed by Usta Erfan and he knows him from start to finish"—that is, he knows where he lives, who his family are, and so on. "He couldn't go anywhere with that stuff! He would be caught immediately."

It was a world that was new to me. It was organized and ruled by trust, and it had its own laws, customs, and rules. The traders' and smiths' respect for these customs and rules was absolute. No one dared violate them. Their word of honor was stronger than any written contract, and they considered that anyone demanding written contracts or paper receipts from them was dealing them a great insult. The expression "You can dunk it in a glass of water and drink it," signifying that a piece of paper is good for nothing, comes from this concept, that one's word of honor is better than any paper. If any person should dare to break the rules of honesty and truthfulness within this society—be it by cheating on the purity of raw material, or not honoring his word—he would be rejected by one and all, and no one would have any dealings with him again.

When I entered this world of craftsmen, it still held the remnants of the old divisions between professions that used to be an essential element of urban life in the nineteenth century. The sheikhs of each guild oversaw most of the society of workers in the city, comprising makers and craftsmen. They intervened to break up fights and disagreements, and punished transgressors for wrongdoing. Thus they contributed in a clear manner to running the city and keeping order. These craft guilds worked as an administrative union in the city.

The pecking order of crafts in the old days had the *sabi* ("boy"), meaning apprentice, at the bottom, and the *ma'allim* ("master") at the top; and above the *ma'allim*s was the sheikh of the guild, or head of the union. All this had its roots in the tradition of the sheikhs of the Sufi sects. The *sabi*, who lived with his *ma'allim*, owed him obedience and respect, while the *usta* or *ma'allim* had a duty to teach the *sabi* the ins and outs of his trade. This process took from five to seven years, during which the *ma'allim* treated the apprentice like a father would a son, taking responsibility for feeding him and clothing him and covering all his expenses. After the *sabi* became proficient at the craft, he would show his work to the sheikh of the guild. Each *ma'allim* had a number of boys training under him, and a *sabi* could not leave his master without asking permission from the sheikh of the guild, explaining his reasons for leaving his master and getting the sheikh's approval. Apprentices received no pay, and it often came about that an apprentice, through constant contact with his master's family, married his daughter and ended up inheriting his craft, his expertise, and his business.

After a while, an apprentice was promoted to *'arrif* ("one who knows"), a level between apprentice and master. At this stage, he received a salary commensurate with his skill, and lived with the master still, for another three to five years, to gain experience, during which—again—he was not permitted to leave. If he were to do so, he would never find another master to accept him, as there is an ethics governing this process. When the apprentice became a master of his craft, after a longer period, he again presented his work to the sheikh of the guild, who then testified to him deserving the title of *ma'allim* or *usta*. Sometimes, the sheikh signed the piece presented to him as an indication that he had passed the *'arrif* on to the next stage. Frequently, a celebration called *al-shadd* was held for a *sabi* or an *'arrif* who moved on to the next stage. Before an *'arrif* became a *ma'allim*, or an *usta*, and became independent, another ceremony was held, called *al-idhn* ("permission"), to permit him to pursue the craft on his own. This was the system and the law that governed the profession, helped the craft evolve, and preserved the status of both shop owners and workers. It also guaranteed that individuals would not transgress or break the laws that were in place, which, in the end, produced magnificent works by great masters.

Unfortunately, all this has now changed. The Sagha is no longer the Sagha I knew in the mid-1970s. Mu'izz Street is no longer the Mu'izz Street of the 1960s. I made notes from all my conversations with Hagg Mikkawi, and noted the names of the major masters of the craft specializing in traditional jewelry, their locations, and specializations, and saved the most valuable pieces from being scrapped and melted down, now part of my private collection of Egypt's jewelry. It is part of the heritage of a nation that would have been lost in flames but for my good fortune in meeting the wonderful Hagg Mikkawi, and his agreeing to give me these pieces at prices I could afford, and frequently pay in instalments. And to this day, I possess a number of valuable index cards devoted to the profession: observations, information, drawings, and comments.

I remember when I would be traveling to an Arab country such as Syria, Jordan, or Iraq, the first place I used to go to was the goldsmiths' and silversmiths' district and the craftsmen's neighborhoods. If I had the money, I would always buy pieces in silver and gold, and take notes from my talks with the tradesmen and smiths. On my return to Egypt, I would start to compare the pieces from there with the pieces in my collection; I would often find resemblances. Naturally, this drove me to try to understand and find out about the migration of tribes from place to place, taking their heritage and culture along with them. I began to read about ethnography, and the effects of these tribes' migrations from place to place, carrying language, clothing, habits, and also jewelry.

One day, I was overjoyed to receive a phone call from a jeweler in Girga. He asked me, "You put a necklace in your book that I have the twin of in my shop. I wanted to find out its history exactly."

I responded, "Open to the back of the book. You'll find a table with the hallmarks on the necklace, which will tell you where it was made, and what year."

Afterward, he thanked me. "It was made in 1940!" he said gleefully. I was filled with joy to think that I had taught someone something useful!

The Wikalas

The main *wikala* in the Sagha is the Gawahirgiya (gem merchants) Wikala, where all the traders in valuable gems used to congregate. It had a big wooden door, about five meters tall, and inset into the big door was a small door they called Bab Khoukha. The deadbolt of the large door was magnificent, all in brass, covered with Islamic engravings, and opened and closed with a clever mechanism—a museum piece, in my opinion. Every time I went into the wikala, I spent five minutes staring at the wonderful historic bolt and its unique design.

The wikala had a garden in the center, surrounded by a square courtyard, around which were set all the jewelers' shops. I always visited Wassef's gem store to look at the old Turkish pieces he sold, or to buy old silver. As desertification swept across eastern Africa, large amounts of silver from the Rashaida tribe and the Horn of African flooded Egyptian markets. The tribes living there sold immense quantities of this national treasure in the markets of Arab countries. I bought important examples for my collection from Atef Wassef at the Gawahirgiya Wikala.

There was a second story at the wikala overlooking the courtyard. There used to be a Jewish goldsmith there called Noubar who made the clasps with steel springs for gold chains. It really was excellent work. There was also an Armenian craftsman on the second floor by the name of Henry, and he was the best at making the tiny gold cases that hold copies of the Qur'an to be worn on necklaces.

Years later, when I went to visit the Sagha and the Khan and pass by my old friends to say hello. I thought I'd pass by the wikala to take a look and feast my eyes on the beauty of the deadbolt there. But sadly, it had been stolen.

At the rear of the wikala there was a back door I used to come in by. Going upstairs, I would find myself face-to-face with old Uncle Abbas al-Talli ("the plater"). The frontage of his store was one of the prettiest I saw in the wikala, like the stores from the 1920s and 1930s. Hagg Abbas was a good man and a skilled craftsman. His store was always clean and tidy, and he always wore a white crocheted cap on his head. I used to like having tea and chatting with him. He spoke politely and respectfully. He was a first-class plater and understood his profession.

This area takes me to the Maqasis Mosque and the Diristawi Wikala, where the craftsmen specialize broadly in making silver trays. All the gifts handed out by ministries and government offices are from here, especially retirement gifts at the end of the tenure of an important employee, or a manager, or a minister, each according to their status. There used to be a Jewish engraver by the name of Eli Damdam, who engraved them by hand with steel styluses in different shapes (now steel engraving is done with lasers).

There was also the wikala of Baruch the dust dealer, the biggest in the area. I found that he used to export the dust after he had extracted the gold and silver it contained in his own primitive way. What was left he sent to a factory in England, where they used the latest technology to extract whatever precious metals were still left in it. This was then shipped back to Cairo, through official channels, namely the Customs Authority. All this were legal and above-board, with government approval.

After the Gawahirgiya Wikala is the Wikala of Abu al-Rus. It used to house the Qasabgi family, who specialized in making the extremely fine 23-karat gold wire—thread, really—used for embroidering the cover of the Holy Kaaba in Mecca. Some of the members of the same family did the actual embroidery, called *taqsib*—from this comes the name of the family, Qasabgi. This family also embroidered the veil for Princess Diana's wedding in 1981.

These very fine gold wires become hard after they are worked, so hard that they cannot be used for embroidery. So there was another family, al-Galla (the polishers), who heated the wires to give them the softness and flexibility needed for the embroiderer to be able to thread them into a needle and work with them. This heating process used animal dung to heat the wires: the heat given off by the dung was gentle on the fine wires, keeping them from melting, which they would if a fire burned too hot.

In the early 1970s, I used to see salesmen from the countryside in Sagha Street and inside the Sagha itself, carrying dung in reed baskets on their heads and selling it to goldsmiths for this heating process. One of the best known of the Galla family at Wikalat Abu al-Rus was Hassan al-Galla, who was also a famous plater in the Sagha. He finished the goldsmithing process by giving the gold piece the required color—whether bright yellow or cool, whether matte or shiny. I used to sit by him as he heated the gold piece gently on charcoal, using dung, then doused it in *nashtiba*, a mixture of sodium carbonate, iron oxide, gunpowder salt, and ammonia. I don't know the scientific name for it, but gold treated this way would come out like the gold in the Egyptian Museum—very bright and yellow.

When I wanted to press something, I used to go to al-Rubi in Khan Abu Taqiya, who had the best known metal press, as I didn't have one. He had dug a great hole in the floor of his shop, about three meters by three meters, and a meter and a half deep, which housed the press. We would chat about the profession while he sat in this hole like some kind of shelter. I gave him the work and sometimes waited, watching him, and sometimes left to run errands and come back.

I wanted to root around after the name of Khan Abu Taqiya ("the cap wearer") and find out where it came from, but I couldn't! It occurred to me that it *might* be because Egyptian Jews lived there, and some of them wore a yarmulke; so perhaps the name came from that. Heaven only knows.

There were two wikalas in the neighborhood facing each other, known as the Zeinab Khatoun wikalas, and sometimes the Aziza wikalas, after the female guard or gatekeeper of the place. I always liked to look at old houses and wikalas with their Islamic vaults and archways, and imagine how this neighborhood looked in the olden days. When I wanted to ask about something, I would stop to chat with the people living there, whether they were shop owners or the people I found sitting outside their homes on chairs in the street. Sometimes one of them would point out his house to me and say, "That's my house there above that wikala. I rent the air, you see, from the Ministry of Religious Endowments!"

I would laugh. "What does that mean, renting the air?"

"On the ground floor down there, this belongs to the Ministry of Religious Endowments, and it's rented out; the air above it belongs to the Ministry, and that's what I rent."

The Donkey Wikala was at the end of the market. I'm pretty sure it's called Wikalat al-'Agati now, after the 'Agati Family, which owns a lot of holdings in it. They say the Donkey Wikala was a place to tie up your ride—donkeys, mules, horses, and camels—for people coming to this important area to buy what they needed. An old-time parking lot! In Muhammad Ali's reign, there were about thirty thousand donkeys used for transportation; each donkey had a license, and its owner had a card that allowed him to work, and a donkey driver was called a *makari*. Among the special laws was one against cruelty to your animal, and not making it carry too heavy a load.

The most important storefront in this wikala was that of Ahmad Murtada, the king of engraving wedding rings. I still remember this artisan with his brilliant skill. We have a saying, "his hands are so skilled they should be wrapped in silk," and that definitely applies. He was the best person to engrave the names of the engaged couple on rings, no matter how thin, and decorate them with a pretty drawing. How talented he was! I had never seen such a level of skill in engraving inside a ring in my life, except for Italian craftsmen. Unfortunately, I didn't manage to keep a sample of his work, which I often had done at his shop for clients who asked me for a special design for their wedding rings. May he rest in peace, that craftsman, that artist!

The Chicken Wikala was pretty much facing Wikalat Abu al-Rus. It was small. I used to get my work polished at a shop there whose owner's name I can't remember at the moment. I didn't like to spend too long there, as it was stuffy, with poor ventilation. I don't know why they called it by that name. Most probably they sold chickens here long ago.

Abdin and the Nubian Jewelers

Nubian jewelry—the important and distinctive jewelry of the south—was absent from this artisanal quadrant in spite of its great importance as a basic part of the jewelry map of Egypt. I used to ask myself, "Where is Nubia in all this? Somebody tell me where the Nubian jewelers are!"

When I asked where Nubian jewelry was made and where it could be found, they all told me, "You need to go to Abdin. That's the heart of the Nubian community in Cairo." Long ago, most of them lived in the area around Abdin Palace, and a lot of Nubians worked in the palace back when we still had a king. There were four or five shops in the Abdin and Bab al-Louq area that produced jewelry for the Nubians who lived in Cairo and as far afield as Alexandria. The most famous of these was Awad Gasser, the sheikh of the Nubian goldsmiths and silversmiths. He was the king. There was also Hassan Ali Muhammad, from Sudan, who had his shop in Bab al-Louq—it's a car dealership now—and Shazli Hamed, from Mansuriya in Aswan; he was from the Ababda tribe. And Abdou Ahmad Hassan, known as Abdoun, was a jewelry maker from Abu Simbel, from the Fadija tribe. He died, and his son kept working until he died; I dealt with his son and we made a lot of copper jewelry, plated in gold, for the Nubian Museum in Aswan.

I remember my first meeting with Awad Gasser like it was yesterday. I walked into the shop and there he was, like some aristocratic figure, sitting before me! He was dark-skinned, in his fifties, fashionably dressed in a suit and tie, and he didn't speak like any of the merchants or craftsmen I had ever met. He was well-spoken in a way that showed he was well-bred and a man of some status. When he finished with the clients who were in the store to buy gold for the trousseau of a Nubian bride, come especially from Aswan for the purpose, the store was empty. He looked at me with great courtesy and said, "At your service, Ma'am." He was very like my father: dark-skinned, well-spoken, polite.

From that moment, I struck up a years-long friendship with him. He told me that he had been born in the village of al-Geneina wa-l-Shibbak in Egyptian Nubia and belonged to the Fadija tribe. He started to learn the craft when he was fourteen years old, from his brother. He spoke at length about Nubian jewelry and its different designs, and which villages' women wore which type. The designs were different for every tribe. I made notes of all this and went home to copy it out onto my index cards, together with a rough sketch of the jewelry in question. Whenever I had some money, I went to him to buy a Nubian piece. After a few visits, he said to me, "I'm going to bring you some things I've kept at home for a very long time. Silver from my ancestors' era. I want to show it to you."

We made a date, and I went to him at the appointed time, bursting with excitement to see all that he kept hidden at home and didn't display. He had asked me to come later, when there were no customers in the store. Then, he brought out a sack about sixty centimeters high and emptied it out on the floor. I thought my heart would stop. Nubian silver treasures, pieces made at least fifty to a hundred years ago!

I bought most of my Nubian collection from Awad Gasser, and in addition acquired valuable information from him about these pieces, and about which Nubian tribes wore them—Ulayqat, Fadija, Kunouz, Mahasi—in addition to the techniques used in making them. All this was a great help to me in my first book. You know, most Nubians wear 21-karat gold, while silver was worn by people in poorer regions, which makes sense of course.

I learned from him the difference between the jewelry of Egyptian Nubia and Sudanese Nubia, and even the differences in design. I will never forget this man. When I found Nubian jewelry with fish patterns, I asked him, "What brings fish to your Nubian designs, Mr. Awad?"

"*Bashmuhandisa*," he said, smiling and using the polite form of address to an engineer or architect, "most of them are fishermen. They like their women to wear fish."

One of the Nubian rings I'm very fond of is a simple one known as the Sidi Ibrahim ring. It is lovely and inspired me a great deal in my designs: I have used that magnificent composition in many rings and bracelets. A bridegroom gifts his bride three or four Sidi Ibrahim rings set with different stones to bless the marriage. The other favorite ring in Nubia is the Mangouri ring, always with five domes of silver—you know, five is a secret and blessed number.

How I loved Nubian jewelry, with its unique designs and a meaning behind every piece! A bracelet in the shape of a stylized breast to encourage the flow of milk, worn by nursing mothers. The most beautiful piece of Nubian jewelry is without doubt the *khilala,* which is hung on a woman's shoulder to pin the traditional Nubian wrap, the *toub,* to her gallabiya. Marvelous compositions of crescent moons, stars, houses, and sometimes fish, ending in a long chain, at the end of which the women hang a red wallet, embellished with wonderful geometric patterns in bright colors such as green and blue.

Because of the way the Nubian tribes are spread out across the Egyptian-Sudanese border, in small, scattered villages and hamlets, it was hard to find craftsmen to live there permanently. Life circumstances, too, left their mark on the jewelry worn in these villages.

I learned from Awad Gasser how Nubian jewelry was made, from the technique to the fineness of the gold that needed to be used, and how in the past century this profession used to be confined only to blacksmiths, called *tabiti* in those days. Most Nubian craftsmen toward the end of the nineteenth century and the start of the twentieth were blacksmiths by profession, and most of the techniques for making Nubian jewelry were based on hammering on steel molds of the required shape. The most widespread earrings in Nubia are the *'uksh* earrings, with their immense size, and the *fidawi* earrings, which I found in paintings of Akhenaten with his daughters sitting beside him, who wore almost the same design. Also, the *sa'fa* ("palm frond") necklace from Nubia is very close to a necklace drawn on a temple wall.

In Nubian jewelry, there is very little welding, which is always kept to a minimum. The smiths used to move from place to place, among Nubian villages, carrying everything they needed on their backs: their tools, anvils, and so on. They would lay a fire on the ground, and use a handheld bellows to melt the metal. They would go into the village and sit in the village square, and word would get about among the women that he had arrived, so they would come and crowd around him, each of them holding something in her hand. They were traveling smiths, and a single smith would do all the work that the village people wanted: broken jewelry needing to be welded, or simple pieces he could fashion as he sat there. An itinerant factory on two legs, they went from place to place, earning their living.

Sadly, Awad Gasser—this refined, aristocratic man—died, and the shop was taken over by his son, who turned to radical Islamism and sold everything to do with his father's work because he thought it was *haram*.

During this period, I also met Dr. Ali Zein al-Abidin, a professor of applied arts and researcher into the art of Nubian and popular jewelry: his two books were the only reference for this art. I stayed in contact with him for long years, until just before his death, and I learned a great deal from the information he included in his book.

Workshop Dust and the Shashangis

Here I need to talk about something important in our craft: the industrial waste it leaves, including dust, sanding materials, old cloths, and water for rinsing. The dust of the workshops, which is swept up daily—I often see how careful the craftsmen are of it and how they keep it in a safe place—well, when I asked what that dust was worth, my friends at the Sagha took me to the world of the dust dealers, the world of the artisans who extract the gold and silver from the dust of the workshop, collected annually. I wanted to understand this world, so sometimes on my break I visited the dust shops in Harat al-Yahoud to find out how gold and silver are extracted from workshop dust collected over the year, and the processes it goes through: burning the dust, grinding it, and then using mercury to extract the precious metal. It is dangerous for the health and is done in a primitive manner. In Europe, too, factories keep everything that was used to make jewelry, such as sanding materials, old cloths, and water for rinsing, and all this is also burned and sifted through to extract the precious metal.

Shishni in the Sagha is the determination of the fineness of gold, and a *shashangi* is the person who specifies the type and fineness of gold or silver in an ingot, using a basic chemical method.

Salah Yousef, a young university-educated man and the best-known seller of equipment and tools, was the first to open a store selling equipment for jewelers. I would sit with him on my lunch break or when I needed to buy equipment. He introduced me to the people in the neighboring stores, and discreetly supplied me with advice on how to deal with them. We talked shop and he would show me all the new equipment he had bought from abroad and the latest technology in the world of jewelry making. Sol, as I call him, is still a friend and my trusted resource in this world called the Sagha. I didn't have the budget to visit exhibitions abroad in the field back then.

I knew all his apprentices by name. Once I went into his store—it was very narrow, about two and a half meters wide, and long—and found one of the apprentices missing. I think his name was Muhammad. I asked after him, and he said, "I let him go."

"But why, Salah?" I asked. "He was shouldering some of the work with you!"

He said, "I saw him eating baked pasta from the cart on the corner that sells pasta with meat."

I laughed. "So what?" I didn't understand why someone would be fired for eating baked pasta.

"*Bashmuhandisa*," he told me, "he can't afford that pasta on his salary. He must be stealing from me. If someone who works for me suddenly starts showing signs of riches, it means he's stealing from me."

So many things I learned from mingling with all these friends, workers, and traders! Salah was also the one who taught me the code: the language used by workers and traders among themselves when they didn't want customers to understand them. *Yaft* meant "good," instead of the regular *kwayyis*; *'ashfour* meant "bad," instead of *wihish*; *hat al-gift* meant "shut up," instead of *uskut*; *al-dafsh ashfour* meant "the client is bad," instead of *al-zuboun wihish*; *al-dafsh yaft* meant "the client is good," instead of *al-zuboun kwayyis*; *dabbar ishtiqala* meant "get a commission," instead of *i'mil hesabak 'ala 'umoula*; *fa'as al-dabsh* meant "get rid of the customer," instead of *ikhlas min al-zuboun*. As for numbers, they were *ahadi, shnayn, shalousha, abu-rabi', khamsa, shisha, shisha w'ahad, shmouniya, shmouniya w'ahad, 'enetra*—which were very different from the standard Egyptian Arabic numbers. The term *nibista'* meant "let's go eat."

The world of this craft, its craftsmen, and its craftsmanship is a world I entered while still young, and it left important traces on who I am, and in me a soft spot for a world that will always and forever have a place in my heart.

The Hallmark, Weights, and Measures Authority

I had to get the pieces I made hallmarked to guarantee the nature of the metal used, whether silver or gold, and its purity. It's the law: no product may be sold in stores or to the public without reference to an authority for governmental oversight to assay the fineness of the metal—16k, 18k, 21k, or 23k for gold, and 60k, 80k, 90k, and 125k for silver. The authority tasked with this business was the Hallmark, Weights, and Measures Authority, an arm of the Ministry of Supply.

The first step to get licensed to practice silversmithing and getting the pieces from my workshop hallmarked was for me to pass an official government test to be qualified. The exam consisted of a series of questions about the nature of metals and the fineness figures of the precious metals for sale in the market, and an eye test to make sure my eyesight was good. The exam hall was full, with about forty workers waiting to get licensed. I was the only girl among them.

I passed the exam, which was held at the office headquarters in Gammaliya, and thus I became licensed by the government to practice my craft. This was in the late 1970s. I had become the only girl in Egypt who held a license to practice silversmithing and goldsmithing!

I didn't have anyone working for me yet who could take my work to the Authority; I had to do it all myself. The Authority was based in an old building overlooking Beit al-Qadi Square in Gammaliya. I went at eight o'clock in the morning and stood in line in front of the window where they handed out tin boxes to put the jewelry in that needed hallmarking. Then I stood in line with the workers in front of the deposit window, which was locked with a padlock. I handed in my work and got a receipt for it; then, after three to four days, I would come back and retrieve it from the same window, hallmarked. All this takes place in a big hall in the Authority. At 8 a.m., you would find at least fifty to sixty workers carrying their boxes of jewelry to be hallmarked, be it gold, silver, or platinum.

Around the same time, fruit sellers and greengrocers had to get their scales (back then called *qabbani*) checked at this office, to oversee their suitability for use. Also, all the iron weights equal to one kilo, half a kilo, and a quarter kilo were checked for accuracy. In earlier times, the weights were

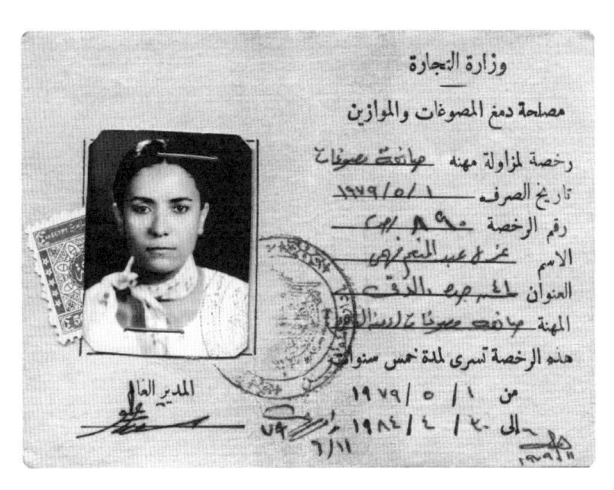

My license to practice silversmithing and goldsmithing, 1979.

an ounce, half an ounce, and a pound, and this was also when I saw the old volume measurements of a *qadah*, a half *qadah*, and a quarter *qadah*; there was also the *ardabb*, the half *ardabb*, and the quarter *ardabb*, measures made with great artistry and ornamented with nails on a base of metal.

It's said in the history books that historian Abdel Rahman al-Gabarti's father was one of the most accurate adjusters of weights and measures, and made sure the weight was correct. In the 1970s, I used to see vendors sitting outside the Authority to test their weights for the sale of fruit and vegetables.

The employees at the Authority heard about "that university girl who stands at the window every morning to hand in her work." I was called in by the assistant manager of the Authority, who said to me, "Madame, when you come in to get your work hallmarked, go to the office of Mr. So-and-So and take a seat there, and they'll help you hand in your work." This made things somewhat easier for me, as I no longer needed to stand in the morning lines: I went inside and sat down in an office full of civil servants, and one of them would take the box from me, hand it in, and come back with the receipt. I don't mind telling you that standing in line outside the Hallmark, Weights, and Measures Authority with the workers really didn't bother me, because I always had the feeling that I was part of that world, and was determined to learn everything related to my job.

After a while, I had made friends with everyone who worked at the Authority. I was an oddity to them: a university graduate working with her hands, and with a jeweler's license, to boot!

Opposite this office was the department where the jewelry handed in was sketched. Of course, this gave me access to a treasure I could never have dreamed of in my entire life: in 1916, during the reign of Sultan Hussein (1914–17), a law was made that all Egyptian gold or silver must be hallmarked with the fineness of the metal, and there were precise locations specified for all these hallmarks, to prevent falsification. This meant the Authority had to sketch all the pieces submitted to them so as to specify where on the piece the hallmark was to be located. During my morning wait for the official receipts, I met a fellow alumnus of the Faculty of Fine Arts, Madame Hala: it was she who sketched and recorded these drawings. The Drawing Department at the Hallmark, Weights, and Measures Authority opened up a treasure to me of drawings of old Egyptian jewelry, recorded by the Authority when it hallmarked them, since the 1950s.

I submitted a request to the Authority to get photocopies of these drawings, which I considered to be documentation of the jewelry designs of this period, and likewise the pictures hanging on the walls of the senior officials depicting the designs and history of the hallmarks, and jewelry pieces dating back to 1918. These were important and valuable documents for this profession.

The people working at the Authority were all acquaintances of mine, and often I came by there to say hello and to look at the large caches of confiscated contraband jewelry. All the staff knew of my avid interest in goldsmithing and silversmithing. Occasionally there would be a gold-smuggling operation, and it was the Authority that was responsible for assessing the value of the seized goods, which were held by the state and sold at public auction at the Authority annually. They invited me to attend that auction, and I came to one or two, but unfortunately the pieces on display were mostly commercial pieces with no artistic side to them at all.

I remember a funny story: I received a phone call from someone working at the Authority in the late 1980s, telling me that a quantity of ancient Egyptian gold, about 1.5 kilograms, had been seized at the airport from an American woman. "It's here at the Authority now, and we're opening it tomorrow. If you're interested, a committee from the Antiquities Authority will be coming, and we'd be honored if you wanted to come look at the cache."

Naturally, this was very intriguing to me. The people working at the Authority knew of my interest in important historical pieces. The next day, I went early in the morning to Beit al-Qadi. There was a committee from the Antiquities Authority, and another committee from Hallmark, Weights, and Measures, and me. They opened the sealed package after taking it out of a safe. And imagine my surprise when I found nothing but a collection of pieces by the famous Greek goldsmith Ilias Lalaounis! He makes copies of ancient Greek jewelry. I said, "Stop! These are modern pieces. They're no more antique than I am!"

I left them and walked out. I found out afterward that this was the jewelry of an important American official who worked at the State Department, a woman who had been on a business trip to Cairo. Heaven only knows what happened after that. But the jewelry was returned to her, with an official apology from the Egyptian Foreign Ministry to the US State Department.

I must thank all the officials of the Hallmark, Weights, and Measures Authority throughout my constant work with them, and my repeated visits for all this time, for access to the important historical material which was invaluable to me. I wrote about it in my first book, published by the AUC Press, on the history of traditional Egyptian jewelry. I know my way around a jewelry piece now: I can tell what year it was made, what region it came from, and the fineness of its metal. For instance, English letters were used in hallmarks from 1916 to 1940, when the Authority was run by British managers. Afterward, Arabic letters were used from 1940 to 1982.

My relationship with the Authority taught me a great deal about the process of exporting and hallmarking jewelry and the laws governing it. When my financial affairs improved, years later, I tasked one of the workers in my shop with the responsibility for getting jewelry stamped. I also gained experience in exporting my pieces, too, as a lot of Arab countries began to request an Azza Fahmy exhibition: I never liked to take a piece out of Egypt without going through the official process. I had to go to the airport dozens of times to get approval for exporting my pieces: I became a jewelry export expert, and an expert at standing at bureaucrats' windows. The employees working in this process always helped me and made my task easier, maybe because I was a woman.

People in Egypt generally buy gold and silver at the gram price announced daily on the market, as an investment, but to me, it was art. I like to design pieces that mix gold and silver, influenced by what I saw in medieval Ayyubid jewelry. I was the first Egyptian to mix gold and silver in the same piece. However, the laws governing the hallmarking of pieces in Egypt at the time stipulated that each piece had to be made of a single metal. This law put a stumbling block in the way of a lot of exports from my company, because the government would not allow the two metals to be hallmarked together. After three years of effort, I convinced the employees of the Ministry of Supply and Local Trade, responsible for the Hallmark, Weights, and Measures Authority, to propose a draft law to the People's Assembly to agree to hallmark two different metals in the same product. We succeeded in getting the law into the People's Assembly for discussion; the Assembly convened; and they approved it unanimously. I heard from the people I worked with on this issue at the Ministry of Supply that this law was unofficially dubbed the Azza Fahmy law! And so I became the first artist in Egypt to use gold alongside silver with the government's blessing.

All the buying and selling side of this profession I had to do myself. This came in very handy, especially after I founded the Azza Fahmy company. I became an expert: I even knew by heart how many hallmarks each piece required, and what they were called! That made it hard for any not-so-honest employee to cheat me. I had a small notebook where I took down everything I spent, a bit like a grocer's ledger. For ten years, I took it everywhere with me, writing everything down; when I got home, I would add it all together and write down and record how much I had spent.

3

BUSINESS AND MOTHERHOOD

Marriage and Children

A few months after I graduated, I took a job designing the home of famous composer Baligh Hamdi—a small apartment in Zamalek with one bedroom and a hall with a piano, at which he wrote his music. I knew a branch of this family very well from Helwan: Dr. Abla Hifni, a dear friend and former dean of the Faculty of Education in Zamalek, and her husband General Husam Hamdi, the brilliant officer who taught at the Military College, Baligh's brother. They were part of my close circle in Helwan. Baligh wanted to renovate his little apartment in Zamalek, and they asked me to meet him to reach an agreement. I was twenty-three. It was my first interior design job, and for such an important Egyptian composer! I was thrilled and enthused. The appointment was made to meet at his family home, where he lived with his mother, Auntie Aisha, and his sister, Safiya Hamdi, who used to be an inspector of artistic works at the Ministry of Education. This was a ground-floor apartment in a building overlooking the Nile in Zamalek.

They invited me to dinner, so that we could get to know each other. Abla and Husam came with me. The impression I came back with after this visit was wonderful: I liked the family a lot, and felt they were very similar to ours. Dr. Mursi Saad al-Din, Baligh's brother, was at that dinner as well. I felt that I had become part of a family I had known forever and felt familiar with.

I viewed the apartment, and Baligh explained his requirements to me. I began to come up with ideas for his tiny apartment. I visited his family several times; my favorite times were talking to them about work before I went to the Ministry of Information. I would arrive at 9 a.m., have breakfast with them, talk about what was needed, and then go to work. They were a delightful family, close-knit, and very fond of each other. His mother, Auntie Aisha, was a model mother. I learned that she had been a member of the Wafd party, and was friends with Safiya Zaghloul, the "Mother of the Egyptians" and wife of Saad Zaghloul, the adored nationalist Egyptian leader and advocate of independence in the late nineteenth and early twentieth centuries.

After a while, about three months in, I was sitting there with Baligh explaining something I was going to do at his apartment. He looked me in the eye and said, "Azza, will you marry me?"

Truth be told, I was struck dumb. Of all the questions I had ever thought he'd ask me, I wouldn't have imagined this! I was quiet for a time and said, "You are all a wonderful family and I like you all very much, but I know nothing about you as a person. Give me a chance to get to know you and then I'll tell you what I think."

When I went home to my mother at the end of the day, she said, "I have to get the opinion of your paternal and maternal uncles." Baligh was thirty-six at the time. Well, the uncles categorically refused. They said it was an unequal marriage and wouldn't succeed. They said we were incompatible, with very different lives. Of course, the enthusiasm and vigor of youth, and what came into my head and what I thought, led me to say, "How can they reject someone they haven't even met?" I was young and reckless, inexperienced, with poor judgment; that's how I see it now. A while later, they said, "Do what you want. You're a free agent, and you're the one responsible for your life."

So we got engaged, and I started to get to know Baligh better: his life, his friends, what he did and with whom—I had only known him for the few hours we had spent talking about work. The first to congratulate us was the Lady of Arab Song herself, Umm Kulthum. She wanted to speak to me on the phone, and when I heard her awe-inspiring voice on the line saying, "Congratulations," I dropped the receiver! To this day I can't forget it. It's something I can't describe—the strength in her voice, broad and deep. I went to one of her concerts where she sang "Faat al-mi'ad" (It's too late), the song that Baligh had composed for her. I was sitting at the front. It was something truly mind-blowing to see her singing on stage, and witness the audience's interaction, and their love and admiration for this unrepeatable phenomenon known as the Lady.

The battle of my family rejecting Baligh began to calm; I calmed down too and took to thinking rationally. Was this the man I wanted? Months passed, and I didn't learn anything new about his life. Breakfast and/or lunch, talks and discussions about music and its history, more discussions of traditional song and modern vocal technique. He was a genius, a prodigy in every sense of the word. He was deeply Egyptian, with a clear vision, and left his own stamp on everything he did. He respected ancient heritage and how it should be reused: Sayed Darwish and the singers and performers like him, Egyptian folk rhythms, reusing these with Umm Kulthum and Abdel Halim Hafez. He had conviction in what he did, understood it well, and was genuine. I deeply admired this facet of him. But what made him tick? I was no closer to knowing! Personally, we were no closer than we'd been before.

Credit where it's due: his brother Mursi Saad al-Din wasn't happy with this engagement. He came out once and said to me: "Azza, think. Will you be happy in this marriage?" His honesty earned my boundless respect.

After a while, I could tell it wasn't going to work. I decided to be honest with Baligh. I remember that day well. He had a rehearsal at the Institute of Arabic Music with Abdel Halim Hafez. I had been there that morning explaining something about finishing up with the apartment. He said, "I have a rehearsal now; let me drive you to the Ministry of Information."

I got in next to him. He had a little red sports car. I felt like the actress Miryam Fakhr al-Din in one of her movies, riding next to him, with my hair blowing in the wind. We arrived at the Ministry. It really only took a few minutes. "Remember, Baligh," I said, "when you asked me about us getting married, and I said give me a chance to think? I need to tell you that I think this relationship isn't going to work. I'm very sorry." And I rushed out of the car, not waiting for an answer. He was staring and looked stunned.

And so this short story ended with Baligh and the family I was so fond of. It was a brief engagement, which I later analyzed like this: The family had chosen a girl who was well brought up, from a conservative family, wanting Baligh to marry and start a family with a wife who could give him children and keep his household intact, surrounded by a close-knit, pleasant family who were fond of one another.

I've since been married twice in my life. The first time was in the late 1960s. I had just ended a relationship that wasn't a relationship, which had lasted five years of my university education, the best time to enjoy friendships and hanging out. I was introverted. This person and I never met face to face; he never even held my hand. It was all over the phone. He controlled all my movements. I was only allowed to move in the family's social circles: the family, my home, my university, and my closest friends from Helwan. That was all. No trips, no movies, no theater, I couldn't make a move without his permission. Most young men in university can't be trusted, especially in their attitudes, and you need to be careful of them. Now, I can't even believe it myself. How did I end up living the role of Amina, the subservient and submissive wife of over-controlling husband Si al-Sayed in Naguib Mahfouz's *Trilogy* for five years of my life?! I was probably naive at that time—like an idiot, I was happy to be controlled by this lion of a man!

When I decided to go on a trip to Italy with the university, breaking the rules of the game and throwing all his commands to the four winds, I took on a completely new worldview. The Italian journey opened me up to the beauty of life. I enjoyed the company of young people my age, open-minded and fun. When I came back to Cairo, a light had come on in my head. I saw my colleagues at university with new eyes. A close friend of mine, Ihsan Nada, the jewelry artist, and her fiancé at the time, Ahmad Rabie, became part of my basic circle. I started to go out to the theater, the movies, the opera, the Pocket Theater. More joined the gang, and the circle expanded a little. I experienced part of the cultural circles of the 1960s and the "revolutionary tide." I met my first husband at that time. He was a cultured leftist who could talk about anything, and had information and answers for everything—a walking encyclopedia. Music, he knew. History and politics, he knew. Philosophy, literature and poetry, he could discuss well. Anything that crossed your mind. I was massively impressed with him.

Now I wonder: how, in my twenties, was I so smitten, so impressed, with people just because they could talk about everything and answer every question in my head at that time? Frankly, I was bowled over by this type of man, and felt that my happiness in life lay in choosing the right partner who I felt understood everything in the world and was culturally open-minded.

In the mid-1960s, there was very little travel; but young people were permitted to travel and work in Europe in simple jobs—restaurants, offices, factories. This young man went annually to work in the vineyards of Bordeaux in France, so famous for their wine. He came back to ask for my hand after his summer job in France, and his engagement gift to me was an iron wolf trap. He had found it when he was digging in the fields. How thrilled I was with the old trap! It dated back to medieval times. A real museum piece! I hung it in my bedroom and he told me, "This is my engagement gift to you."

My mother, of course, lost it completely when she saw the gift, which I showed her, beaming and puffed up with pride. She stared at the trap, not knowing what to say. Of course, I understood from her face what she wanted to say. When his family came to ask for my hand, they bought the *shabka* themselves and brought it with them. But at the time, I'm telling you, I was completely in love with that ancient trap. (Stupidity at its finest.)

After we were engaged, he earned a scholarship to study for his PhD in Italy. After a while, he became involved in the leftist movements that were widespread in Europe at this time. Altogether he spent about five years between Italy and France. Time went on, perhaps more than two and a half years, and as the saying goes, "Out of sight, out of mind." There were constant arguments between me and him, and at the time it wasn't so easy to communicate with someone in another country as it is today (with mobiles and email): we had to make international telephone calls or write letters. At the time, Europe was for him the opening to a new world. The student movement in France was flourishing, and he also found himself there. He refused to come home, and wanted me to join him; and later, he decided to join the armed guerrilla groups in South America, which were then at their height. Guevara was everyone's leader, and his image hung on every young person's wall, and appeared on their t-shirts as well. At that time, I had just started to see my path ahead and to get to what I wanted to achieve; my work in jewelry began to crystallize, to take shape, to become clear; and I couldn't see myself toting an AK-47 and forging through the forests of South America!

We started to take different paths. At the time, we had groups of friends in common, and I grew closer to another man in the group. The rift between me and my fiancé began to grow wider. I decided to resolve the confusion by going to France in a true attempt to find out what our relationship was coming to. "Girl," I said to myself, "your fiancé is a respectable man, and he has a lot of qualities you admire. You chose him. You must go and make the relationship a success. You have to try."

So I did. After a while, I felt that each of us really was on a different path. I decided to break up, and I told him. I came back to Cairo and began to focus on my jewelry work. My relationship with the other friend grew, and we married. We were married for seven years without children: something made me hesitant. Then I realized that children are the most wonderful thing in the world. They are real happiness and joy. They gave me what was missing in my life. I had Fatma and Amina, with three years between them—even that was planned, because the books said that this was the ideal age difference between children! I had to lie in bed for a long time, so I read everything on childrearing from start to finish: nutrition, psychology, developing a child's personality. This marriage lasted for about seventeen years. In the end, it didn't work out for many reasons. The marriage failed, and we broke up.

Harraniya

I had to face life on my own with all its responsibilities and with the two girls. We had built a house in a village outside the city in the countryside on the Saqqara Road, in a place called Harraniya. I took the girls and moved out there, and started what I call the Harraniya stage in my life, which lasted ten years.

At first, it was a challenge to make Harraniya work. My work and workshop were very far away; the house had no furniture, and I had to furnish it piece by piece; there were school fees, and I needed, like every Egyptian parent, to help the girls with their homework. The house was built on a plot of about two feddans. I had to take care of this land and benefit from it by planting all the vegetables we needed. I tried to learn how to plant summer and winter crops, and how to plant without pesticides—in other words, organically.

I had fruit trees: limes, oranges, tangerines, and date palms. How could I benefit from this expanse of land in my daily life, and save up some of the crop to sell? Early in the morning, I used to go down to the land with the farmer we'd hired, see what he was doing, and give him the instructions and requests of an agricultural engineer whose help I had enlisted on the advice of some friends, so I could grow things right. He came to see us once a month, and I

The house in Harraniya, 1980.

had a notebook in which I wrote down the instructions and precise times for certain steps that had to be taken, such as pruning the trees and getting rid of insects by spraying insecticide, when to sow the arugula, parsley, and dill, the jute mallow, fava beans, onions, and garlic. All this was homegrown.

We also bought a water buffalo, chickens, and goats. I thought of making cheese like my mother did. Of course, I ended up not doing it and the project failed. The house was behind the village, on the Sukkari drainage canal, opposite the important compound established by the great architect Ramses Wissa Wassef. The villagers threw their garbage and dead animals into the drainage ditch, blocking it, and I had to solve this problem. I made friends with all the irrigation engineers in the area and knew them all by name. I also had their telephone numbers in case the canal got blocked. I went to them in a faraway village half an hour's drive away to have them unclog the ditch at least four times a year.

Then there was electricity and its problems, and laying a cable to illuminate such a big house, and how to guard the house! I hired guards from Saqqara and Shabramant armed with licensed rifles, because they worked for the Ministry of Tourism to guard this historic area. Naturally, every so often they brought me something from I don't know where, some statue or artifact they got from their co-workers at the archaeological dig, trying to sell it to me! I finally got them to understand that I was an artist, not a dealer in stolen antiquities, and they gave up after realizing it was no use trying.

I was responsible for the farmer I hired to cultivate the land—his health, his family, his children. One of the responsibilities was the three guard dogs they kept, organizing their food and vaccinations. After a while, the girls started pestering me for a dog, so we got a boxer and they promised to take care of him. But in the end, the responsibility for the dog fell to me. I could barely keep up with feeding and vaccinating him, and in the end he became sick and died.

In the house, the living room had a marvelous fireplace. I designed the tile around it myself at the workshop of Samir al-Gindi, the famous ceramics artist. We had to lay in a supply of wood for the entire winter season; we kept it in a room behind the house. It's bitterly cold out there because it's an open area, all farmland around the house. I don't even want to tell you about the various flying bugs and the oversized mosquitoes. We also had to organize getting rid of rodents, mainly mice, which had to be done regularly, or else the house would be overrun!

My best times with the two girls were when I got back from the workshop, all sitting on floor cushions around the blue-tiled fireplace with its gorgeous Mamluk designs. We were served supper on a big old brass tray, and we ate and chatted, and they told me about their day. I told them about my day, too: who had visited, what I had done, what I had sold. We would build the fire up, adding wood each time it burned low.

My name had become better known, and I had more acquaintances from neighboring Arab countries: Sudanese, Libyans, Syrians, and Iraqis, as well as Egyptians; professors, doctors, researchers. I decided to hold my first New Year's celebration at my house, in the lovely eastern hall, with its beautiful ornamental marble floor and a little fountain in the center. How I enjoyed the three or four New Year's celebrations at that unique house! Traditional food, traditional clay pots: everything was homemade. I do believe my guests enjoyed it.

I want to tell a story I just remembered. I had a chauffeur from the village by the name of Khalil, a plump, cheerful, and trustworthy young man. He drove the girls to and from school. I usually went to my workshop in the mornings, driving my Volvo to Boulaq al-Dakrour myself. One time, Khalil had to leave early after he drove the girls to school, because someone close to him in the family had died. Abdallah the caretaker called me on the landline—cell

With my daughters Fatma and Amina at the house in Harraniya, 1990.

phones hadn't been invented yet—and said, "Who will bring the girls home?" There was only fifteen minutes left till school let out. Qadriya, the wonderful woman who served as the girls' nanny—who played an important part in my life as someone responsible to care for the girls, without whom things would have been very hard, and who was like one of the family—suggested a way out: Abdallah could go and pick the girls up. I agreed to the idea, as I didn't have any other solution. So Abdallah went and picked the girls up from school, and when I came home Qadriya told me, laughing. "Amina came home riding the donkey with Abdallah, and Fatma walked alongside!"

Long years passed. One day I was chatting with Amina and remembering our years living in Harraniya, swapping stories and memories. The story of her riding home from school on a donkey with the caretaker came back. Suddenly, her eyes filled with sorrow and rage. "If you only knew how I suffered at school from what you did! Some of the kids made fun of me, and I got mocked and teased for ages over that thing with the donkey!" I felt so guilty at having failed that girl and forcing her to have a hard time at school.

But truly, it was just a practical thing to save the day: there was nothing else for it. Seeing my face and how I reacted, Amina smiled and said, "Mummy, those are spoiled rich kids. Forget it. I got over it myself and decided to laugh about it." Then she said, "You ought to see me if this happened today—you'd see what I'd do to those mean kids!"

"Now that's a strong girl," I said to myself. That was when I understood the full meaning of bullying, how much it hurts and affects children, and how one should not dismiss these things or take them lightly. I'm sorry, Amina. I really couldn't help it.

The issue with women who have a life like mine is the constant sense of guilt and a continual sense of falling short or failing their kids, and not giving enough. I always tried to convince myself that it mattered more to spend quality time, not quantity—in any case, I had no other choice. Over time, I tried to spend as much time with them as circumstances permitted, to make our time together matter. I tried to concentrate on culture and upbringing, and choosing the friends who surrounded us wisely.

In the summers, we went to England to stay with a dear friend, Soheir Kamal, who lives in central London. She had a spare room where we stayed, and we used to spend about two weeks holidaying there. The first items on our lists were the museums: the British Museum, the Victoria and Albert Museum, and the Natural History Museum. We also visited the seasonal exhibitions and the famous parks, spending a day with my friend Christine Green, the Egyptologist, and her son James. Our Oxford Street shopping was limited. Sometimes I also brought the girls' close friends, Inji Husni and Karim, with us.

For long years, I was invited to represent Egypt at a craft show in Britain. I used to enlist all these young people to help me with sales, and I made a habit of bringing along a craftsman from a different profession, such as tentmaking or glassmaking or pharaonic relief carving to work in front of the visitors. I became acquainted with the best craftspeople from Asia, Africa, and America at that fabulous exhibition, and made friendships which have lasted until today. The team of children used to help with everything. The Oxford exhibition was a wonderful time with the children, fun and educational for us all, opening up a world of leading craftsmen from all corners of the world.

Ten years after I moved to Harraniya, I had acquired a decent amount of experience in all types of summer and winter farming. I also came to know

Portrait of me in Harraniya, early 2000s. Copyright © Randa Shaath.

all the diseases that afflicted the crops. I took the books on agriculture out of my late father's library and started to read them; I also planted the flowers my father had liked. I grew familiar with the differences between planting citrus and palm trees, with tree pruning, with the proper time for everything, and what to do for a palm tree to make it bear fruit. I used to bring in a *nakhal* (palm tree person) to assist us at pollination time (there are male and female palm trees). Drip irrigation took up a large portion of our land, and I learned its pros and cons. I also needed to get involved in irrigation in general, and cleaning the public ditches, including dealing with the relevant government offices. Truth be told, in the end I was completely exhausted, and still couldn't keep up. The issue was that there were other responsibilities: my home, my daughters, and my business.

The things I used to love about Harraniya began to disappear. Unregulated housing started creeping closer to us, and state-built bridges blocked off our view of the great pyramids, in front of which I used to sit on my bedroom balcony and meditate. That beautiful home and the land around it was a management job all to itself, and my pressures mounted as our business expanded. I had to start thinking about leaving the world of country living outside the city and going back to living in a regular apartment in Cairo.

After ten years in Harraniya, we moved into an apartment in Dokki, opposite the Goethe Institute, on the twelfth floor, with a rectangular balcony overlooking the Nile. I lived there for twenty-five years.

All these things and the journey of my life, how I lived, and the choices I made, weren't easy. The journey into maturity that I went through was hard and very often burdensome. Unfortunately, there are pros and cons to everything in this world. After a while, I felt that something inside me had hardened. I don't know quite how to describe it, but I think I lost my softness and vulnerability: I had to set it aside because of these circumstances and this lifestyle. I had become serious, sometimes too serious—maybe even stern and forbidding. I didn't laugh or smile often like my mother did. This type of life affected me: it made me severe and businesslike, and I mercilessly trained myself. "Don't get worked up," I always said to myself. "Don't let it upset you. Just think calmly, and everything will work out."

I never made any allowances for my mood. Not in the mood today? It didn't matter, I worked anyway. Bored? Fine, no problem, I worked anyway. Sick? If it wasn't so severe that I was flat on my back, I'd tell myself, "Work through it, girl, and drink lots of lemon juice." I always had to keep going. I couldn't let things grind to a halt. Everything that needed doing had to be done. I really do admit there never was anything I had to do that I left undone. The many weighty responsibilities, the decisions dropped in my lap, made even my human interactions businesslike, and the daily business of living killed a great deal of life's romance.

Finally, I have understood where this unattractive trait came from. I try to be aware of it—I swear, I'm trying—but nature wins out. Now, whatever situation I find myself in, when I remember, I push back that nature and I try to do better. When I'm sitting and chatting with Amina, she'll often stop and look at me and say, "Mummy! Smile!" And I'll laugh and smile lovingly at her.

> I have no tears to cry,
> Nor wings to fly.
> In my heart is the weight of a mountain
> And a bird's fragility.
> —Fouad Haddad, Egyptian vernacular poet

Overalls

My first fifteen years in this profession demanded using powerful acids, especially nitric acid diluted in water, to remove all the residues that might interfere with the welding. The acid is put in a beaker they call a "boiler," and we dip the jewelry pieces in it each time they're welded. When the acid sometimes splashed onto my clothes, it left holes all over; in the end, to save my clothes, I took to wearing overalls, like manual workers wear. I was thinking practically, and it was a great solution.

I chose nice-looking overalls worn by workers in America. My first pair was brought to me by an American friend visiting Egypt, and I was delighted with them, they were so practical. I took to asking anyone who came from America to buy me overalls with shoulder straps from Sears, which sold for twenty-five dollars. The best gift I could get from abroad was a pair of blue, or striped, denim overalls, which really did save my clothes for a long time. I was always in my overalls and sneakers, marching straight ahead. I had no sense of alienation or anything odd. I always felt that you must think practically and do what suits you as long as you're not harming anybody. I went everywhere in my overalls, even to the bank. It seems to me that I spent fifteen years straight in overalls and sneakers, as far as I can remember.

After years of being attached to that uniform, I began to design similar overalls in the same cut, but in different fabrics, with an artistic and traditional side to them. I wore those for long years as well; they still hang in my closet, and I have a personal relationship with them. They're part of my beloved history. They remind me of the past and I treasure them; I can't bring myself to give them away.

Even my personality has changed because of my job and always being around workers, especially in my early years in Khan al-Khalili. I had to look a certain way: baggy trousers, a blouse long enough to cover any curves, hair severely pulled back, and no makeup at all. There was no place for taking care of my appearance in my long years in the world of the craft and craftsmen; quite the opposite. I had to wear clothes that I didn't mind getting spoiled—with holes from the acid, or stains from machine grease and from sitting in forging shops and pressing shops and rolling mills, and on chairs or stones dirtied with grease or the black residue from forging metals, where I sat waiting for my job to be completed. The overalls solved all these problems for me. But something happened inside me: caring for my appearance or looking smart no longer meant anything to me, and I now threw on whatever and went out. In fact, my daughters—some time after I had stopped working with my hands and focused instead on perfecting my designs, which had become my mainstay—often told me, when I was going out to the office or to meet someone, "Mummy, how can you go out of the house looking like that? You're the most famous designer in Egypt! Take some care with your appearance!"

It really didn't make a difference to me. My appearance was never a problem or any kind of issue for me. Now, for the last few years, I've been trying to change this aspect of me. I'm not young anymore. I need to wear things I like and jewelry I'm fond of, and stop walking around like a hobo, and quit thinking that nice things are wasted on me.

I have fond memories that I always recall now with a smile: walking out of work at the Sagha and going to visit close friends, I used to be still wearing my overalls—I mean, I didn't go home to change before visiting. Zeinab Shaalan and Badriya al-Ghanem, two of my closest lifelong friends, used to say, "Azza, please! Not on the white couch in the grease-stained overalls! You'll get it dirty!" We remember it now and laugh.

Now, after all these long years, now that I have a factory of my own and female employees, when a woman comes into the factory wearing something too tight or revealing, I say, "How can you come to work looking like that? You need to dress in a practical and decent way."

After a while, I had some money and I bought an old used Fiat 126 to get around, sparing myself the endless bus rides. At first, I was embarrassed to go into the Sagha by car, even though it was a very modest car! I felt it was too ostentatious to flaunt it in front of all the workers who knew me, as they were used to seeing me on foot, carrying my work bag. For long years, the final stage of finishing a piece of jewelry had to be done outside our workshop in Boulaq because we didn't have the equipment. I used to collect everything that had to be done elsewhere—polishing, gemsetting, and plating—into a big bag, load it into my little Fiat, and head for the Sagha. I would park the car in a lot next to Wikalat al-Ghouri and cross the street from the Sagha. Then I would call in at the specialist workshops to get jewelry polished or gems set at the Chicken Wikala at the top of the Sagha, and I would leave the pieces at old Uncle Ahmad the polisher's; I would give him a specific number of pieces and asked him to finish them at once. Then I would go over to the gem setter's to get the gems I was carrying set into jewelry, once again, counting out the pieces I gave him; then it was on to Erian Henein's to get some pieces plated in gold, according to my clients' requests. Then I'd sit at Erian's and chat to pass the time until the others finished the work I had left at their shops.

Erian was a good friend, and I enjoyed talking with him. He always had interesting and useful information for me. His family were all artists: one brother was the famous sculptor Adam Henein, and his other brother, Nessim Henein, was a researcher at the French Cultural Center, and had written important books on cultural heritage. Then finally, if there was time, I would go to Hagg Muhammad Mikkawi's stall to see him or go and chat for a bit with Salah Yousef.

Then it was time to make the same tour in reverse, collecting all my work, putting it in my bag, and going back to the parking lot. I used to leave my car in the care of Ahmad the parking attendant, whose whole family were parking attendants—he and his brothers were responsible for this whole parking area. He was a nice young man, always smiling. I knew him for thirty years, up until his death. Ahmad was one of the people who made my life easier during my Khan al-Khalili years. I had no problem at all leaving the car with him and taking off running.

Sometimes I had hunger pangs at night when I finished my work, so I would stop at Halwagi's, the best known falafel vendor in al-Azhar. Halwagi was a tall, plump, smiling man in his fifties, always sitting. I never in my life saw him stand up. He sat with his awe-inspiring presence in front of the frying oil, wearing a gallabiya and a white apron, a crocheted cap on his head. He wore white all over, "white as jasmine," as we say! I would order an *'igga* sandwich from him, which I liked very much: like an omelette made with falafel and parsley. I would watch admiringly as he made it and stuffed it into a small loaf of white pita bread, then handed it to me with a big smile, saying, "Bon appetit, *Bashmuhandisa*." I learned how to make *'igga* from Hagg Halwagi. He gave me the recipe with a smile, and now I make it at home (one egg, a spoonful of raw falafel paste, and a lot of chopped parsley). The venerable man had a policy that he stuck to: if you ordered an *'igga* sandwich and he started to make it, and you later changed your mind as to the number—"Make it three!"—he curtly refused: "Leave some for others to eat." All his customers knew this of him.

I just remembered a scene at Halwagi's: there was always a red convertible parked outside the store, just like the cars we see in the movies. I thought it belonged to someone going into the Hussein Mosque, or sitting at the Fishawi Café, which was almost adjacent to his store. Often when the Hagg was frying the falafel, there was a handsome young man by his side helping him: he wore a white apron like him and passed him things. I found out later that this young man was his son Ahmad, who was a university student. Years later, I happened to see this young man driving that red sports car through the streets of Cairo, like a scene from an old movie of heartthrob Abdel Halim Hafez! I was confused for a moment. I knew Ahmad Halwagi very well. Then I laughed in delight. At that time, the class divide wasn't so rigid, and a university student felt no shame in helping his father with his profession, even if his father was a falafel vendor.

Years later, I passed by Halwagi's for the *'igga* sandwich I was so fond of. Unfortunately, it wasn't there any more. There was another sign for a different vendor. I grieved. He was part of the area's history.

And this brings to mind old Uncle Hafez and his brother Ahmad, the fruit vendors who had a cart on the corner of the Gawahirgiya Wikala. Hafez was from Sohag in Upper Egypt, from the village of Kawamel. He had amazingly fresh, crisp tangerines. He was tall and thin, wore a turban, and was always well turned out. He always said good morning to me. "Fresh tangerines today, *Bashmuhandisa.*" I would tell him, "Keep three kilos for me to pick up on my way back." I always came home with a bag of tangerines. Also, there was the guy who sold the beautiful crispy pita bread at the mouth of Harat al-Yahoud. I often bought fresh bread from him.

Finally, I would return to the parking lot, retrieve my keys from Ahmad the parking attendant, and go home at about 10 p.m. When I got home, I would take down all my expenditures throughout the day for my accounts. When I look now at these notebooks in which I took down what I'd spent, I laugh. Everything was in piasters, and a very few pounds. It was a different world back then! Having to go through all these different stages of making a piece of jewelry, which I was forced by circumstance to carry out myself, gave me a lot of experience in the field, as well as a knowledge of the smallest details of every stage and trade secrets.

The one who taught me how to engrave things onto my pieces was Hassan the Engraver, the top steel engraver in the neighborhood; he engraved pharaonic and Islamic designs on steel. This was, of course, before today's laser machines were invented.

My avid interest in this profession eventually made my mother believe in what I was doing. It was hard for her at first to understand how a university student with opportunities doing interior design for friends' houses could reject all that and decide to live like a worker. It made no logical sense to her at the start. She didn't dismiss it out of hand, but still, she didn't give her enthusiastic approval. There was more of a state of "wait and see." Eventually I decided, without making a fuss about it, to open my own workshop and, of course, Helwan was the place that was available to start out.

The First Workshop

I tried to find a place near my home, so I'd be close to where I rested my head. I had the opportunity when my mother told me that Angele, the owner of our building, was renting out the room underneath our kitchen balcony because it was now free, and the rent was three pounds a month. Now that was great for my budget! Three pounds I could afford.

Angele was an Armenian–Egyptian lady who owned the apartment building where we lived, in a distinguished area of Helwan, opposite the famous Glanz Hotel, where the upper sets of Egypt wintered, coming to Helwan for its dry climate and the famous sulfur springs, which were said to cure multiple ailments.

I rented out that small room underneath my mother's apartment. It was glassed-in on three sides and had a separate entrance. It overlooked a big garden of citrus trees—oranges, tangerines, and limes. I went downstairs from the kitchen balcony in my mother's house, down a spiral iron staircase to the door. My neighbors in the rooms facing mine were students of the Helwan Secondary School from various Arab countries. These included the sons of the ruler of Yemen at the time, Imam Hamid al-Din, and every day we heard their staff calling them in the morning, "Wake up, Prince Ahmad! Wake up, Prince Muhammad!" All my Yemeni neighbors were slight of

164　BUSINESS AND MOTHERHOOD

build; at home, they wore a kind of sarong around the lower half of their bodies in traditional stripes or checks, and on top an undershirt.

I was thrilled. At last, a place all my own to work in! The room was about 3.5 by 3.5 meters, so more or less square, floored in cement tile. I put in a square table which I bought secondhand, and a chair to sit on that I bought from Madame Angele for another three pounds, in addition to a rocking chair for any guests that might come. I still have it.

I bought equipment for my work—a bellows and a butane gas canister, and the most basic tools: a hammer, a file, pliers, a saw, and a pair of clippers. All the joy in the world filled me as I stayed up until midnight or even later, working on pieces of jewelry I adored! They were naive and simple, but there was something different about them.

In summertime, I opened most of the glass windows of the room, and a breeze would flow in, laden with the fragrance of the orange and lime trees growing in the garden, nurturing my spirit. I was floating on air with happiness.

The late, great filmmaker Atiyat al-Abnoudi was one of my closest friends. Atiyat used to travel to Europe and North Africa for documentary festivals, where she always wore pieces that I had designed and made by hand. She was my first model! On their visits to Cairo to attend seminars or discussions, young foreign movie directors admired her jewelry, so she asked me to make pieces for them. At the start of my career, Atiyat's circles of friends were a financial lifeline for my business.

The circles expanded slightly, and with them my love for knowledge and desire to learn more of the techniques of this craft. I often visited the Egyptian Museum on Tahrir Square, the Islamic Museum in Bab al-Khalq, and the Coptic Museum in Old Cairo to sketch the jewelry they had there and try to plumb the depths for new designs. The first collection I produced that had its own specific character was the one I designed under the influence of the Fatimid water-jar filters, which I had admired greatly when I

My earring design here, called *shibbak al-ulla*, draws from that of an earthenware filter found in the neck of a Fatimid water jar.

visited the Islamic Museum, and immediately reimagined as earrings. Similarly, the Mamluks' great oversized copies of the Qur'an, which were made especially for mosques and schools, benefited me a great deal in terms of their calligraphy and their gorgeous golden ornamentation.

I had very much admired the signatures of the master craftsmen on their museum-worthy pieces there. The copper twinned with silver, the ceramics, the wood—all would have written somewhere on them "Made by So-and-So," or "Made by Ma'allim So-and-So," or "Made by the Lord's humble servant So-and-So." I believe they were proud of their products. An interesting thing I realized when I looked at wooden pieces is that the master craftsmen who inlaid and carved—and sometimes painted—colors, signed their name *al-Mizawwaq*, "The Prettifier!" The name came from the craftsman making his pieces pretty! They added it the end: "Ma'allim So-and-So the Prettifier." Al-Mizaawaq became the name of many of these families or artisans though, by the way, many of the gorgeous museum pieces were never signed by the great men who made them.

Occasionally, when I was stumped by a technical issue that I couldn't solve, I went back to Hagg Sayed's workshop in the Khan to resolve it. Things went on like this for about two or three years.

I held my first show at an art gallery owned by the Ministry of Culture in Zamalek in the late 1970s. This was the first jewelry exhibit to be held in Cairo in a governmental gallery; only painting and sculpture were ever exhibited at the big art shows. Jewelry, up until then, wasn't considered an art worthy of being shown at exhibitions or galleries, but was treated as a mere craft. I sold some pieces, my income increased, and I had a modest sense of success at what I was doing. I remember the centerpiece of that exhibition was a copy of a famous Ayyubid piece on show at the Islamic Museum. My uncle, General Abdel Farrag Fahmy, bought it to encourage and support me.

My circle of friends and friends of friends grew. There began to be a small market for my products. My insistence on learning and getting information on jewelry making and how it related to technology, as well as the history of the craft and my reading of articles on the subject, only increased. The books available in Arabic on this subject were limited; at the same time, I was rushing on ahead like a rocket, wanting and needing more knowledge, and understanding more and more. Some of my friends began to give me books in English about the craft and its terminology, which they brought in from abroad, but I had a problem: what English I had learned at Sohag Preparatory School and Helwan Secondary School was enough to, say, give an interview for a magazine, to express myself and get across what I was talking about. Government schools at that time taught good English. But reading a book, and understanding its technical jargon and artistic terminology, was beyond me. I needed quite another level of English for that.

I decided to take action. I would improve my English and learn the terminology for my chosen profession. I needed to understand these books and absorb their ideas and information; I could benefit from them, and improve. I said to myself, "The best thing for it is to translate an important book; that will help me to learn better."

I bought a big dictionary, as well as a dictionary of technical terms, to help me on my way. I started with my first book, by Philip Morton, on the art of making contemporary jewelry. It was a gift from a friend who had bought it on a trip abroad. I took to reading, opening the book and translating each term, writing terms down in Arabic so I could memorize them. It took about two years to translate, because I was too busy to devote myself to it. I was working at the Ministry in the morning, and at my first workshop in the evening. I can't tell you how much I learned from translating an important book about jewelry, all the technical terms, and even a greater understanding of how jewelry making related to art and sculpture, and its importance.

My knowledge grew, and my English likewise improved to the point where I could understand most of the foreign reference books my friends had taken to giving me in this field. The best gift I could be given and which made me happiest was always a book on the art of jewelry. I still keep my old translation of that first book in my handwriting. I'm very, very fond of it, and it reminds me of an important stage in my life.

Now that my finances had improved, my travels abroad increased, both for work and for shows. A major point in my travel program was to visit specialized art bookshops to buy books about jewelry. You can't imagine the amount of excess weight I had to pay for on my return to Cairo, carrying these artistic treasures. I have about four thousand books about craftsmanship, jewelry, and traditional art from every era. It's a rare library, specializing in every aspect of this art from many regions of the world, wherever there are tribes and peoples that wear important traditional jewelry. Now I'm blessed to be able to read and understand these English books without issue. My translation of that first book, which did, admittedly, take some time, allowed me to overcome the hurdle of technical jargon, and granted me the freedom to read all the references and books that enriched my cultural life and my information about the craft.

Toward the end of the 1970s, on an important cultural visit to America on an exchange program with a number of artists, writers, and Egyptian opera professionals, I exhibited my collection of traditional art at the Smithsonian Museum in Washington DC for three months. On the itinerary was a visit to the fashion library of the Metropolitan Museum of Art in New York, located in the museum's basement, where they also had a display of a great many samples of traditional costumes from different countries—Japan, Mexico, India. It was a library for students, researchers, and designers. At the time, the assistants to the famous designer Yves St. Laurent were there, sketching ancient Japanese costumes for him. I was overjoyed to realize that my own library of jewelry and crafts was larger than theirs, and richer. I said to myself, "Bravo, Azza! Bravo, Azza!"

The Boulaq al-Dakrour Workshop

When work picked up, I found that I needed to expand my workspace and open a workshop in central Cairo. I didn't need to do everything myself anymore. "I have to bring in one or two craftsmen to help me," I thought, "to make chains, clasps, and so on." My budget allowed for me to get a workshop in Boulaq al-Dakrour, the crowded area on the other side of the train tracks from Mohandiseen. It consisted of two small apartments facing each other on the ground floor of a six-story apartment building overlooking the Zumur Canal, which separates Boulaq from Mohandiseen. I also had to make a decision to quit my job at the government, as all this while I had been working at the Ministry of Information in the morning, only becoming a jewelry maker and artist in the afternoons. I rented the two apartments from Hagg Mahmoud, a government employee with his own business besides his work. His family were all day yelling and noisy, but oh well.

I was moving forward by self-propulsion, enthusiasm, and one success after another. I didn't have a system or business plan. Things developed quickly, and demand for this kind of jewelry increased. I had certainty and passion on my side. All this pushed me forward and gave me confidence that I would succeed, that I'd make it.

I began to feel that I needed an accountant to help me out. I hired a man who took to coming by every two weeks to pick up the notebooks in which I noted down what I'd spent, together with my sales figures, and every so often he made out a balance sheet with our financial situation. My finances improved a bit more, and I decided to quit my government job and devote myself completely to making jewelry. On 23 June 1974, I received a document confirming that my name was no longer on the roster of employees of the Ministry of Information. I had quit.

At that time the director of the British Council, Dr. Norman Daniel, was one of my clients. I had been introduced to him by my friend Atiyat al-Abnoudi; the British Council had funded a number of her documentaries. My friendship with Dr. Daniel and his wife Ruth lasted for a long time; he always asked how my work was going and followed my successes.

This was when the master craftsmen and silversmiths of the Khan were my teachers; every time I had technical difficulties making a piece, I went to the Egyptian and Armenian smiths to help me solve it. My ideas and designs developed quickly, but I was really starting to struggle with making my ideas a reality. I had been exposed to so many museums, exhibitions, and art books that my creativity had skyrocketed, and the ceiling for my designs became higher and higher. But my mind was running ahead of my hands. This came down to the proficiency of the master craftsmen of Khan al-Khalili. I would never deny or belittle everything they taught me—but I still needed more technical skills. My life's dream was to study the art of jewelry making at the Royal College of Art in London. Unfortunately, this was impossible, especially financially. But the dream of a better education never went away, as I was desperately in need of it.

London and the Scholarship

One day, Dr. Daniel and his wife Ruth invited me to dinner at their house and asked me how I was doing. I said, "My ideas have outstripped my skills." It was plain as day. A month or so after this meeting, Dr. Daniel sent me an invitation to meet him at his office at the British Council. I went, not knowing what was up. Just like that, he told me that he was giving me a British Council scholarship to study jewelry making at one of London's major institutions, the Sir John Cass College of Arts and Sciences, part of the City of London Polytechnic (now part of London Metropolitan University).

I couldn't believe it. Was I really going to England to study properly? I swear I was actually crying as I walked out of his office. I was so thrilled and touched by this man's support and his faith in me and what I was doing, and still unable to believe I was going to London to study. I didn't work in the government anymore, as I had quit. And I didn't have the right to a scholarship from the British government. But this man had intuited, with his generous spirit that truly loved Egypt, that this girl really did need more knowledge and education, and that she was serious about the art she produced. Dr. Daniel had secured me this scholarship on his personal responsibility, full of confidence that this would raise me up to a higher level in my career.

I went to London, having completed all the documents necessary for the grant. The day after I arrived, I went to the head office of the British

Overseeing the work of Usta Saeed, one of my craftsmen, Boulaq al-Dakrour workshop, 1974.

At Boulaq al-Dakrour workshop, 1974.

Council in the center of London. I got all the information from them, and tips on living in the big city. They had an office that specialized in helping grant recipients with a guide to the families that were prepared to rent out their spare rooms to expatriate grantees. I found a place in Islington, from where I had to take two buses for an hour to get to the Polytechnic. The landlords were a husband and wife, both professors of anthropology at university, with a little girl.

The Polytechnic had nine main departments for jewelry making. Before I went to London, I had settled on three topics of study: enameling, engraving, and embossing or creating reliefs, but when I got there I found so many other options that could all help me. I ended up selecting nine subjects, and of course this led to a complete transformation in my technique.

Winter in London is no fun. When I went into the Polytechnic in the morning, the sky was gray, almost black, and it was dark when I left at the end of the day. On the weekends, I had a long list of museums and exhibitions I needed to visit. My intense focus on learning and educating myself in a city full of everything that could improve me technically and help me in any way made me like a sponge, wanting to absorb everything it possibly could in such a short time. My goal was knowledge. On Saturday mornings I did my shopping and cooking for the whole week. Sunday was for museums and libraries.

This period absolutely transformed my career. The greatest technical masters in casting, etching, coloring, and shaping were here in London, teaching me. I could execute virtually any design that crossed my mind with my own hands in a scientific manner with proven theory behind it. They knew how to explain things technically: what happens, what to do about problems I might face, and how to avoid these in the first place.

The scholarship period over, I came back to Cairo with greater confidence and a sense of competence. Now I could execute more difficult and complex designs. My mind and its designs were now closer to my hands and their ability, with a much better understanding of the techniques of the profession. The dean of the Polytechnic wrote to Dr. Daniel after I came back to Cairo, saying, "Never in my life have I seen a girl with such enthusiasm for learning the profession."

I will never forget this generous man who believed in my potential and worked to get me this scholarship, which had the greatest effect on my technical knowledge. Dr. Norman Daniel lived with his wife Ruth in Egypt after he retired; Ruth died and was buried here, and later her lifelong companion died and they lie side by side in the soil of this Egypt that they had loved.

My professional abilities advanced by leaps and bounds after that time in London. I became able to make more difficult pieces, and this was reflected in the way I ran my workshop. Often the workers who worked with me, when I asked them to execute a design I had done and wanted made— usually one that was more difficult or complex—would say to me, "It can't be done, *Bashmuhandisa.*" Before the scholarship, I couldn't contradict them. But after my return from London, I was able to say, "Yes, it can. Get up and I'll show you how it's done." And I would sit down at the *tazga* and carry out the design. This kind of thing made the workmen respect me as a master craftsman, who could do everything and for whom nothing was too difficult.

Azza Fahmy's more refined career started from that moment. I began to think of making a name, a brand, for Egyptian jewelry. I worked with my hands and executed my own designs for about twenty years running. At first, I brought in a worker to do the things that took me a long time and weren't creative, such as chains. Afterward, it was two workers, and then they multiplied. After twenty years, I had fifteen workers sitting at that *tazga*, as well as another group assisting them. When I used to work with my own hands, I signed every piece I made myself, like an artist signing a painting. And because I'm fond of palm trees, I engraved two palm trees and the name "Azza Fahmy" along with the year. I take such great joy in that silly, childish palm tree that I used to engrave on silver pieces! When I happen to come across a piece from that period, my heart flutters. The tall tree, with its roots in the ground and its head in the sky—the palm tree—is Egypt to me, which I love: standing tall and proud. I really miss making pieces with my own hands now. It's so much fun. Unfortunately, my life became too busy to keep making pieces myself, and now I've ended up only designing them, not carrying them out.

In 1994, the great Egyptian moviemaker Youssef Chahine asked me to create the jewelry for his film *The Emigrant*, which created a furor when it was released, even being banned for a while, because its story was adapted from the Biblical story of Joseph. I had another experience working with the genius Chahine: *Destiny*, produced in 1997. It was set in twelfth-century Andalusia and was about the Arab philosopher Ibn Rushd. Both movies involved a collaboration between myself and the movie's costume designer, the great Nahed Nasrallah.

After I finished designing the movie's jewelry, I was asked to show my designs to the great man, or "Joe," as they called Youssef Chahine. I went into the apartment where his office was to show him the jewelry I had designed and found myself in an office-cum-kitchen, with a desk and chair in one corner of the room. The other corner held a gas stove, a fridge, and a kitchen table—it was a really cute little kitchen! I started showing him my ideas, but after ten minutes he closed the portfolio and said, "That's enough already! I brought in the best person in the country to work with! Like I'm going to know better than you! Go ahead, ma'am, I approve everything you designed!"

When he saw my confusion and that I was staring at the kitchen, he said, "What? You're surprised that I'm working in the kitchen?"

"Yes," I said.

"I like to cook," he said, "so I put my office in the kitchen. What's wrong with that?"

"There's nothing wrong with it," I responded. "In the end, each of us needs to do what they like." But I'll tell you something: that occasion opened my eyes. I learned something very important from that day: you have to do what you feel, and what you love, even if your office ends up in the kitchen.

Ri'aya—My Friend with the Braid

My friend the artist Abdel Ghani Abu al-Einein, who earned and truly deserves the title "the people's artist," and his wife Ri'aya al-Nimr, came into our lives and taught us what folk art really means in every little detail of our lives, starting with clothing—village gallabiyas, Bedouin dresses, the *milaya laff*, the burqa, a netting or mesh face veil, sometimes with a decorative piece over the nose, not to be confused with the contemporary burqa worn in the Arabian Gulf, to jewelry, to *mashrabiya*, to decorated benches, to the Primus stove, to the oil lamp. A magical world that links you to your country and homeland, and opens up your mind to things, planting seeds in you that later bear fruit. She called him "Enein" and he called her "Umm al-Enein"—"two eyes" and "mother of two eyes."

I got to know them in the late 1970s. They had a house in the traditional style in Harraniya, and their small museum, which held all the Egyptian and Arab folk heritage they had collected, was an education for me. Together they had founded the Siwan House Museum in Siwa Oasis, as well as working together to lay the foundations for the Folk Art Center in Cairo. Ri'aya was a beautiful Egyptian woman, and I always think of her. She wore traditional Egyptian costume, village or Bedouin, her black hair behind her back in a long braid. She had her clothes made by seamstresses from the villages in the Nile Delta who made the traditional women's gallabiya. I was stunned by this woman's Egyptianness. She always wore traditional Egyptian jewelry or folk or heritage jewelry from another country. In my eyes, at the time, she was a unique example of a cultured Egyptian artist. She always explained Egyptian heritage and its elements to us, and spoke with pride about her clothing, for which she bought the Egyptian cotton fabric from ordinary stores. Her colors were always flattering and well-matched, and she added rickrack braid where appropriate. She kept the original countryside design and respected it. From this lady, I learned to wear traditional costume, that is, the village gallabiya. I couldn't afford store-bought dresses at the time, so I created a pretty style for myself which I liked a lot.

My father had left us some land near Damanhur, forty feddans in Hosh Eisa. My brother Ali cultivated the land and sometimes my mother went to visit him. I asked her to find the seamstress who made the village women's gallabiyas, having learned to wear such clothes from Ri'aya. I bought cotton cambric and lawn cloth—which we call by their French names, *batiste* and *linon* respectively—and rickrack braid in complementary colors from the notions store, then had them made into dresses by the countryside seamstress and wore them when they were brought home to me by my mother. I loved them to no end, and people thought they were nice. Ri'aya al-Nimr truly taught us something, and we learned a lot about Egypt from this great lady. She introduced Shahira Mehrez and me to the seamstresses of the Eastern Delta, where we had our clothes made.

I remember that Hussein Bicar, the great Egyptian artist, who was a personal friend, wanted to draw me. "Mr. Bicar," I said to him, "you draw elegant ladies in furs with their hair done at the hairdresser's! I don't have all that stuff. Look for yourself at what I'm wearing!"

"Pretty lady," he laughed, "I see the real Azza in her village gallabiya." He drew me, and I still treasure that drawing. It showed me in a pink countryside-style gallabiya with white polka-dots, made of quality Egyptian lawn cloth. It really did capture my spirit. My mother had that gallabiya made for me by a seamstress near our farm in al-Abqa'in, in Hosh Eisa.

Ri'aya and Abu al-Einein's Harraniya home, and their little museum there where they collected examples of folk art and crafts that you couldn't ever imagine in addition to various heritage costumes and folk shoes, was where I found things that I only later realized were important: Primus stoves of all shapes and sizes and brands, and the needle to clear blockages in the gas jet; the types of Turkish coffeepot used in each of the villages, and teapots and tea trays—a record of a wonderful artistic world of anthropological crafts. My acquiring these things and using them today at my house is thanks to Ri'aya. I don't actually use the Primus stove, of course, but the brass trays and the traditional enameled teapot, all those I use.

We spent many Fridays and holidays like Shamm al-Nasim at Ri'aya's Harraniya home. I met the leading Egyptian intellectuals there—all the brilliant artists of the good old days including the artists behind the classic puppet show *al-Leila al-Kibira* (The Big Night).

I devised a personal style all my own, learned from dear Ri'aya: a village gallabiya cut in any number of traditional styles, in different color combinations and fabrics I chose myself, combined with village, Upper Egyptian, or Bedouin shawls. I learned the shops that specialized in these products, like Ouf, which is still in business, on al-Azhar Street. Definitely, my love for folk costume was planted in me by Ri'aya, and I also took my love of wearing traditional clothes from this great Egyptian woman.

After Ri'aya and Abu al-Einein passed away, their relations donated their collections and acquisitions from throughout their lives to the Bibliotheca Alexandrina. There is a section there bearing their name and comprising most of what they collected.

This reminds me of something. On each of my trips to a place with special heritage, I have brought back a traditional costume typical of that area for my granddaughter Thuraya Moussa. I think now, as I'm writing these notes, that I unconsciously wanted to fill her with a love for this great art, to plant the seeds of appreciation of this art in her just as Ri'aya planted them in me.

My deepest appreciation and gratitude goes to the spirit of this artist and researcher with deep roots in her country, and to her husband, a great artist who drew our attention to things that we lived with every day without being aware that they had artistic and heritage value.

The 1970s

The 1970s were an important formative era for me, with a circle of artist, intellectual, and writer friends who played a vital role in molding my character. When your circle is made up of all the different arts—sculpture and painting, for instance, as well as cinema, journalism, and the literary world—you will naturally learn from them and be affected by them. There were Egypt's poets, Abdel Rahman al-Abnoudi and Sayed Higab, friends I came to know closely; the Cinema Club, founded by Mustafa Darwish, where we watched the best of European and Russian film and different schools of filmmaking, including Italian cinema—I especially remember *La Dolce Vita*. Experimental theater, too, had a place in my life: the Pocket Theater, where I watched the Theater of the Absurd, and the Puppet Theater in its heyday, when its director was my friend Ragi Inayat, and where I watched the unique, unforgettable live performance of *al-Leila al-Kibira* with puppets by the great artist, my friend Nagi Shaker, and directed by Salah al-Saqqa.

Opening up to culture and history and reading books from the people around me inspired me to bring what I read, admired, and loved into my artistic designs, to let people enjoy them just as I was enjoying them! The first verse of poetry I used was a design on a keychain. It was a verse by Tunisian poet Abu al-Qasem al-Shabi:

Unhappy, unhappy, unhappy is he
With a delicate soul that
Trembles with compassion like me.

Also, there was the experience of knowing Egypt's great artists, such as painter Kamal Khalifa, with whom I went on trips to Alexandria to meet the two great painter brothers Seif and Adham Wanli at the famous Café Elite, where intellectuals, poets, and artists used to congregate and engage in deep artistic conversation with the greats of that generation.

This was when I really let loose with linking literature and jewelry. I created a collection of Salah Jahin's famous quatrains, his *Ruba'iyat*, on jewelry, and I always engraved many palm trees on the back of each *Ruba'iya*, with my name and the year I made the piece. This collection had a great impact. I discovered that the whole world's philosophy could be found in Salah Jahin's *Ruba'iyat*. Each of us finds ourselves in one of them; people felt that their lives, what they did, and who they were, were represented in each quatrain. A client would come in and request a particular *Ruba'iya* for a person they felt it applied to. This made the collection incredibly popular, and for years afterward, people kept requesting a reissue. Here are two of my favorite *Ruba'iyat*:

I want to live, even in a forest wild.
Wake and sleep naked as a newborn child;
As bird, beast, human, insect, as a fly!
Life's beautiful, even as a plant—that's why.
I am the one who dreamed the impossible dream.

Saw the moon, leapt high aloft to reach its gleam.
Whether or not I caught it in my flight,
Who cares? My heart's thirst was quenched with delight.

I made a necklace from a line by Palestine's great poet, Mahmoud Darwish, for Mother's Day:

I long for the bread of my mother,
And the coffee of my mother,
And the touch of my mother.

My trips to Amman, Jordan to visit my Palestinian–Jordanian friends at the time of the Intifada and the rise of the major poets of the Occupied Territories inspired me to create many pieces, some of which were sold to benefit the Intifada. I liked the Palestinian poet Tawfiq Ziyad and made a piece using his poem "I Call on You":

I call on you;
I press your hands;
I kiss the dirt under your shoes;
I say I will sacrifice myself for you;
I give you the light of my eyes
And the warmth of my heart.

I realized the great treasure and immense wealth all around me. I realized how lucky I was to have been born in this part of the world, with the sheer size and quantity of ancient and modern heritage and culture that surrounded me. This was a veritable Ali Baba's cave of treasures for me—successive discoveries without end.

My collections and designs came thick and fast, inspired by exciting subjects. For instance, there was the Symbols collection, where I showed the protective signs worn by the women of the Arab world, displayed on their jewelry and clothing and in their homes, and the sayings and talismans they wear around their necks and on as many pieces as they could in their daily lives; we included an explanation of what lay behind each design.

The Design Studio by Azza Fahmy

In 2012, I had an opportunity, through a European Union grant, to take part in training young people and helping them create different kinds of art connected to our heritage in various fields (filmmaking, theater, and painting). I applied and was accepted. The grant lasted two years. The idea I presented was to train forty-five young people to understand and absorb the significance of different objects and sites that were part of our heritage, and then turn them into contemporary pieces of jewelry. I received hundreds of applicants. I chose forty-five to train with me, mostly young women.

I chose Aswan as the location for the training. I adore that city and hold it in my heart; I always experience it as a place filled with peace and positive energy, especially sitting in front of the Nile and looking at the great granite boulders tumbling over each other in incredible formations. This is when I feel that my friend, the late great sculptor Adam Henein, who selected Aswan as a location for his Sculpture Symposium, truly had a point.

We chose five great teachers from the major schools of jewelry making in Europe. They came to Aswan, and each of them spent fifteen days there teaching. The group of young teachers were selected by a committee which I headed, after which we sent them to Aswan to see this inspiring place with its Nubian houses, traditional markets and products, and the people of the southern Nile Valley. They made sketches to turn into jewelry under the supervision of each important European trainer. It was a marvelous experience, which produced modern pieces with a traditional heritage flair. It was a great success, and we held several exhibitions at cultural centers in Cairo. The experiment was new, and it produced artists and young people with a keen awareness. After a while, I felt that those young people were in need of continuing quality education at the same high standard, so I decided to open a jewelry-making school in Cairo to teach and prepare underprivileged students to travel to Europe.

In 2013, the Design Studio by Azza Fahmy was opened in collaboration with one of the major schools in Italy, the Alchimia Contemporary Jewellery School in Florence. This was where Amina had studied for a year before she went to England. We collaborated on devising the curricula, and two Italian teachers came to act as instructors. I funded the school out of my own pocket, and we started out in a place that we founded with very modest resources, but we always made it beautiful. I felt that the young people of Egypt were in dire need of innovative, high-quality artistic education, a lack that I had felt and experienced long ago when I compared my Khan al-Khalili education with the scholarship I had received from the British Council.

Now, the Design Studio by Azza Fahmy is the foremost jewelry design school in the Arab world. Most new young designers in the Egyptian market are products of this wonderful school, of which I'm very proud. I am also happy with the Egyptian, Arab, and foreign instructors who teach there. Part of the student body over the years decided to go into teaching, and so, after a few years, we began to have Arab and Egyptian instructors. I'm as giddy as a little girl at the end of each year when the students at my school exhibit their final projects at a show. We invite everyone we know. I look at the results

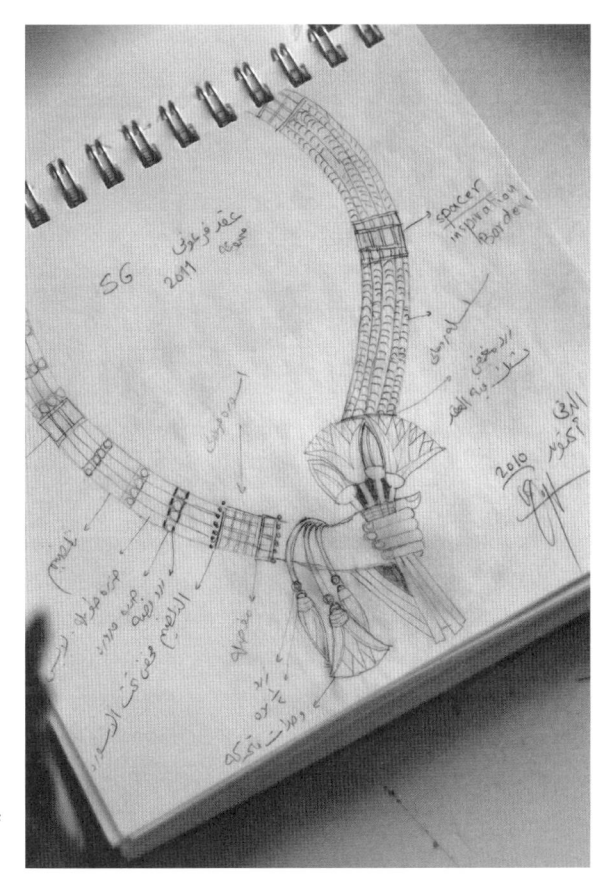

My sketch of a pharaonic necklace, "Hands of Friendship," 2012.

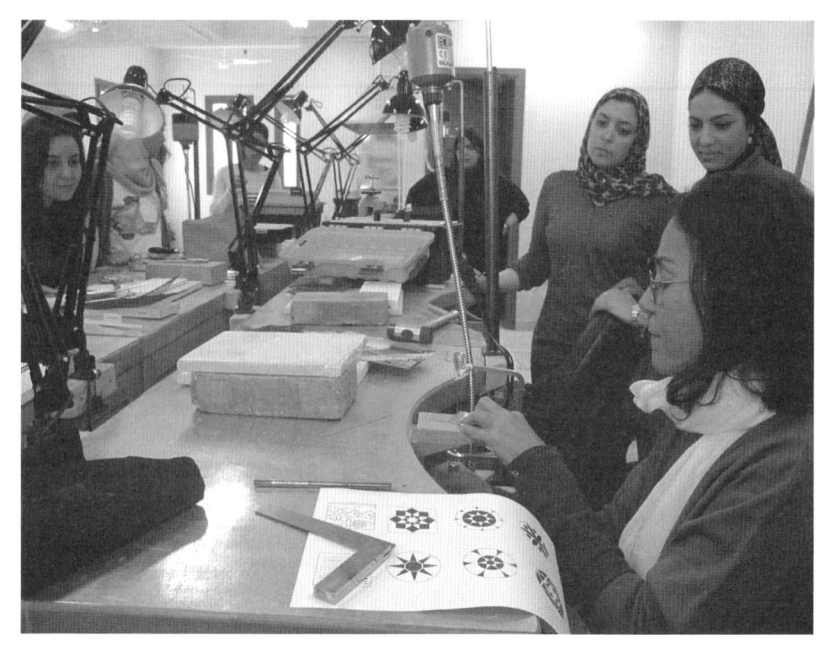

The Design Studio by Azza Fahmy, Historic Cairo, 2016.

achieved by these students and say to them in all truthfulness, "I wish I had had someone to give me this opportunity and teach me well at the start of my career like you have!" I say it from the heart. The matter of good education is something like a sticking point for me.

You know, I tried to get over this issue by getting an MA or a PhD. I asked my company, after President Sadat's economic Open-Door Policy in the 1970s had started to affect the country—to let me go to Florence in Italy to spend a month there every summer and take a course on jewelry making. I chose that city because it's so famous for art, bursting with magnificent sculpture, painting, and architecture. The Medici family lived and ruled there, and it is where the Renaissance blossomed and where the giants of that period lived and worked—Giotto, Raphael, Michelangelo, Leonardo da Vinci, Botticelli.

My visits to this incredible little city continued for three years, as I spent a month there every summer to take courses in specific specializations of jewelry. I can't describe my delight to you in that city, whose squares all boast statues of the giants of the Renaissance, and which contains the Uffizi

Museum and the famous Ponte Vecchio bridge, with the little stalls on both sides displaying the most fabulous old Italian jewelry. I cleansed my eyes with the most beautiful art and filled my mind with the works of the giants of the Renaissance. Just existing side-by-side with these immense talents and seeing them every day added another dimension to my artistic repertoire. When I came back to Cairo and passed on the course I had taken to the workers in the factory, training them on the techniques, this made me very happy and filled me with joy. In this way, I went some way toward solving the issue I had with my lack of education.

When the American University in Cairo granted me an honorary doctorate, it gave me the feeling that I wasn't so bad, after all—I'd achieved something in the field, and now they call me Doctor. I believe fully, with all my heart, that good education is the most important tool we can give our children to reach a high level of understanding, achievement, and progress. It is the indispensable weapon that we need to focus and give our children.

I've worked on myself a lot, in different aspects. I've always wanted to understand new things that might add to my general knowledge about women

The Design Studio by Azza Fahmy, Historic Cairo, 2016.

in general, and about working women and their issues in particular, and how they can overcome obstacles and make their lives easier. Whenever I had the chance, I attended lectures, conferences, and workshops to enrich my storehouse of information on this subject. I really did benefit a lot, and broadened my horizons of thought to learn about women's issues and difficulties as well as the paths to resolving them. It was all so useful to me.

In September 1995, I was able to attend the United Nations Fourth World Conference on Women, which was held in the Chinese capital, Beijing. The conference declaration stated that it was "determined to advance the goals of equality, development, and peace for all women everywhere in the interest of all humanity." I was selected to attend the great event, which was the biggest women's conference at that time, bringing together 30,000 women from all over the world. I asked Dr. Hoda Badran, the leader of the Egyptian delegation at this great convention, to allow me to bring my daughters with me—I couldn't leave them behind. In addition, I wanted them to have the chance to attend this unique event and benefit from this massive conference. I brought Fatma and Amina along, together with their lifelong best friend, Inji Husni. To me and them, the Beijing experience now represents a watershed in our lives, which left its mark on who we were. The girls learned a lot from their visit to China and from attending such a big conference discussing women's issues and issuing some recommendations for addressing them. I was affected a lot by attending these seminars too—I got a better understanding of women's issues (specifically of women who work), and how to find some solutions for the pressures women face daily.

Fatma, Amina, and Inji were some of the youngest attendees at this international encounter. While we were there, we visited the Great Wall of China and the Forbidden City, and of course we did some shopping at the famous silk market in Beijing, which sells the major international brands you can find in Europe at unbelievably low prices. "Made in China" can be found on many brands from international designers.

In Beijing Airport, waiting for our flight back home, I can't describe to you the size and quantity of the luggage checked in by the Egyptian and Arab women from the conference—mountains and mountains of suitcases piled up on top of each other. I heard a story when I got back that I'm not sure is true: they say the jumbo jet bringing back the Arab women taking part in the conference had to be towed onto the runway with chains because it was so heavy.

My First Book

When Atiyat al-Abnoudi saw the sheer volume of index cards and sketches that I had produced over twenty years, and the meticulous notes and comments I had made on the pieces I had drawn, she said, "All this could be a book on Egypt's traditional jewelry. It's got to be published! It could explain the main regions of Egypt—the Nile Delta, the Nile Valley, Nubia, the Western Desert and its oases, and the Eastern Desert and its tribes—how the jewelry took shape and was influenced by these regions, who made it, the techniques used in making it, and all the stories behind every region and its production."

My dear, lifelong friend gathered up all the cards on which I had spent my life writing observations on the jewelry I bought and acquired by way of technical or design or historical study, observations on the resemblances between pieces from different regions, the names of the pieces as pronounced by the peoples and tribes who wore them, and how they were used. I worked with her for about two years on transcribing this material; she did the writing and editing based on the stories I told her about these regions and pieces. We met once every week or two, and she asked me questions and I told her stories. This faithful friend deserves the credit for producing this important book, because the book would not have been possible without her, at least not at that time. The process wasn't easy! Back then I wasn't free to work on the book; I was busy with my own work, and she was working on other important things too.

The pieces of jewelry of all kinds, with their great diversity, needed to be photographed, we decided. We started the process of getting them photographed by professional photographers, most of them friends or the children of friends. I enlisted them to help me, as they only charged me what I could afford. All of them were excited about the project and quoted me sums within my budget.

We felt that the American University in Cairo Press was the best publisher for the book, especially an art book like this one. We paid them a visit, Atiyat and I, and they were convinced that the book was important. They asked us to create two portfolios to show them the concept and its level. I did, and they approved them with high praise. I signed the contract, delighted. I needed to give the Press—where my friend Nabila Akl worked (the director was Mark Linz at the time)—my photographs, in addition to the Arabic material translated into English. My friend Nehad Salem provided a good literary translation, and it was edited by the AUC Press. The book was published as *Enchanted Jewelry of Egypt* in 2007, and in a new edition, *The Traditional Jewelry of Egypt*, in 2015.

The process of gathering the material for the book, starting with Khan al-Khalili, through writing, photographing, and publishing, took twenty years in total, and it is now the most comprehensive reference on traditional Egyptian jewelry in the hundred years from the late nineteenth century to the late twentieth. The production process for the book added accompanying photographs of the landscapes and inhabitants of these regions, whether villagers, Bedouin, Nubian tribesfolk, or people from the crowded urban areas, and the book would not have been complete without them.

The layout team I worked with were my dear German friend Christa Dupke and her assistant Thuraya. The photographs from different regions were taken by my American friend Barry Iverson, as well as Tareq Hifni, the son of my friend Nadia Mursi. Some of them I had taken myself on previous visits to the Dakhla and Kharga Oases. By the way, I'm very fond of photography, and I think I have a decent eye. The archives of Dar al-Hilal, the publishing house, and the magazine *al-Musawwar*, as well as the archive of the newspaper *al-Ahram*, were among my important sources for references, where I worked for days getting historical photographs that the book needed. I bought a photograph collection from them that added an important historical dimension to the book.

I had to cover regions such as Siwa and the Eastern Desert, including the southern Red Sea, and photograph them. I believed that including photographs of these places would give an additional dimension to the book, especially when we explained the nature of the region to the reader and the reflection of this nature on the jewelry worn there. From my understanding and study of jewelry over fifty years of my life in the craft, place and jewelry are intimately connected. The jewelry of the Nile Valley and Delta is influenced by the Nile and the green environment; delicately made, influenced by the characteristics of the crops, the greenery, and the water. The delicate technique of filigree, with its fine wires, is frequently used there. As for the jewelry of the desert, it reflects the harsh nature of the desert: most of it is made of large plates of silver or other metals.

I had to visit those places at times when the weather would be suitable, especially the desert—it was no good visiting the desert in summer. This included the Eastern Desert and the southern Red Sea—Shalatin and Halayeb, and Gebel 'Elba (the land of the Beja people), where the customs and manners of the Nubian tribes resembled those of the Ababda people and the Bishari tribes in their customs and manners. This covered important areas of the book on interrelated regions, and I needed to see all of this with my own eyes and record it on camera. This was a region I had never been to, and I had no good pictures of the place that would be any use in the book, so I decided to go and take pictures.

Of course, the first thing we had to do was get security clearance. Everyone in our party had to be Egyptian, because of how close it was to the Sudanese border. I chose Tareq Hifni, a talented young photographer, to come on the trip. The only person I trusted with the job of taking us there was Amr Ali (the poor dear who died too young). He always used to nag and tell me, "Auntie Azza, you have to come to the Gebel 'Elba and see what it's like there! It'll give you so much information and I'm sure it'll inspire you!" I met this wonderful young man—whom I considered one of the best young Egyptians, a real patriot who loved his country—through my daughter Fatma. He was a graduate of the American University in Cairo and chose, like some of his colleagues, to move out to the desert, to the nature reserves in the Red Sea where people go diving and to live and start their own business ventures—a different life for different young people. He always seemed to me like a lion protecting a part of Egypt that was important to him—that is, the nature reserves and the environment of the Red Sea.

Amr reminded me of the ancient Egyptian artist who first noticed the way the vulture sat in its nest with its wings extended forward to shade its chicks inside, protecting them from the blazing sun. That artist used the bird as a symbol for protection, putting it on temple doors and using it for important jewelry made for Egypt's great kings, Ramesses II and Tutankhamun. That bird was called Nekhbet, or the Protective Mother. I made a necklace for my pharaonic collection that I am very proud of, which I called Nekhbet.

"Nekhbet"—This is a vulture collar necklace that I designed in 18-karat gold with sterling silver. It showcases intricately designed vulture wings that mimic the Nekhbet Wing. In ancient Egyptian religion, Nekhbet was the goddess protector of Upper Egypt.

I'm even happier when women come to me and say, "I want the Nekhbet necklace." They actually say the name in the ancient Egyptian language. Can you believe it? That, to me, was a great success. In my opinion, Amr Ali was the Nekhbet of the Red Sea. He was the protective mother, the guardian of the nature reserves there, and the protector of the environment in the Red Sea. May this wonderful young man rest in peace. From him, I learned the value of our beaches, our sand, our shells, our fish, and the wild animals that live there. Every time I pick up a shell or a piece of coral, I think of him. He always barked at us: "Shame on you! Leave the natural environment alone!" He died young after leaving his mark and a fond remembrance in this important region of Egypt.

I arranged with Amr that we would set out at the start of winter, before the rainy season, when there are floods. This was in early October 2004. We started the journey from Hurghada in the four-wheel-drive vehicles used in the nature reserves, accompanied by a young team of guards of the reserve whose job was to record, study, and protect these areas. With us was also Dr. Samir al-Sunbati, a senior reserve official.

The trip took about a week. We drove about 750 kilometers south of Hurghada, until we got near the town of Halayeb near the Egypt–Sudan border. I wasn't sure that the inhabitants of these regions still kept the traditional objects worn by their parents and grandparents. I had collected some over the decades, many of which were sold at markets in the towns of Daraw and Aswan, either because people were having a hard time financially or because the new generations had stopped wearing stuff that was out of fashion. So I thought, to be safe, I'd take the examples I had in my jewelry collection with me on my trip there. I put my jewelry from the Ababda, Rashaida, and Bishari tribes in a bag and took it with me.

Our first stop was planned to meet the Rashaida. Their name comes from being the descendants of Zubayda, the wife of Caliph Haroun al-Rashid. They have branches in Saudi Arabia, Yemen, Eritrea, and Ethiopia. They are traders, especially in falcons, and particularly the peregrine falcon, the best of the Arabian falcons sold in the Arab Gulf, which they train. They speak Rashid-accented Arabic, and do not hold Egyptian citizenship.

The protectorate guards knew where they could be found. We crossed great distances to look for them and find where they had last been seen setting up camp—they were nomadic, moving around for trade. At last, we found a group in Wadi al-Nadayet: we saw tents pitched in the far distance. How small they were! They grew bigger the closer we came, until we arrived at a certain point. Then our guides said, "We can't go any closer. There aren't any vehicles parked."

I really had no idea what that meant. It turned out that if the men of the Rashaida were home, their cars would be parked outside their tents. If there were no cars, it meant that they weren't home, only women and children. This, flatly, was a firm boundary: No Entry. Forbidden Zone. The young men accompanying us asked me to go to the tents on my own, without even a photographer.

I picked up my camera and walked alone in the direction of the tents. Suddenly, dozens of little girls and boys came running toward me, tiny dots that started getting bigger and bigger. The girls wore cheerful colors and patterns, with pretty faces and smiles, and kohl around their eyes; the boys were dressed in light violet and blue, all the same color, both amzamyah and breeches. It was an odd observation. I found out afterward that violet was the color of grief, which they wear in sorrow for leaving their homeland and extended families.

The children took me to the tents, where the women were sitting. I was greeted by beautiful women with big black eyes and coal-black curly hair with a wavy fringe over the forehead. It was an exotic, peculiar beauty with a striking charm. There, I met Habbouba ("Grandma," as the Sudanese also call their grandmothers). She was wearing a *zamzam* or *shinaf*, which is a nose ring, and a *sa'fa*, which is what the Rashaida call a bracelet. I asked the women after we had had our coffee if I could photograph them. "No, impossible," they said. "Only photograph the children," though they also allowed me to take a photograph of their Habbouba.

Rashaidi women are strong, making and decorating their own tents. Each tent is named for its female owner—*Beit Zahra* or *Hosh Zahra* (Zahra's house, Zahra's courtyard), *Beit Gamila* or *Hosh Gamila*, and so on. They are good at macramé making and selling the necklaces, beads, and macramé they make. Their names, too, are special: Hamda, Husna, Naf'a. Quite a number of the children wear leather amulets around their necks. The men bring these charms from Sudan. Women wear what they call a *qan'a*, a kind of veil whose beauty I have never seen equaled, either in materials, colors, or variety of design. It is a long expanse of fabric hanging down to below stomach level, embroidered with silken threads at the forehead and the openings for the eyes, and with colored fringes. The headscarf is worked with orange beads. When a Rashaidi woman goes out, she wears a black headscarf. She wears no necklaces: the *qan'a* is her adornment.

I sat with the Rashaidi women for two hours. After asking them a lot of questions and getting the answers I needed, I picked up my camera and left. Then we traveled for another four hours on rocky roads through the mountains and the desert, heading for the Ababda and Bishari tribes in the Gebel 'Elba. We arrived before sunset—this was important so that we could pitch our tents before darkness fell and set up our sleeping arrangements, as there was no electricity. I was awestruck as we approached the mountain, which looked mythical—a gigantic size, rising up in the empty space, all alone, covered with thick trees, the peak shrouded in mist and clouds because of being so high. The guards told me it was 1,437 meters above sea level, and I learned later from the young people that this height helped the rare plants that grow there, plants not found anywhere else in the deserts of Egypt.

The trees grow thickly there, which is why the Ababda and Bishari call it "the forest." You feel you're farther south in Africa: the trees and the wide open expanses remind you of African landscapes. The *siyala* tree, a kind of acacia, has branches and leaves at the top that remind me of the hair of the Bishari men, which is pinned up with a wooden comb that they call a *khilal*. The reserve officials with us told me that a large number of medicinal and fragrant herbs can be found on Gebel 'Elba. The Bishari tribe have a great respect for the *siyala*, and would never cut it down—this tree shades them in the summer heat, and they collect the dry branches to warm themselves in the biting cold of winter. You always find piles of firewood around their huts.

The region is rich in natural resources such as metals. It's a pastoral society, with rain year-round, although scarce, and they rely on wells. The Bishariya hold their celebrations and weddings on the mountainside, performing their dances with swords and shields. They are fighters, and it's said that long ago it was they who defended the region against invaders seeking to loot the gold mines centered in the Alaqi Valley, or Gold Valley, as they call it. It's said that in the times of our ancient Egyptian forebears, there were twelve gold mines in the area.

They have their own tales and legends about the relationship between beasts and humans, which is why the bracelets of the Bishari women take sharp triangular forms all around—spikes, really, which can cut a person if used as a weapon. Curious, this relationship between jewelry, the environment, and social circumstances. How does this all come together to create a final shape of a piece influenced by all these things? (I was delighted to write about this in my book.)

Night fell, and we sat around the fire to keep warm. It was very cold. Old Uncle Hussein Abdel Sayed, who was Bishari and also Ababda at the same time because they intermarry, was making *gabana*, their coffee spiced with cinnamon, cloves, and cardamom, in a special clay pot brought in specially from Sudan. I asked him, "What kind of jewelry do the women wear here?"

He took to drawing shapes in the sand with a finger, and I told him the name of each shape. Laughing, he took to saying, "Doctor, you know everything!"

I went into the tiny tent, just big enough for me, and went to sleep. I covered myself with three blankets, it was so cold. As I was falling asleep, I heard the Bishariya around the fire speaking a language I couldn't understand. Later, I learned that this was a language called Nabarawi—entirely oral, with no written form.

At dawn, I woke to the sound of people chattering around the tent. I made out the voice of Dr. Samir al-Sunbati, with two Bishariya, saying loudly, "We'll trade you the lady doctor sleeping in the tent for forty camels."

I poked my head out of the tent flap, laughing. "So that's your game, Dr. Sunbati, plotting against me?"

Camels are very important to the Bishariya; they bring good fortune. There are various types of camels. The thoroughbreds are racing animals, and they are decorated with talismans of blue beads to ward off the evil eye. There are *malaki* (royal) camels, for transporting possessions, trained to carry luggage during travel. Camels are extremely patient and loyal to the end; they are also hot-tempered and savage when the situation calls for it. A Bishari's relationship with his camel is a strong and important one. He knows what it wants and what it suffers, and he knows how to treat it when it falls sick. Camels are branded with their tribe's symbol to avoid conflicts arising when a camel herder has large numbers that may mingle with other tribes' herds. I learned that Bishari camels are branded with an H. The women here receive paid their bride-price in camels. This woman is worth five camels, another is worth ten, and so on, depending on the situation. They tell me that the inhabitants of Gebel 'Elba go to the Atbara River in Sudan after the spring rains to let their camels graze there; in winter, when the rainy season starts, they come back home.

The Gebel 'Elba trip, the information I got from the women of the Bishari and Ababda tribes, and the photographs, were very important to me in my book. The Ababda and Bishari intermarry and are interrelated in many ways. The jewelry of this region is greatly influenced by each other's tribes, and is very similar to the Nubian jewelry and the jewelry of Sudan. In times past, the main gold market they had dealings with was in Daraw, in the Nile Valley, where there is also a huge camel market for camels brought in from Sudan via the ancient Forty Day trade caravan route.

For marriages, the Red Sea Ababda used to make a trip of several days on camelback through the heart of the desert to the Daraw market to buy their gold jewelry from the goldsmiths there who specialized in these types. Now, you drive from 'Elba to Daraw in four or five hours.

The Ababda and Bishari women wear a piece of fabric six meters long, which they wrap around their body, just like Sudanese women, called a *toub*. They prefer bright colors such as turquoise and fuchsia. Men and children wear amulets around their necks by way of ornament, inscribed with Qur'anic verses, or prayers written on cardboard wrapped in fire-treated leather engraved with geometric patterns. (I found similar amulets in the Omdurman market in Sudan.) These charms are made by sheikhs called *al-Sharif* or *al-Faqir*, mostly from Sudan.

One amusing thing I remember from the trip was when I asked Amr how to relieve oneself at 'Elba, and he pointed to the high mountain. "You have two choices," he said. "Mountain No.1," and he gestured to the mountain. Then he pointed to a smaller mountain. "And this is Mountain No.2," he laughed. "Pick whichever you like!"

The Ababda and Bishari tribes are not dark-skinned, but olive-skinned. Their features are like European people's, and they are generally slender and as tall as bamboo, which I think is caused by their constant moving about the deserts and mountains, their reliance on milk for nutrition, and their diet, which is low in carbohydrates. The main occupation of these tribes is herding, and they trace their history back to Zubeir ibn al-'Awwam. In his seminal study *al-Khitat al-tawfiqiya al-jadida*, Ali Mubarak Pasha suggests that the Ababda and Bishariya are most probably the descendants of the Beja people, based on the similarities between their racial characteristics and habits. He adds that they inhabit many parts of the desert between the Red Sea and Nubia, and the mountain peaks and valleys, and that while they speak Arabic, they also have another language (Nabarawi).

I paid a visit to Souq Shalatin, the biggest market in the southern Red Sea area, where mainly Egyptian and Sudanese goods are sold, and where traders from Sudan meet in large numbers coming by way of Darb al-Arba'in. This trek, with wells on either side, including time to stop and drink and rest, takes about forty days, and it is the major trade route through the region. The main trade is in camels and day-to-day needs. The Sudanese *toub*—the length of fabric that the Ababda and Bishari women wrap around themselves—is sold at the market. I couldn't find any silver jewelry or a silversmith in the market, but I found an amulet-maker who made them out of animal hide, especially goatskin.

The chance to be in the market also allows people to swap news between the tribes coming from all directions to buy what they need, bringing the news of everything that happens around them: who has had a child, boy or girl, who has died, who has married, and so on. They told me that they squat in big circles, with the village elder in the center, holding his pointed stick, which he uses to draw signs and symbols in the sand. This meeting is called the *siknab*, a Nabarawi word meaning "news"—that is, a meeting to swap tribal news. (Their version of newspapers and news programs!)

We couldn't go into the Halayeb Triangle because of the political situation at the time, but Amr told me a nice story about the way the people of Arab countries get along, no matter what their governments say. During the border dispute between the Egyptian and Sudanese governments about whom the Halayeb Triangle belonged to, there were great numbers of soldiers, both Egyptian and Sudanese, stationed on the border, on high alert. The divisions stood face-to-face, armed to the teeth and equipped with tanks. At the time, Amr's job was to inspect the natural reserves in the area, and this was in the summer. Summer in that region of Southern Egypt is *blazing*. He was ordered to meet with the military commander in the area to report his business in the city and get this man's approval. When he arrived at the place where he was supposed to meet the military commander, he found the Egyptian and Sudanese commanders sitting side-by-side in their undershirts, enjoying the shade of a tree. In front of them was a backgammon board with a game under way, and they were chatting and roaring with laughter. It's true: peoples are one thing, and governments are something else entirely.

Sinai: Eid and Barbara

I visited the Southern Red Sea two times: once on my trip to Gebel 'Elba to collect more information about the Ababda, Bishari, and Rashaida for my book; and the next to attend the Wadi al-Gemal (Camel Valley) festival, held by my friend Walid Ramadan, who was responsible for the nature reserve. Our company took part in the festival: we exhibited traditional Egyptian dresses and the jewelry worn with them, and I gave a lecture on these garments and adornments. Holding the festival in the reserve itself was a marvelous idea to bring together all the tribes of the Egyptian desert and oases. It was the biggest ever festival for the people who lived in the deserts of Egypt. Every tribe and oasis exhibited its own art, music, songs, traditional dishes, folk games, and dances. Twenty-seven tribes from all over Egypt in one place! I was delighted to attend, and I learned a lot from meeting the people and the tribes, and collected so much information from them about their habits, customs, and traditions.

When I was there, I made the acquaintance of Eid Abu Suliman, a friend of my daughter Fatma and Amr Ali. Eid was the son of Suliman Eid Salem Abu Nagazi, the sheikh of sheikhs of the Tarabin tribe in South Sinai, who ruled the region back when it was occupied by Israel. The youngest of his brothers, Suliman was nevertheless chosen to rule the tribe, one of the largest in all Sinai, on the strength of his levelheadedness and wisdom. Eid was married to Barbara, a Swiss–Danish woman, and they had two daughters, Yasmin and Tamara, currently at university in Europe. Eid Abu Suliman was one of the best young men you could find in the Tarabin tribe, and he knew every secret of the Sinai Peninsula: its valleys, plains, and mountains.

About a year later, in 2008, I was invited by Eid and Barbara to spend New Year in the Sinai desert with them and some of their tribesmen. It was a great experience. I had so much fun, and it was a wonderful time. Also, I learned a lot from the six days I spent there. I took down a lot of things that were said, and information from Barbara, from Eid, and from the members of his tribe who were hanging out with us. Sitting around the fire at night for warmth in the terrible chill of the night, as I asked question after question, made me so happy, and gave me so much information about the tribes in Sinai.

We camped at Gebel al-Barqa in a huge cavern. Eid told me that the place was his and Barbara's discovery, their secret cave away from prying eyes. This was where they came every New Year's Eve to celebrate the new year with his tribe. After the celebration, they blocked the cave mouth with dry branches to keep anyone else from discovering their party spot before they left. They call it al-Barqa, which means "glittering," because it's surrounded by sand dunes that glitter in the moonlight. Barbara told me about the Suwara festival at the full moon, the only time when women gather together with men in traditional costume. They stand in rows facing one another, the women and the men, and the men recite poetry. It's a family reunion. The Tarabin from the mountains bring dried dates and the coastal

Tarabin bring dried fish; the families exchange gifts of dates and fish, and the young men and women meet each other for potential marriages. Barbara told me that she attended it once in her life, and she believed that the Mazayna tribes still practice this ritual.

I wanted to visit the Serabit al-Khadem area, which had been famous for its turquoise and copper since pharaonic times, so we drove over there. The Bedouin women in that area have a most unique character. They wear their hair in braids that they wrap around their foreheads in a marvelous, special look. It was brought home to me how much movie designers learned from these personalities, their style of dress, and the forms of their jewelry.

Bedouin women are artists in what they wear. The environment surrounding them is desert, with few resources. Jewelry in Sinai is scarce and limited, so a Bedouin woman makes up for it by decorating and embellishing her dress and veil. Each girl embroiders her own wedding dress before marriage, with fabulous artistry. The tribal girls are known for the skill of their embroidery and the personality expressed in it. They wear their dresses on their wedding day; most of these garments are embroidered with brightly colored cotton threads in various shades of red and yellow on black fabric. If her husband should happen to pass away, during her mourning period, a woman embroiders a blue mourning gown, a sign to the village of a time of sorrow. After a while, if she wants to marry again, she embroiders a fresh gown, half in red and half in blue, to signal to the tribe, "Get ready!"

The burqa, or face veil, of the Bedouin woman is the most attractive piece in all Sinai. It is a highly embellished traditional piece, with cultural links to that worn by Egyptian urban and village women, and not to be confused with the contemporary burqa worn in the Arabian Gulf. For a girl, there is a short black veil called a *lathma*, which covers her mouth, and she wears this until she has her first child. After giving birth, a woman then wears a long semitransparent face veil that she embroiders herself. She buys all the necessities from the fabric dealers: light chiffon, colorful silk thread, genuine amber beads and other beading, and old coins, including coins from Britain and Austria. For the rich girls of the tribes, the coins they sew into their face veils are sometimes solid gold or silver. You can often find Ottoman-era coins on these face veils. Over the course of my life, I have acquired a sizable collection of these gorgeous pieces. The social status of a Bedouin woman can be seen from the elements she sews into her burqa, which differs in style from one tribe to another. If a man catches sight of a woman in the desert, he knows her tribe just by looking at her face veil. If he is tired, or finds himself hungry or thirsty, he stands at a respectable distance and asks her for what he needs without approaching her, which would bring the wrath of the common law down on him.

These tribes' burqas are their bank, or savings account, especially the ones adorned with gold coins. They are handed down from mothers to their eldest daughters. There are three types of silver bracelet worn there: *al-Bint wa-guzha* (the girl and her husband), *Daqqat al-'aqrab* (the scorpion tattoo), and *Widn al-quffa*, (the basket handle). This last was so named because it looked like an actual basket handle and was made by my old friend from the Khan, the sheikh of the silversmiths, Hagg Mikkawi.

A Bedouin woman's necklace tells her life story. Every important event in her life is noted and threaded into these beads and this thread. A bead given to her by her mother when she was pregnant; a bead given to her by her husband on coming back from a trip; a bullet from a rifle that she found while out herding goats; a bead given to her by her father at an important family event. The necklace she wears is a record of her life and specific circumstances.

Bedouin women also have a collection of beads for emergencies: amber for crisis and times of trouble—often you'll find a Bedouin women pinning a cloth bag to her necklace, containing a diverse collection of beads: heliotrope, a dark olive-green stone with red specks, which they call "bloodstone," to stop bleeding; a stone for headaches; one to encourage a mother to give milk when it's time to nurse; another for a scorpion's sting; another to ward off the evil eye. There is a poultice, too: the head of a horned viper, a scorpion, and a wasp, all burned together over a flame until they are charred, then pounded together and made into a paste with which a nursing mother's nipple is rubbed. They believe that this combination protects a child from the stings of wasps, scorpions, and snakes. A complete mobile pharmacy, hanging in a bag pinned to her necklace or clothes to use when needed.

The famous necklaces of cloves that Bedouin women wear are threaded after soaking cloves in water until they soften, and are worn in a long necklace that gives her a fragrant scent. Also, there is a shell they call *wardina* which they pierce with a nail and thread through with a string. It is hung on children's foreheads for protection.

I have an important collection of books in my library about the history of beads, their importance, and their connections to human history. I'm very interested in the history of this beautiful product, and I attend many international conferences with people interested in this fascinating subject. At these conferences, I have met experts and specialists from America, Europe, and Southeast Asia, all explaining the importance of this wonderful art, its history, its effects, its influence, and the powerful connection between beads and the people who wear them. I'm also a member of international associations for the art of beads, and I'm always in contact with them, following up on what is written and published on this refined art.

During this trip, we drove by the old emerald mines in Sinai, which were extensively mined in Roman times. They were all in caves too high for me to climb up and view these historical sites.

How I enjoyed my trip to Sinai with Eid and Barbara! The information I learned about Eid's family and about the habits and customs of the tribes was very important and added to my knowledge about the Sinai tribes. From them, I learned the four most important things in a Bedouin's life: water, fire, flour, and wood. Bedouins live on the bread made by both men and women that they call *fitir*, and *'afij*, which is milk dried in the sun and used in cooking. When the wind whips up, Bedouin bury themselves in a hole as long as their body, called a *qarmous*. And in the biting cold of the desert winter, a layer of burning coals is covered with a layer of sand, and they lie on it.

There were no communication networks in the desert of Sinai. When I wanted to call Cairo, Eid took me up to a hill about fifty meters high, not far from our camp. I can't tell you how we got up there in a four-wheel drive! It was like something out of the movies. After a few nice bumps and teeth-rattling bounces, we arrived and I got out of the car on the hilltop, where there is an area—no more than a meter square, which Eid knows perfectly—that you can get signal. "Stand right here in this spot," he said, "and talk."

How I enjoyed the company of that wonderful family! How much I learned about the Tarabin of Sinai! All this was by way of the young Tarabi, Eid, and his wife Barbara. I fell in love with Sinai, the Land of Turquoise, with its distinctive nature and its marvelous mountains with their different shapes and colors at sunset, when I could gaze and daydream at the mountain ranges all in a row in shades of gray and pitch-black, a wonderful inspiration for a painter. I wish I were an artist! I would draw the trees, the springs, the Bedouin women herding sheep and goats through the hills and valleys, standing there in their bright colors, holding their shepherd's staffs—dots of color, red, yellow, and orange scattered about on the background of sand with its different shades. It's a world I took great joy in experiencing, even for a short while.

4
INSPIRATION AND ADVENTURE

Traveling for Crafts

Just as I was methodical about learning my craft and trying to understand everything to do with it, I also had a desire in mind to find out more about the outside world—it was, after all, like ours, with a heritage and civilizations of its own—and see what kind of costumes and jewelry were worn. This, of course, called for reference books and trips to these places, which was hard for reasons of budget and time—I always had so much to do!

One of my blessings is always finding simple and easy solutions to start doing what I want to do. I started by making clippings of everything I saw in magazines and newspapers about the subject I was interested it: articles, photographs, information, news. I attended seminars and lectures on the subject, where I met people in the field. This, of course, gave me some knowledge of Black Africa, the eastern and western Arab world, the Sahara Desert, the Tuareg, Asia and Southeast Asia, and Indonesia, with its marvelous islands of Bali and Sumatra. Over the first twenty years, I collected information and research on the jewelry and crafts in these regions from specialized magazines, periodicals, and societies with an interest in these things, both local and international. I learned the names of the major professors and the important people who specialized in each field.

As I grew more financially stable, I was able to buy reference books for all this. It was something I always budgeted for. On every trip abroad, a priority on my list of places to visit was art bookshops and specialized stores. I'm sure you know how big and heavy art books are, so I also budgeted for extra baggage on these trips. After fifty years of my career, I'm blessed with a beautiful library and technical and craft archive, which is my real fortune, the riches I have amassed throughout my life, in addition to the actual examples of traditional jewelry and costumes and handicrafts. As my sister Randa—an internationally renowned lighting designer, who has the same passion for collecting reference volumes—always says, "When you think of anything to do with an idea you want to work on, you'll find at your fingertips the reference that can help you develop it. It makes things easier."

My collection of books in the Azza Fahmy Archive, I have collected over long decades. I carried them back from every continent, north, south, east, and west. I have read them and learned of the main countries with significant folk artisanship and handicrafts. (My interest is, of course, jewelry, but there are many other things I like: fabrics, wood, costumes, glass beads, and wickerwork.) This art, creativity, and originality opens your eyes to beauty and activates something in your mind, which absorbs and understands them. Afterward, you feel you've gained something, some new ideas, which start to dovetail. I always say, in the Egyptian way, "We put it all together in a blender, turn it on, and mix it up"—it produces something new and innovative, giving us a sense of freshness and joy.

All this drove me to plan to visit these places and see these arts and crafts for myself in their original locations, and to meet the people who were still there and working on them. Some of these trips were thanks to international conferences I was invited to, and others were my own plans. At the same time, everything I collected had given me an idea of the major countries I needed to visit to see everything I liked right there in front of me, to touch it with my hands and understand it. I ended up with a list of important countries known for their artisanship, and I tried to spend my holidays and time off in places that made the work I liked, to combine work and learning with play.

I'll try to tell you a bit about some of the countries I managed to visit, and how I got the chance to go there. (There are still many countries on my list that I want to see! I hope I live long enough.)

Siwa Oasis

I've visited Siwa four times in the past forty-five years. The first trip was in 1966, organized by the students and professors at the Fine Arts School to celebrate the end of studies and the start of our professional lives. We decided to go to Bahariya Oasis—a group of students from the Architecture and Design Departments, about twenty-five or twenty-eight students, as I remember. I don't remember exactly how many boys and how many girls, but the boys far outnumbered the girls.

The budget was very tight, and we couldn't afford to rent a bus. We ended up renting a large truck, and the boys arranged with a contractor to make a wooden frame for the bed of the truck and cover it with heavy fabric to make a kind of room. We put three long benches into it, so that everyone could sit on them.

We all met at a club that was run by the Faculty of Fine Arts, in a building on Ramses Street, next to the railway station, and set out from Cairo at dawn, heading for Bahariya. First, we headed for the desert. There were no paved roads through the desert back then: it was all beaten paths and desert trails, well known to the drivers who worked around those parts. Oh my goodness, there was no end to the laughter and jokes on that trip. You just couldn't compare it to anything else. I swear, the Faculty of Fine Arts crowd are hysterical. We sang, as well, like all young groups on this kind of trip. At that time, the famous patriotic songs celebrating the 1952 Revolution were the best of the best: the amazing poet Salah Jahin wrote the lyrics, the great composer Kamal al-Tawil set them to music, and they were sung by that era's heartthrob, Abdel Halim Hafez.

Among the professors with us on that trip was the great painter Hamed Nada in his capacity as chaperone and supervisor. At night, we lifted the benches out of the truck; then the girls got in first, deep inside the truck, and Professor Nada counted them; then the boys got in to sleep, alternating their positions so one boy's head was at the other boy's feet. The great artist himself was the dividing line between the boys and the girls.

When we woke up in the morning and needed to relieve ourselves, this, too, needed to be organized between the boys and the girls, especially since we were in a wide-open desert area. To do it, the girls got out of the truck first, while the boys waited inside; then it was Professor Hamed Nada's turn along with the rest of the guys. They formed a row of about fifteen young men, with Professor Nada facing them, and burst into song, a line from Abdel Halim Hafez's famous patriotic anthem, "We have only to pass by the desert to make it green!"

First, we took the Fayoum road, and arrived at the first entry to the desert. There was a traffic checkpoint there. The policeman on duty recorded our entrance to the oasis. A while later, after about half a day's driving, we had the feeling that the driver was lost. It looked like he didn't know the way, and the truck started to get stuck in the sand. We spent about a day stuck deep in the sand. After a while, we learned to work together to get the truck out of the sand, by digging and putting thick cloths under the wheels. But I began to feel that none of the other students was taking any positive steps to get us out of trouble. Everyone was just sitting around cracking jokes, and they took to splitting up into groups and kicking a ball around. On top of the truck were crates of oranges and tangerines, so, munching and chomping, they actually did form teams and start a soccer match. Nobody was taking our situation seriously! I don't mind telling you, I broke down and started to cry, especially as I couldn't see anyone taking action. They thought it was funny to measure my height and go, "Okay, which direction do you want to be buried? Facing north, or northeast?" They began to take it seriously when they saw me crying.

Anyway, finally we got out of that area and found our way back onto the paved road. So as not to ruin the trip, we decided to change our plans and go to Siwa. But there was one problem: the traffic authority had registered us coming in and noted down our license plate. However, the traffic checkpoint for the Oasis had no record of a truckload of Fine Arts students arriving, because we had driven out by a different route, one without a traffic checkpoint to make a note of our departure from that part of the desert. (Back then, it would never have occurred to us that the traffic checkpoints had ways of notifying each other that a vehicle had arrived safely at an oasis.)

We got to Siwa two days later. We had stopped off in Marsa Matruh for three hours to rest, leaving for Siwa down roads that were mostly just trails of packed sand. It took forever to get there. When we arrived at the oasis, I felt I had stepped into the Ouarzazate region among the villages of southern Morocco. Stunning desert architecture, and scenery that went straight to the heart. The mud-brick buildings had a unique character.

I don't remember how long we spent there, perhaps four or five days. There weren't any hotels, so they put us up at a government rest house with hotel facilities. We walked through the town, looking at the many springs that Siwa is known for, particularly Ain Cleopatra, Ain al-'Arayes, and Ain al-Shams, next to the temple of the god Amun, which they say Alexander the Great visited on his journey to Siwa. We saw the olive groves, planted by workers they call the *zaggala*, wearing a strange traditional costume which looked like a sack to me, very thick handmade fabric woven on a manual Bedouin loom. I had no interest in any type of jewelry at that time, nor did I know that this was going to be my main occupation; but the general surroundings caught my attention. The architecture was distinctive; I'd never seen anything like it in Egypt. There were little girls, about nine years old, walking through the streets in costumes that seemed foreign to Egypt—beautiful traditional costumes in distinctive fabrics, with their hair in many tiny braids, like the photographs I saw in magazines of the Amazigh peoples of North Africa. Siwa was primitive at the time, with no sign of urbanization.

Aghurmi, the ancient town high on a mound, had traditional houses of unique character, constructed of karshif stone, which is a mixture of salt, sand, and mud. The doors were of olive wood or palm wood. There were two groups of people who lived in Siwa at that time: the Easterners, who lived, as their name suggests, in the east, and the Westerners, who lived in the west.

Four days into our visit, the superintendent of police in charge of the region burst in, waving copies of the national newspapers *al-Akhbar* and *al-Ahram*, both carrying a big story about twenty-five designers lost in the Western Desert, saying that the government had instituted a search for us! Police patrols were even now combing the desert for the lost group. There were no cell phones back then. Some official at the oasis—I can't remember who—notified *al-Ahram* that we had arrived in Siwa. Our families were frantic by then.

What I gained from this visit was the chance to see an extremely special, different, and beautiful part of Egypt. There's something truly unique about it. I came back fascinated and impressed. This was when I bought my first silver ring, with a rectangle that had a palm tree on it. It was stunning. The Siwans call it a *konkit*. I paid five pounds for it, which was an enormous sum at the time. "It's made by Gabgab, the famous Siwan silversmith," they told me. I wore that ring for years and it still holds pride of place in my collection. It was the first ring in my private collection—truly beautiful, with a breath of artistry in the engraving, by someone who could do quality engraving on silver.

You know, up until the day of my graduation, I always wore the same earrings, each a simple gold bead, and a silver necklace around my neck with my brother's watch—my brother who died in the 1973 war. It was a pocket watch that had cost seventeen pounds from Ataba and it had the brand *al-Turmay* (the tram) written on it in Arabic. I still have it. What I mean is, I was never one of those girly girls who primp and preen, and I didn't even think of jewelry in those days.

My next trip to Siwa was twenty years later, in 1987, to view the jewelry of that unique region. By then, I had started to work in jewelry making and had developed an interest in finding out what the people of Egypt wore, and I had prepared myself with all the information I needed about the oasis. I was interested in Egypt's traditional heritage and wanted to know what Egyptians chose to wear, especially the desert dwellers, and in particular those of Siwa, who have a style of jewelry that's different from the Egyptian style in general.

I headed out full of hope of finding how Siwan jewelry was made in the oasis and what techniques were used there. I thought I would go and find the Siwan silversmith, sitting on the ground creating jewelry for the oasis. Unfortunately, the image existed only in my mind: I was deeply disappointed to learn that all of Siwa's jewelry was produced in Alexandria, at old Uncle Amin's, next to the docks! Afterward, you know, I kept looking for this old Uncle Amin until I found him and went to visit him in his shop. I spent about three hours there, looking at the jewelry he made for the Siwans, and took information from him that I wrote down. I bought some pieces from him, too. He was training up his daughter as an apprentice to help him with the engraving. She was a really good engraver; I still keep a piece of her work. Siwan silver jewelry is made of 80-karat and 60-karat silver, and sometimes out of white metal, or "horse silver," as they call it in the profession.

My third visit to Siwa was in the early 1990s, as I wanted to learn more about Egypt's traditional jewelry. I found that things had changed a bit. There was a hotel, where I stayed and met Abdallah Baghi, a Siwan who used to be the headmaster of the school there and who belonged to the well-known

Baghi clan. With me were my two daughters, Fatma and Amina, who were very young at the time. Abdallah later became head of the local Educational Department. He was a great help to me back then, and told me about life in Siwa and the people's habits. His contacts helped me to be invited to one or two people's homes, which was otherwise very hard to arrange. "Things have changed a bit," he said.

In the 1960s, on my first visit there with the university, Siwan girls used to be offered for marriage from eight or nine years of age up to about twelve. How could you tell? By the fact that they began to braid their hair into about twenty-six little braids. This meant that a little girl was ready and being offered for marriage. An engagement would take place by means of the traditional recitation of the Fatiha, the opening chapter of the Qur'an, by the two families, after which the girl would be set aside for the boy with a common-law contract until they were both of marriageable age. Sometimes, an engagement could last for ten years. The fiancés only met at festivals and on special occasions. On their wedding day, it is the groom who undoes the bride's braids. Sometimes, in some Siwan families, as soon as a girl was born, there was a specific boy she was meant to marry.

Women braided their hair into sixty-five braids, and each woman had her own style. Older women wrapped their braids around their heads like a cap that they call *takoshet*; a married woman braided in a form called *tosht*; and little girls, *tabu-tabu*. I learned that women washed their hair in Siwa with a type of fine clay that comes from smooth mud, which is full of beneficial minerals. You know, in North Africa, in Morocco, they have the same habit of washing their hair with fine clay.

All the women had kohl around their eyes, and they say that men wear kohl on their wedding day. A man puts on kohl from his wife's kohl holder. On a girl's wedding day, her mother, her maternal aunt, and her female relatives are the ones to braid her hair. However, usually, the process of braiding a Siwan woman's hair is done by a woman called a *tarraza*, who does it professionally,

On this third visit, I spent about three days in Siwa. In that time, I learned a lot of information from Abdallah and from the families whose households I managed—with difficulty, through people close to Abdallah—to visit; they spoke Egyptian as well as Siwan, an oral language related to Amazigh. This language has not been taught in schools, in contrast to Amazigh in North Africa: on my most recent trip to Morocco, I found that Amazigh is taught in the schools of the regions where the tribes live in the upper and mid-range Atlas Mountains. All the street signs in Morocco, and the signs on important buildings, are written in Arabic, Amazigh, and sometimes French.

For my most recent trip to Siwa, I prepared carefully. I did a lot of reading and research and also made a list of questions I was going to ask the more experienced people in the oasis. I went armed with some information, having read Ahmad Fahkry's two books about the Egyptian oases, which said that the Amazigh Siwan tribes had learned Arabic in the era of Muhammad Ali, in about 1820. Before that, they only knew Amazigh.

When I first arrived in Siwa in 1966, some of the old people living there knew only a few words of Arabic. They say that at the turn of the twentieth century, there was a single family that specialized in translating for strangers who came in caravans from the Nile Valley or North Africa to trade and barter for dates and olives. The sheikh of this family was named Sheikh Alkabar. When I asked Abdallah Baghi about the major and famous dishes, he told me about Makhmakh, that is, purslane, which grows wild naturally in the fields.

It was on this visit that I bought my first collection of Siwan silver. It represented the major pieces a Siwan girl wears for her wedding. Most of a girl's fingers are adorned with rings of different shapes on her wedding day: square, round, rectangular, and so on. Each of these has a name, and a size. They call a ring a *mahbas*, the plural *mahabes*, which means "stopper." I have written about this in detail in my book about traditional Egyptian jewelry. I bought the *ta'laqin* and the *aghraw*, the two most important pieces in the jewelry of Siwa: one worn on the head, the other on the chest. I don't want to bore you by getting too technical about the types and names of Siwan jewelry, but this is the research I did on this visit.

Then I asked if there used to be silversmiths in the oasis long ago, making its pieces? Of course, the familiar answer was "Gabgab." He had been the major silversmith of Siwa in the 1940s, they told me, and it was said that his sister assisted him. He died in an accident, I think a motorcycle crash. The pieces made by this brilliant artisan are some of the most important and wonderful examples of silver made in this oasis.

One day, two foreigners arrived in the oasis, on the pretext of research and development. They deluded the people of Siwa into thinking that they were there to conduct educational and medical projects, and they lived there for more than three or four years. The woman dressed in Siwan costume and braided her hair like the Siwans. They bought most of Gabgab's work from the prominent families, and they also bought all the tools he used for jewelry making. They left Egypt, taking with them an important part of the history of desert artisanship and jewelry. What I heard is that this historic collection is now on display in a museum in Zurich.

Long years later, I requested a meeting with the Swiss ambassador to ask him about the possibility of getting this collection of human history repatriated. Naturally, the man laughed and said, "All this stuff left your country with your approval! It was labeled as a collection of exhibits for a show on the jewelry of the Siwa Oasis!" What a great shame.

On that visit, I bought Siwan dresses, a lovely collection: the gorgeous black wedding gown they call *nashrah aztaf*—strangely, Siwan women wear black gowns on their wedding day for good luck—and the same gown, but in white, which they wear on the second day of the wedding; they call it *nashrah dakhwaq*. When I look at the ornamentation of these gowns, full of tiny shell buttons, which play a large part in each piece's design, and the colors of silk thread around the neckline, branching out from it like the rays of the sun in the direction of the sleeves, I'm immediately put in mind of the ancient Egyptian drawings of the sun's rays on pharaonic temples. The colors used by Siwan women are the colors of the natural environment that surrounds them and which they see and are affected by every day. There's green, the color of palm fronds; and yellow, orange, and red, the color of dates as they change at different stages of ripening before they're harvested.

The collection of Siwan shawls being offered for sale at that time were gorgeous museum pieces. This is the item that Siwan women pour all their artistry into. In chiffon embroidered with silk threads of a type they call *hurr*, which they buy from the cities, such as Alexandria and Cairo, the shawls are covered with designs in square, triangular, and circular shapes, which I learned were symbols that had been borrowed by different civilizations from each other. This shawl is called *taruqa't* in Siwan.

A Siwan woman's veil is a marvelous creation. The number of lines of embroidery differs according to the financial situation of the woman wearing it, up to a maximum of sixty. In regular veils, the lines range from thirty to thirty-seven lines on average, with a minimum of eighteen. An interesting thing I noticed is that Siwan women and girls have eighteen ways to add buttons to their dresses or veils.

The shawl for Siwan men, which I like a lot, is called *jird*. I bought one and I used to wear it all the time in winter. It's a giant shawl in white wool, over two and a half meters long, which Bedouin men wrap around their bodies several times in winter to ward off the chill. The Libyans call this shawl a *jird* as well.

The people of Siwa believe in the evil eye, bad energy, and spirits. A well-to-do Siwan woman will fill her veil and dress with amulets, sometimes of low-grade (60-karat) silver, or white metal, hanging from her veil or dress by a string. Some have *Ma sha Allah* ("what God wills") written on them, said to ward off the evil eye, and sometimes the image of a five-fingered hand, as five is a lucky number, and sometimes fish. These low-grade silver amulets gave me tons of inspiration for pendants and earrings.

Dr. Ahmed Fakhry's book on Siwa was one of the major references on the subject, and I learned a lot of historical information about the oasis from it. The illustrations he published are wonderful pictures of the special traditional costume there, quite different from the traditional costume of the rest of Egypt.

The *toub* is the most common type of gallabiya in Siwa, and women wear it daily. It's cut like the voluminous *hashimi* of the Arabian Gulf, or the costume worn by Beni Udayy in Asyut. The difference is that it has a rectangular embroidered section around the neck, called the *touq*, or choker. My dear friend Nevin al-Tamman, a wonderful person I met in the early 1990s, was one of the first women from Cairo to visit this oasis. She did embroidery projects with the Siwan women. Her courage is indescribable. She had a daughter, Tamtam, who now manages her successful business. I always think of her parking her old-model Land Rover outside my gallery, which was a Mecca for tourists visiting Cairo. She brought me handicrafts from Siwa to display in my gallery and told me stories of how she took baby Tamtam in a basket and headed off for Siwa to work with the women! She spent the night on her own among the palm trees in the middle of the oasis alongside her little Tamtam. She brought me Siwan breeches and *toubs*. How often I took the embroidered cuffs of those Siwan pants and sewed them onto my jackets! How many compliments I got! This was back when I had the time to design my own clothes and enrich them with traditional elements. She also had a lot of embroidered collars made for me by Siwan women, which I added to the designs for dresses I wore. People told me they were beautiful.

My fourth and last journey was in mid-2004. I went to take pictures for my book with the AUC Press, and I was accompanied by my American photographer friend Barry Iverson, and my dear German friend Christa Dupke, who did the book layout. We took all the photographs we needed, spending a week there; I used Abdallah Baghi's silver collection to model on the women of the oasis, since the girls and women there no longer wear traditional jewelry, but wear modern gold or plastic instead.

My design for my Desert collection, launched in 2002, came from my interest and study of desert jewelry in general: Egypt's Eastern and Western deserts and oases; the Sahara Desert south of Morocco, where the "blue men," the Tuareg tribes, live; and the Indian deserts of Rajasthan—I've worked on all these regions. I enjoyed the process of reading and research, and it bore fruit in the form of a collection that people still talk about today. We used Fatma Ghaly, my daughter, to model the jewelry for the ad campaign, as we couldn't afford a professional model. I'm grateful that the collection was a success. In it, I offered modern women a taste of what desert jewelry is like with its distinctive character in a contemporary style.

The Oases

In the early 1990s, I decided to go on a trip with friends to visit the Dakhla and Kharga oases. They were regions I hadn't visited before and which it was important for me to see. I had opened the al-Ain Gallery in 1982 along with my sister and my ex-husband, the father of my children. It was the first gallery in Cairo exhibiting the work of artisans (jewelry, furniture, and brasswork). This store was a destination for a great many traveling traders with no stores of their own who sold antiques. They would come down to Cairo to sell an old-style radio, a gramophone, swords and daggers, and frequently desert dresses. These men toured small towns, buying things from middle-class and upper-middle-class families, things they no longer used.

I met a man called Ahmad from Bahariya Oasis. He had heard of my interest in traditional jewelry and costume. He used to come to my little workshop in Boulaq al-Dakrour carrying a sack of thick fabric in which were gallabiyas from the oases. At the time, the most luxurious gallabiya could be bought for a hundred pounds. Few people cared about this heritage in Egypt back then. Some galleries sold these things, among them Shahira Mehrez and Azza Fahmy. There were old embroidered gallabiyas of museum quality, some with faded colors, and occasionally newer embroidery that usually wasn't up to the standard of the older stuff. Sometimes he would pull an old rusty tin box out of his pocket, open it, and pour out the contents: nose rings (*shinafat* or *khuzam*, and called *gutr* by the people of Bahariya). I consider these pieces, made of low-grade gold—12-karat—to be some of the most wonderful and beautiful Egyptian jewelry. They are made using a granulation technique, one of the most difficult in all jewelry making, a descendant of the old Islamic jewelry craft in Ayyubid and Mamluk times. Ahmad would collect all the women's old and broken *gutr*; some of them he was asked to repair and return, but some were for sale. There were different sizes. The large ones cover about 20 percent of a woman's face, and most of her mouth. When a woman from the oasis wanted to eat, she would use one hand to lift up the nose ring. Ahmad used to tell me that when most women took off their *gutr* for repairs, they got a kind of headache, and would be frantic to get it back to wear it again. I never understood this or found any explanation for it except that it must be a psychological thing.

In the oases, they also have an important piece of jewelry that I often find deep in Upper Egypt too, and it's also worn by the village women of the Nile Valley. They're called *saqya* earrings, and look like a *saqya*, or waterwheel, because all around the circumference are little formations like the buckets of a waterwheel that go round and round, filling up with water as the wheel turns. These earrings were made in 21-karat gold, but I noticed that the part of the earring that goes through the ear was fixed to the main body of the earring with a piece of lead. This made me curious; I didn't get it. How could such a cheap metal as lead be used to seal something in 21-karat gold? The antique earring dealers used to call the earrings with lead in them "genuine" or "original" earrings. Of course, because I'm in the craft and I work with my own hands and I know about these things now, my eyes were always drawn to the small details that other people might not notice. Later, I

With my daughters in the village of Mandisha, Bahariya Oasis, 1990s.

made the connection of the combination of these two metals (gold and lead) and the copper bracelets that people with rheumatism wear for pain relief. I read a little about metallurgy and how different metals interact. I think this might be why. Ahmad would also sell me braids made of wool or silk, ending in lead pieces. Often I braided them into my own hair, in a long braid at my back. They call them *rishrash*. I still have a collection of them.

All these things, which I bought for my collection of heritage Egyptian crafts, made me want to go and visit these remote locations, to see for myself their clothing, their jewelry, and their crafts. I wanted to see the things I'd bought and acquired for real, in their own environment, and use my camera to take pictures. So I decided to visit Dakhla and Kharga.

In the winter of 1991, I visited the Dakhla and Kharga oases with my friends Sherifa Barada and her sister Fatma and her children, and, of course, my own daughters, Fatma and Amina, were first on the list. Dakhla, which literally means "going in," is so called because it's deep inside the desert, and Kharga, which literally means "going out," has that name because it's on the outer edge of the desert.

The Kharga and Dakhla trip started from Cairo, stopped at the Bahariya Oasis, then went on through the desert to Dakhla, and from there to Kharga.

We stopped for a few hours in Farafra, but I didn't go in there, as they told us at the time that it was a very poor oasis where I wouldn't find any costumes or jewelry. I took a great many photographs and got information and made observations about the garments and their embroidery as well as the types of jewelry they used that I wrote down. On this trip, I also sketched a type of pot with a special shape for which the oases are famous called a *jarra*, the most beautiful piece of pottery there. Toward the end of the seventeenth century, a family came here from Qena and made it their home, where they began to make pottery in many distinctive shapes and forms, each of which had a particular use: the *qadous*, or bucket, for waterwheels; a *mahlab* used for milking cows; a *zibdiya* for keeping butter; a bread oven called a *souma*.

We visited al-Bawiti, the capital of Bahariya Oasis, and went from there to another famous village, Mandisha. I visited the hot springs there and took a dip. Another day, we spent the whole day in the village of Bashandi, the center for making dresses *(toub)* and embroidery. Coins and shell buttons are the basis for these garments' designs. I sometimes found real old coins, but often they were what we call in the trade *khiryat*, bought from Harat al-Yahoud and made of white metal. The traders brought the fabric from Kerdasa, in Giza, and sold it to the women of the oasis. I attended the weekly market: old women from the oasis sitting and selling vegetables, wheat, and corn, wearing a *gutr* in their noses.

In general, the jewelry from the oasis is low budget except for the *gutr* nose ring, mainly made up of necklaces of beads. On her wedding day, a woman wears seven necklaces: a necklace they call *sinan Farouq* ("Farouk's teeth," referring to King Farouk, with beads that do look like teeth) and sometimes *sinna dahab wa sinna louli* ("a tooth of gold and a tooth of pearl"). Then, a necklace of imitation coral made of *hanib* (their word for glass), and a *faqish* ("shatterer") necklace of glass so light and fragile that it shatters like an eggshell if you press it with your finger. Its name comes from the root meaning to break or crack. There was the clove necklace, made of red glass that looks like cloves; a glass necklace; and a necklace of "false coral" in roughly zigzagging glass. I learned that a divorced woman wears a necklace called the divorcée's *baghma*, to make a public announcement of her status.

The women of the oasis make their own necklaces and buy the beads from traders, who bring them in from the big cities. There is also an adornment of white metal, a pendant about 10 centimeters in diameter, worn by the women of the oasis for protection, with primitive drawings on it of people and sometimes with "Sultan of the Jinn" written on it: they call this *al-louh*, "the panel", or *jalajel*, "bells." It shows a lot of influence from the jewelry worn for the religious–magical ritual of the *zar*. A married woman from the oasis wears two anklets of white metal, one of each ankle, called *hajoul*, "hoppers" (singular *hajl*). Kohl is important to women of the oases. They make it themselves by burning cotton soaked in oil, and keep it in a handmade kohl holder, a beautiful traditional piece from the region.

We arrived at the capital of Dakhla, Mut, which is named after the ancient Egyptian goddess Mut, the mother of gods and goddesses. We didn't stay there, though, as there wasn't a hotel where we could spend the night. We visited the famous Bagawat Necropolis, the oldest Coptic burial site in the country. Unfortunately, there wasn't time to really take a proper tour before it got dark.

We visited the village of Balat in the Dakhla Oasis, with its wonderfully distinctive mud-brick architecture. There was a noticeable feature about the houses; they had wooden lintels inscribed with the name of the family and the date the house was built (for instance, AH 1163—about AD 1770) and sometimes verses of the Qur'an as well as the name of the homeowner and the craftsman who made the plaque. There was also a wheat mill, and it is said that the village was called Balat, which means "palace," because it has the ruins of the Sultan's palace.

I had to visit the village of al-Qasr in Dakhla Oasis, dating back to the Mamluks; it was a unique example of Islamic architecture. I had read that it was the first desert village to welcome the Arab tribes that had immigrated to Egypt. It had an ancient mosque and an important courthouse; it had been called by that name, which means "the fortress," because the ruler had his headquarters there. It was truly a unique example of desert Islamic architecture, and it needs to be taken care of and preserved.

It was very important for me to get to these places and see them for myself, to see how these people worked their crafts and what they had and made there. I made notes of all of this, with rough sketches of pieces I saw. Naturally, jewelry is not made in remote areas, but in towns and cities, in specialized workshops, and transported by traveling traders to the people who live in those regions, whether deserts, oases, or remote villages.

My early dreams, and my naive imaginings before working as a jewelry maker myself and getting to know a lot of wonderful remote places, were affected by American movies, which gave people a false idea about remote areas and the Bedouin and nomads who inhabit them. Hollywood shows them all wearing Arab headdresses and riding horses and donkeys. I thought I'd find people working the traditional silver and gold they wear in these remote regions, but all this broke up on the rocks of reality with my repeated field trips.

When we had finished visiting the oases, we went straight across the desert to the Nile Valley, heading for Asyut. From there, we drove alongside the Nile northward to Cairo.

I remember now that having Fatma and Amina along on all these trips was important for them. It left a deep impression of Egypt upon them, as they saw people in their real-life locations and how they lived, what they wore, what their houses looked like, and their habits and customs. I always felt that this gave them a deeper and more intimate connection to their homeland. When Amina went to England to study in Birmingham, the professor was giving a lecture about the history of traditional jewelry arts and showed a slide of something that looked like a gold earring, saying, "This is an earring from the Middle East." Amina raised her hand, right in the middle of the talk, and said, "No, sorry. It's a nose ring from the Egyptian oases." Talking to her on the phone that day (we talked every Monday, when she gave me her news), I was thrilled to hear the story, and my eyes filled with tears. I felt that I had achieved something; I had implanted an interesting tidbit of information in her mind to connect her with the land of Egypt, her country.

My Beloved Levant

Visiting Damascus, the City of Jasmine, had been a dream of mine for years—Aleppo, too. My dear friend Nidal al-Ashqar—the first lady of Lebanese and Arab theater and a cultured artist, she is the daughter of prominent Lebanese writer and thinker Asad al-Ashqar (1908–86), the one-time secretary of the Syrian Social Nationalist Party—was someone I had first met forty years before, when Dr. Samir Sarhan had invited her to Egypt to give a reading of poems by Mahmoud Darwish at the Cairo International Book Fair in early 1984. Dr. Sarhan was director of the Egyptian

State Publishing House for many years and launched a number of initiatives including the "Reading for All" series. Nidal had heard of my work and came to pay me a visit at my gallery with her friend May Jumblatt, the wife of Lebanese politician Kamal Jumblatt, and daughter of Shakib Arsalan. She also became one of my circle of friends in Beirut, and we met many times in her chosen fortress-like home in the Druze Mountains region: a mansion built out of rock and stone like a fairytale castle. She had selected traditional furnishings, lighting, and rugs—every corner had its own kilim, carefully chosen. I had never seen anything like it. I was so happy to be friends with this great person, a maker of history. She filled you with a spirit of determination, defiance, and fortitude whenever she talked about her life and the hardships she had faced: a long history of suffering and struggle. But she had never lost her sense of beauty and grace, her Arab origins, and her distinctive elegance. How much I learned from this wonderful, intelligent person about the designs and history of European jewelry during our talks about her collection and also about the ancient heritage of the Arab and European crafts that filled her home!

I grew closer to Nidal and, to me, Beirut *was* Nidal. I only went there when she was in town: to get away from the pressures of life and work, I would take short breaks where I traveled to see her. We laughed a lot, talked politics, theater, and folk art, and she always called me "the sophisticated peasant"! She taught me traditional recipes from Mount Lebanon (she's a great cook), and I always came back to Cairo loaded down with a year's supply of olives and olive oil from friends' farms, and Umm Ahmad the cook's spinach pies, all put together by Nidal herself. I think that Cairo, too, for Nidal was Azza Fahmy; it's a strong friendship that has lasted over thirty years.

I fell deeper in love with Arabic poetry listening to Nidal reciting it. The first time I heard her in person was at the Mahka, the open-air exhibitions of handicrafts and folk art, theater, music, and other cultural events, at the Cairo Citadel. She recited "No Compromise" by the poet Amal Dunqul. Another time, I was at the Baalbek Festival in Lebanon. She had invited me to hear her reading poetry by Samih al-Qasem, Mahmoud Darwish, and Tawfiq Ziyad. I was sitting beside the best of Amman society, my Palestinian–Jordanian friend Ali Manku, may he rest in peace. He burst into tears when Nidal read Mahmoud Darwish's poetry on Palestine.

When my daughter Fatma was getting married, I wanted to make her a gift of a beautiful heritage piece to remember me by when I'm gone from this world. I decided to choose a classic Arabic poem and have it embroidered on a tulle shawl from Upper Egypt. On one of my quick trips to Nidal to decompress and unwind, I told her this as we breakfasted on her long balcony in Beirut, full of flowers and plants that she cared for herself, and twittering birds in cages. Nidal jumped up at once and headed for her big library, bringing back the book of *al-Mu'allaqat* (the suspended odes). She said, "Take it from Imru' al-Qays's poem, where he wrote for his beloved Fatma!"

My dear Fatma, less coyness and coquetry!
Are you emboldened since your love is killing me?
You have but to command: my heart will make it be.

The shawl turned out a masterpiece. My friend Dr. Nawal al-Messiri had it embroidered on Shandawil Island, near Sohag in Upper Egypt, and the poetry from *al-Mu'allaqat* glittered on it.

This was when my friendship with Nidal started, and it continues until now. I worked on two of Nidal's productions, two important plays by the late Syrian playwright Saadallah Wanous: *The Rituals of Signs and Changes* in November 1995, and *Historical Miniatures* in 1998. She directed them, and I designed the costumes and jewelry. It was a wonderful experience with a brilliant artist. I learned a lot from her and I met a great many of the cultural figures and poets of Lebanon and Syria through her. *The Rituals of Signs and Changes* was performed in Cairo at the National Theater and was a great success.

At the beginning of 1993, Nidal sent me a copy of the play to Cairo so that I could read it and get acquainted with the characters and events. I worked on preliminary sketches for costumes and jewelry for about a year. Then she asked to meet face to face. I went to Beirut, and we met, going into more detail about colors, designs, and jewelry that could be suitable for the play. After lots of discussions, we decided to visit the original location where the play was set. It was set in Damascus in the nineteenth century, and the characters and costumes had to be historical, of course, from the same region.

In the summer of 1995, Nidal drove me from Beirut to Damascus. Our dear friend Mona Kniou, a lighting designer and associate professor, came with us. She later became someone with whom I love discussing art and culture whenever I'm in Beirut. Nidal is the star of stars in Syria. When I walked with her through the beloved streets of Damascus, everyone said hello to her: store owners, salespeople, women in the street, all said, "Welcome, welcome, Lady Nidal!" We visited a great many people who dealt in traditional fabrics in the Damascus market because our goal was to choose some of the traditional Syrian fabrics they call *al-saya* to use for costumes. I came to know the secrets of old Syrian weaving, and Syrian machine embroidery in traditional designs, called *aghabani*. I took many samples and swatches of fabric to design the collection. We did a lot of walking through Damascus's old markets. You can almost smell the history as you walk through them—places like movie sets. Narrow streets with the character of historic Arab cities; windowless walls, tall and long; and suddenly, you'll turn to find a door or small opening through which you pass to find the house's large square courtyard, open to the sky. You find yourself transported to another world, a world with bitter orange trees and an ornamental marble fountain built in the center. The floors of the courtyard are worked in marble and mosaic tile in wonderful geometric patterns. You can hear the splashing of water from the fountain and see the colors of the traditional wooden doors set around the courtyard, leading to the rooms of the residents of this fabulous place. In the rooms, there is handpainted Damascene furniture in bright and cheerful colors, ornamented with gold. I can't describe adequately to you how, suddenly, your nerves are calmed and you're filled with peace at the sight. I felt so happy in this historic place. It felt like I've lived these lives before, and that I must have been there for sure.

Damascus is full of traditional coffeehouses. The Nufra Café, where I sat with Nidal, has storytellers from whom we heard folktales. The *hakawati*, or storyteller, sits on a high chair with all the listeners below him, calling out in admiration at the way he sings the old epic poems. They say in the old tales that the bitter orange tree married the jasmine tree and had a child, which was Damascus. You can smell the perfume of the jasmine planted in the courtyards of big houses—a scent that gives you a strange, pleasurable sensation. Damascus, or *al-Fayhaa'* ("the fragrant city"), the capital of the

Umayyad State, the biggest state in Islamic history, is the city of oranges and jasmine. Now I understand how the Syrian poet Nizar Qabbani said of his wonderful house in Damascus, "Do you know what it's like for a person to live in a perfume bottle?"

There was the famous Bitter Orange restaurant in the old city, where I dined many times on the best Syrian cuisine and the famous dishes of Aleppo served there, such as lamb with cherry jam, and where I met some of the most important Syrians—intellectual politicians and businessmen, artists and creators. And there was the fabulous Umayyad Mosque, the fourth most important mosque of the Islamic period, with its famous courtyard and Byzantine artwork, including gilded mosaics, marble inlays, and geometric shapes, unmatched by any civilization, dating back to Roman times. It is built on a site that originally held one of the largest temples in Syria; afterward a cathedral of John the Baptist was erected on the same site, and his head was buried there. I took many photographs of the decorations and incorporated them into my designs, and my daughter Amina also used them in some of the jewelry she designed. I wanted Amina to share what I was seeing, and I also wanted to explain to her some of the wonderful aesthetic sides of these historic places, and how to look at them and draw inspiration for pieces of contemporary jewelry.

I fell in love with Damascus It is the oldest capital city in the world and the one where the world's most powerful civilization was born. I decided to visit it again, as it had so many things to add to me as an artist. How I enjoyed the street food in the narrow alleyways of the city, strips of grilled meat and *ayran* (a yogurt drink) next to the courtyard of the Umayyad Mosque and listening to the call to prayer as we ate. There was more than one muezzin calling, each call overlapping with the sound of the others. When you are in this ancient city, it's like you're sitting in a grand opera auditorium, with the music of the calls to prayer echoing in the background.

I went to Syria many times with Nidal to work on the play. On one of the visits, I decided to bring Amina along and show her the wonderful examples of Islamic art, Umayyad architecture, the handicrafts, and everything to do with daily life. We visited al-Ghouta on the edge of Damascus, said to be the greenest and most fertile oasis on Earth, full of fruit trees and Damascus's wonderful apricots, and the Rif Dimashq governorate, a center for handicrafts, especially the mother-of-pearl inlay on wood for which Syria is famous.

Nidal took Amina and me to the northeast of Syria, where there are villages and forts on the side of the mountain. We looked down from the mountain peaks to see the sea and the far-off Latakia port. She took us to Ma'loula, the village 1,500 meters above sea level, where Aramaic, the language of Christ, is still spoken. Nidal stood in the main square of the village and recited verses by poets of the Occupied Territories, Samih al-Qasem and Mahmoud Darwish, and some lines by the great Iraqi poet Badr Shaker al-Sayyab, which I later made into a necklace that was one of my best-selling pieces.

Your eyes are two palm groves in the hour ere dawn,
Two windows, looking onto a far-off moon.
Your eyes, when you smile, make the vines burst into leaf
And the lights dance like many moons in the river.

On our next trip, a year later, Amina and I went to Aleppo. We headed north to that wonderful city, the oldest in the world. Dear Aleppo, how many civilizations have come and gone on your soil! It was on the Silk Road, which used to pass through Central Asia and Mesopotamia. White Aleppo was called by this name because its buildings were built of Aleppo stone, which is light in color. Its inhabitants say that Aleppo is a Syriac name, from *halba*, meaning "the white one."

On our drive, we passed the town of Ma'arrat al-Nu'man, where the famous blind Arab poet, thinker, and writer Abu al-Alaa' al-Ma'arri, the author of *Risalat al-ghufran* (the message of forgiveness), was born and died. Then we arrived in Aleppo where, 1,100 years before, a famous poet of the Arabs, the pride of Arab poetry, al-Mutanabbi (915–65), had lived. I used some of his poetry in my designs, including the line that says:

The horses, the night, and the wilderness know me.

We stayed in a big old house built in Aleppo's distinctive style, converted into a hotel. I experienced history in this place, which dated back to the fifteenth century. Aleppo's tall, old homes, embellished with marvelous ceramic tiles and with marble floors and central fountains in their courtyards, are wonderfully inspiring for all kinds of art. I'll never forget the sound of the famous pistachio fruit opening in the morning. When still unripe, they make a gentle *click-click-click*. The sound came to me through the windows at dawn, between sleeping and waking.

My most important visit in Aleppo was to see the famous covered market, the biggest commercial market in the Middle East. As you approach, you see the domes filling large expanses as far as the eye can see, covering the gigantic souk. All the traditional Syrian handicrafts are sold there, including olive oil soap, which I never let run out in my home. I put it by the sink to wash my hands with, and I used to wash my hair with it—a habit I picked up from my mother—before we were introduced to shampoo. There were traditional silk fabrics of all types and designs, an ancient craft handed down from generation to generation, from grandfather to sons and grandchildren, the famous Damascene silk that used to be exported to Europe, especially Venice and Florence in the Renaissance. I visited the workshops and watched the complex process of silk manufacture, and understood why it cost four hundred dollars a meter. There were the famous traditional bath towels, and there were dried fruits of every type—apricots, peaches, eggplant, bitter orange—in addition, of course, to Aleppo's marvelous pistachios. A stroll around this market was the ultimate pleasure. Imagine how one feels walking through this ancient, historic market, knowing that al-Mutanabbi bought his necessities from this very place. You're walking down the same paths he trod! I hear that the Aga Khan Foundation plans to rebuild the market after its destruction in the war. I was delighted to hear that news.

Aleppo has a famous Sagha, well known for goldsmithing since ancient times. They have their own traditional designs, such as gold Aleppo chains, which they make in all sizes and thicknesses. You can buy gold chains by the meter there, after which they're weighed. I took my daughter Amina to the traditional folk markets in Aleppo, and she helped me with a great many important little things during the trip, such as carrying the cameras and recording interviews with the goldsmiths and the traders. I believe that this trip left a valuable impression on her regarding our Arab heritage: the covered market, the Aleppo Sagha, the many Armenians who work as goldsmiths, the best-known Aleppo designs, and the jewelry influenced by the ancient diamond-studded pieces from the Ottoman Era.

I recorded many interviews with the goldsmiths of Aleppo in the Sagha market, such as the Istanbouli family, one of the biggest goldsmithing families in the city. I listened to the history of Ottoman jewelry and how it came to them. I recorded interviews with Armenian–Syrian goldsmiths. All these meetings and interviews were important for me to get to know the types of jewelry there and how it was made, and also the designs and the general character of traditional Syrian jewelry.

I heard old tales about Madame Araxie, an Armenian lady married to an Aleppo goldsmith, who had a great talent for designing old Turkish jewelry. Araxie designed all the jewelry her husband made and it is now sold in the Aleppo markets as historic pieces with artistic value at astronomical prices. When a jeweler there has a piece designed by Araxie, the price is different, and they say, with pride, "Because this is Araxie's work!" I also learned how this profession is managed. It has powerful guilds, with membership fees and regulations and monitoring to ensure respect for the profession, adhering to specific rules for the production process.

Naturally, I wouldn't skip telling you how much I enjoyed their ice cream, which they call *bouza*, made out of all kinds of fresh fruit for which Damascus is famous: cherries, berries, apricots, plums, and peaches. Also, I'd like to say a word about how smart and economical Syrian housewives are. They cook everything and there's a use for everything: nothing is thrown out. The marvelous Aleppo cuisine, influenced by Armenian cooking, is mind-blowing. I learned that I could put jam, especially cherry jam, on meat dishes—sweet and sour!

My relationship with Nidal and our discussions resulted in an important jewelry collection on which I put the most beautiful Arabic poetry and called it "Poems around Your Neck." In all honesty, it was Nidal who came up with the name; she also helped me with some of the choices. We exhibited this collection in Cairo at the Manastirli Palace, as well as in Dubai and Bahrain. Nidal attended and recited the poems herself. I used a lot of pre-Islamic poetry in the pieces we created, and also poetry from the early Islamic period.

His gaze I see affection in;
Onlookers see my love for him.
I'm helpless not to speak his name;
He's helpless not to do the same.
—Omar ibn Abu Rabie (644–711)

If only those we wish for on our own
Would wish for us when they are all alone!
—al-Abbas ibn al-Ahnaf

You whose name people link with my own,
Because of you, how my burdened heart groans!
No one can comfort me when I'm alone;
When you come, all are here, and I'm home.
— Ibn Zaydoun, in praise of Wallada bint al-Mustakfi

She is the story of my love.
—Ahmad Rami

I'm also very fond of pioneering free verse poet and playwright Salah Abdel Sabour's (1931–81) poetry, especially the poem "People in my Country." Unfortunately, I haven't ever made anything with this great poet's work on it. I regret it, and I'm always thinking of this poem, wanting to put it on a piece I design:

People in my country are predatory, like hawks.
Their song is like the shiver of winter through the treetops.
They kill, steal, drink, belch—but they are human.
They are placid and kind with a double-handful of cash in hand,
And they believe in destiny.

The Sultanate of Oman

Over the years I've become an expert in the origins and designs of Arab jewelry, what is worn in this country and that. I pretty much know by heart the different types of jewelry in the Arab world and North Africa, so much so that if someone merges two pieces from two different countries, I can immediately recognize that it's not an original piece, but a composite. I remember once that the Palestinians, after the Oslo accords—that is, after they got Gaza—wanted to build a museum of jewelry and costumes and enlisted my help as a jewelry expert to assess the jewelry that had been collected for the museum. Some of the pieces were partly original Palestinian with additions added from the nearby countries of Iraq and Syria. Really, I was thrilled to know most of the designs of Arab jewelry and where they came from. This was thanks to long experience and continually looking at different jewelry pieces, which filled my head with a huge cultural repository of the jewelry designs in our Arab world, and traditional jewelry in general.

I laughed when an expert from France came to Cairo to help us structure the company. My daughter Fatma had met her in Paris when she was studying for her MA. We sat and talked for about three hours and, before she left for France after our work was done, she said, "This woman," meaning me, "is a walking archive of jewelry! You need to download her brain and put it in folders!"

The Sultanate of Oman is one of the most famous Arab countries for silver and wonderful silversmithing. I have been there about four times: the first time in the mid-1980s, thanks to a British friend whose husband worked in Oman. She said to me, "How is it that you haven't seen the silver in Oman? Why, it's one of the major silver centers in the Arab world!" Back then, only a very limited number of visas for Oman were available. This friend arranged for a visa for me through her connections in Muscat, and I went there for a week.

The Matrah market in the capital was my first stop, with many small shops selling Omani silver. I spent about three days there, going from shop to shop, inspecting the pieces and asking the salesmen questions, salesmen who would sometimes take me to the silversmith who had made the pieces in another location.

There was no skipping a visit to Nazwa, the famous silversmiths' city. My British friend drove me there, a few hours from Matrah. The entire town worked in silversmithing! I spent two days in Nazwa visiting the silversmiths' workshops from morning to night. Question after question! Their tools, and in fact the whole industry, was primitive in terms of silversmithing, but

Omani silver jewelry is some of the strongest and most beautiful in all the Arab world. Back then, I wondered at those silversmiths, sitting comfortably on the ground, creating these magnificent pieces. Now I have some Omani pieces in my collection that I love. I've learned a great deal artistically and technically from studying them.

Like everyone else, I admired the Sultanate of Oman a lot because I could see how its people carefully guarded and preserved a large part of their identity. Sultan Qaboos played a great part in the country, preserving its character and identity, including requiring traditional costume (the *dishdasha*, a kind of gallabiya, and the turban they call a *kamma*) as business attire for all. One of the best-loved and most beautiful items, the one which Oman is most famous for, is the dagger. Daggers are made of solid silver and occasionally gold. The royal family has a collection of different, special, distinctive daggers with curved ends, called *bou-saidi* daggers after the ruling family of Bou-Said.

Abha, Saudi Arabia

In the early 1990s, I received an invitation from Princess Noura bint Abdel Rahman, wife of the ruler of the region of 'Asir, Prince Khalid al-Faisal, the founder of the Arab Thought Forum, to visit an important heritage site in the south of Saudi Arabia to study the craft situation there and try to assist women's organizations in the country. I was thrilled to receive this invitation, especially as I had been wanting to see this region. It was important to me, and its geographical location and proximity to Yemen meant that its architecture, costumes, and jewelry were highly influenced by that country. I have a large collection of books about all these regions: the Tihama mountains, Jizan, and Najran. The terrain is mountainous, and the people who live there are much influenced by the great civilization of Yemen. The city of Abha is the capital of 'Asir, and that was my first stop. Princess Noura oversaw my itinerary and the places to be visited and studied. My next stop was in a town called Khamis Mashit, the biggest market in the region, extremely famous for selling heritage silver pieces, and the second city of the province after Abha, the capital.

They picked a Friday for me, the best day to visit the souk, to which hundreds of people flock from neighboring regions and tribes to buy their necessities. As we were driving there, we passed by mountain ranges with gorgeous nature and traditional architecture, which is a blend of Yemeni architecture and that of African countries. The fronts of the houses are brightly colored, painted by the women in this region in an important art form called *al-qatt*. They explained that wonderful art to me, which is characteristic of these mountainous ranges, where women play the main and only role in producing beautiful façades embellished with lots of symbols. They have passed this art down from generation to generation, with well-kept secrets of color blending that they tell privately to their daughters. They call the designs by many names: *al-khatma, al-kaff, al-batra, al-arkan, al-banat, al-maharij*. Each drawing has its own character and significance, tradition and associated beliefs, handed down from grandmother to mother to daughter, and the art is still practiced today.

On the highest peaks, driving down winding mountain roads, we saw villages at the bottom of the valley with colorful façades and unique architecture. I saw women drawing and painting on the walls of their houses with handmade brushes of goat hair. The natural colors in the environment around them, of rocks and plants, are the main elements of the work: turmeric yellow, indigo blue, clover green.

We arrived at the famous weekly market. I went inside and stood there, stunned at the sight. I really couldn't pull myself together, it was so beautiful. The whole market consisted of goods in different colors: yellow lentils, brown lentils, red paprika, green henna, black pepper, even the people were different colors! There were male traders wearing the traditional *madas* slippers of Saudi Arabia, which they sometimes also call *zubayriya*, because they used to be made in a region called Zubayr long ago. These men look like they just stepped out of a big art-photography book of the type sold in Europe and America. Their skin was dark, and their hair was long and black, braided into two plaits; their black eyes were adorned with kohl; and on their heads were crowns of sweet basil and other aromatic plants, twisted together in a crown they call *al-'asba*—the headwrap—and sometimes *al-mashmoum*—the thing you smell. They wore necklaces of flowers. It was really astonishing. It took my breath away. They wore colored cloths, checked or striped vertically and horizontally, wrapped around their waists. Some had a belt in a contrasting color, and sometimes a dagger. All around was nothing but colors and more colors.

I had been thrown back to the eighteenth century. A book in my library about this region explains the customs and architecture of these tribes, calling the people who live in these mountains "the men of flowers"—which they really are. I'm always overjoyed when I've read a book about a certain region, and then go there and see the people for myself, right in front of me. We walked through the market, flanked by mountains of flowers and sweet basil, for which these regions are famous. They are bought for men to wear around their heads, and they perfume the place with a sweet smell. The combination of this traditional, artistic, wonderful sight with the sweet perfumes—I really can't express it in words. Words fail.

I took so many pictures. After that, we left the market and went to the famous silver market. This is the biggest traditional silver market in Saudi Arabia. I went into the first big store to look at the country's heritage of traditional jewelry so as to present my report to Princess Noura on the state of the craft. The exhibits were all Indian! "What's this?" I asked the salesman.

Of course, he lied to me, and spun a yarn about "this is what the Bedouins wear!" and "This is what they wear in the mountains!"

I said, "No. I want something Saudi."

He couldn't say a word. Of course, he knew I'd seen through him.

I moved from stall to stall, all next to each other. Unfortunately, Indian wares had saturated the market, and there was hardly any Saudi work, just smatterings. Nearly everything in the market at that time was new Indian stuff with a patina to make it look old, sold as Saudi heritage work.

They managed to arrange a visit for me to a silversmith in the Tihama Mountains. Down a road that wound through breathtaking mountain peaks, a drive of over an hour, we went to a house at the bottom of the forested valley. I sat with this craftsman an hour, asking him questions and finding out the techniques they used. His specialty was daggers. He squatted on the floor doing all the jobs of making them, including welding, right there on the floor. Amazing! I took some pictures and left.

I went back to Princess Noura with my report. I sat with her for about an hour explaining the results of my visit. My main advice to her was, "Please record what remains of the Saudi jewelry pieces in private collections before this part of human heritage is lost for ever." I have to confess that I fell in love with the beauty of this special, wonderful mountainous region of Saudi

Arabia, so thickly forested, with its gorgeous location and architecture, as well as its unique crafts. I came back to Cairo with my decision made: all the cards, pictures, observations, and heritage pieces I had collected over twenty years, I was going to work on and start a serious filing system for a book that would bring together this information about part of our great heritage.

And I did. That book has gone into more than one edition.

North Africa

How I fell in love with the northern strip of our beloved continent! What captivated me was the difference in cultures, their variety, and the distinctiveness of each. Around fifty years ago, we spent the summer as a family at our home on the North Coast. On the roads leading there, I used to notice the Bedouin women herding their sheep in eye-catching costumes with large flowers in bright colors, a belt of bright blue or eye-popping fuchsia around their waists. (I later learned that these were sold at Ouf in al-Azhar.) Their hands were adorned with a pair of broad silver bangles they call *damaleg* (they were the work of Hagg Mikkawi in Cairo). I was always happy to see these women on the road.

When I took up jewelry making professionally, I wanted to find out more about the people who lived in the northwestern region of Egypt, starting at Sidi Barrani and Salloum, home to the largest tribes in the Western Desert—the White Awlad Ali and the Red Awlad Ali. This urge grew too big to ignore, and the scope of my interests grew along with it. I ended up making my way from there into Libya, Tunisia, Algeria, and Morocco, and then down to Mauritania and the Sahara Desert, where the Tuareg live, the "Blue Men." I always liked their blue garments and distinctive turbans in the same color. Their women have astonishing and distinctive jewelry with basically geometric designs and patterns. I was dying to see all this with my own eyes. Some of it, I managed to go see for myself, but some of it didn't work out for various reasons.

I visited Libya once, and Tunisia three times. I went to Morocco three times, but Algeria, unfortunately, I never had the chance to see. However, I was content with the books and information I got about Algerian jewelry, especially that made in the tribal region in Beni Yenni, their capital of silversmithing, and Tizi Ouzou, where the most popular tribal jewelry is made. It is distinctive in its use of colored enamel and the addition of many pieces of coral. Their jewelry is unique, with an unusual feature: it designates a woman's marital status. An unmarried girl has different and simpler jewelry from a married woman. Divorcée and widow, mother, mother-in-law, and daughter-in-law: all wear different pieces. As to the grandmothers, after a woman's grandchildren are born, she wears a massive chain they call an *anbashaak*, with different charms pinned to it corresponding to the number of her children and grandchildren. An orphan girl is covered in expensive jewelry, so that she doesn't feel inferior (a marvelous creative thing I never heard of or saw before). There are names in the Amazigh language for these pieces. For instance, a bracelet is called an *amashlouh*; an anklet an *akhl-khal*.

Libya

My Libyan friend Dr. Farida al-Allaqi invited me to her daughter's wedding in Tripoli. It was my first trip to Libya.

A Libyan wedding lasts three to four nights. The henna night, and seeing the big families and and how they celebrated, was very interesting to me. The henna night is a kind of eastern wedding shower for women only. The wedding itself was a wonder, the sight of the bridegroom's family, from twenty-five to thirty-five women, in traditional Libyan dress, all white embroidered with gold thread, all coming in at the same time through the gates of the bride's family compound to the accompaniment of the tambours of the Libyan folk singers, called *zamzamat*, and the old-fashioned wedding singing troupes. The wide Libyan *toub* iscovered from head to foot in gold; I never saw any other people with the custom of filling their *toub* from top to bottom with gold jewelry pinned to the fabric like brooches. They call a brooch *rashga*, or "a piercer." In addition to this, there were 22-karat gold necklaces hanging around their necks. They call the necklace *khunnaq* ("choker"), and they call the bracelet *hadida* ("a piece of iron"). The big wedding *toub* they call *al-houli*. It is embroidered all over, sometimes topped with a traditional vest called a *farmila*. Dr. Farida told me that during the weddings of important Libyan families, the vaults of the Central Bank remain open until the wedding is done and the women return the massive quantities of gold jewelry for safe-keeping.

I sketched a lot of gold jewelry during my time there. I also visited the Tripoli silver market and acquired a general idea about Libyan jewelry. It was the first time I had seen slippers made entirely of silver for bridal wear. The fish *(huweita)* and the five-fingered hand *(khimeisa)* are common motifs in Libyan jewelry. It was my dream to visit the Ghadames Oasis in Libya and see the silver jewelry of that special place, with its unique designs, but circumstances unfortunately didn't permit.

Green Tunisia

October 1992—the time of the earthquake in Egypt—was my first visit to the city of Tunis. I arranged a visit after learning from my friends, the Khan al-Khalili merchants whom I had dealings with, the ones I bought coral from for my designs, that the source of the coral was Tunisia, and that it came with Tunisian traders to Cairo. I wanted to see the source and learn more, and to expand the use of it in my designs. I called my Tunisian acquaintances and set off for Tunisia, where I visited more than one area where the coral-carving workshops are centered. All this was arranged by friends.

Coral—or red gold, as they call it—is found all along the shores of the Mediterranean Sea in Tunisia, Algeria, and Morocco. This is why much of the jewelry of these countries uses coral as a major element. For years I did business with the Tunisian merchants, until the use of coral was banned internationally, and international stores forbade the display of any type of jewelry which incorporated coral. (An important point to remember: coral on the sea floor grows just one centimeter every hundred years!)

During this first trip, I visited the old city *(al-madina al-'atiqa)* and spent some time in the "Ma'mur" al-Zaytouna Mosque, the first university in the Islamic world, and the second mosque to be built in Tunisia—or Ifriqiya, as it used to be called—after the 'Uqba ibn Nafi' Mosque in Kairouan. The Zaytouna Mosque played a major role in spreading Arab and Islamic culture in the Maghreb countries, and was the first school for thinking, from which the "father of sociology" Ibn Khaldoun, the Moroccan scholar Abu al-Hassan al-Shadhili, and the poet of Tunisia Abu al-Qasem al-Shabbi, the author of *Songs of Life*, graduated.

In November 1999, I went with an official delegation from the Ministry of Culture to organize, supervise, and carry out a major exhibition in Tunis as part of Egyptian Cultural Week. With us on this trip were the actress Laila Elwi, a professor at the Faculty of Applied Arts named Dr. Taha Hussein, and the poet Farouq Shousha, who held poetry seminars and meetings with Tunisian intellectuals. We visited Kairouan, with its fabulous mosque, and spent a day in Nabeul, famous for its ceramics, and Hammamet, to meet important Tunisian artists—ceramics artists, sculptors, and painters—in this famous seaside town. I visited an exhibition held by the famous fashion designer Fulla, who made Tunisian fashion in new and contemporary lines.

Carthage and Sidi Bou Said were on the official visit list. How I enjoyed this wonderful suburb, founded back in the Middle Ages, with its white houses and ancient doors carved with distinctive ornamentation and reliefs, painted blue. We sat in its cafés, bought the *mashmoum* (gardenia and jasmine, in great bunches), and ate *bambalouni*, a Tunisian sweet doughnut sprinkled with sugar or drizzled with honey.

My third visit, at the start of the millennium, was with my friend Atiyat al-Abnoudi on the occasion of the showing of her films at the Carthage Cinema Festival. This time, I went to enjoy movies and visit our Tunisian friends.

Iraq

Iraq, the land of Mesopotamia, the civilization that flourished between two rivers, the Tigris and the Euphrates! I had seen Sumerian jewelry for the first time in the photographs of a book about the history of ancient jewelry, a gift from a British friend. I had the opportunity to visit this marvelous country when I was part of the first conference held by President Saddam Hussein on Arab jewelry and fashion in the early 1970s. It was one of the earliest conferences specifically on that subject.

During Saddam's rule, he announced the establishment of the House of Iraqi Fashion in 1970, managed by Abla Klidar, whom I got to know later, in Amman, Jordan. This cultural establishment played an important part in bringing together specimens of historic Iraqi fashion, which they then developed into a contemporary style. It resulted in a spectacular theatrical performance. This historic show presented a part of Iraqi civilization, and it was mind-blowing. The show toured the world, east and west, the greatest and most powerful advertisement for the arts in Iraq.

I was invited to take part in this conference with my dear friend Ri'aya al-Nimr. There, I met all the Arab artists with an interest in the field, and attended seminars and lectures on the history of fashion, jewelry, textiles, and traditional Arab fabrics. I visited the old Baghdad market with a group of Iraqi friends—stores selling kilims, rugs, and traditional textiles. I bought a Kurdish kilim into which the craftsman had woven his life: a donkey, a camel, a house, trees, and people representing his everyday experience. The colors are bright and inviting. I am very fond of this piece and keep it hanging on the wall where I can see it always. I enjoyed acquiring it, as I consider it a masterpiece.

At the Sagha in Baghdad's magnificent old quarter, I got to know the Sabian silversmiths, and spent three hours talking with them, trying to learn about the techniques they used, including the black enamel they call *nilo*. The Iraqi Sabians are Mandaean: they follow the prophet Yahya and have their own houses of worship: I passed by one of these places, on which was written *Mandi al-Sabi'a*, which means the Sabian Temple. I bought a number of silver boxes inlaid with *nilo* in designs depicting palm trees, houses, and boats on the banks of the Tigris. The silver was engraved with great artistry.

I have many photos of important pieces of jewelry from the collections of Iraqi friends that have truly disappeared. I ate *masgouf* (seasoned grilled carp) for the first time on the banks of the Tigris in an everyday restaurant. The owner put on music by the wonderful Iraqi singer Nadhim al-Ghazali:

Tell the beauty in the black veil
You have made a pious monk frail!

I also saw the traditional Iraqi homes built all along the riverbanks. Their *shanashil* (the turned-wood window screens that we know as *mashrabiya*) overlook the river in a scene still carved in my memory. (Oh, what a pity, what a shame, poor Baghdad!)

I did not see any Assyrian jewelry on this visit. But on my next visit to London, the British Museum's section on Assyrian civilization was at the top of my list. I feasted my eyes on the beautiful, artistic designs. A while later, I made copies of the traditional jewelry of ancient Assyria out of brass and plated them in gold.

I am so grateful that I managed to catch Iraq's civilization and saw it with my own eyes! I saw the renaissance of art and culture there in the 1970s before it was largely destroyed. When I was there, they told me, "If you're that interested in jewelry, you must meet Dr. Saad al-Jadir; he is the authority on the subject. But he's left Iraq now and lives in Morocco. He has written an important book on Islamic jewelry."

Morocco

Morocco stayed stuck in my head, so I followed the Iraqis' advice about meeting Dr. Saad al-Jadir, an architect who had studied urban planning in the Soviet Union and then abandoned that profession to devote himself to collecting, acquiring, and studying Islamic jewelry. He wrote two books that were published in Britain: *Kunuz: Islamic Silver Treasures* and *Arab and Islamic Silver*. I got the name of *Arab and Islamic Silver* and sent for it from a specialist bookstore I work with in London, which sells reference books. The book reached me in Cairo and indeed, I found the author a towering authority in his field. I wrote to the publisher to find any information or an address for him, but unfortunately they had none, as it had been a long time since the book was published.

I didn't give up. I was adamant about finding this man. After a while, through some friends in Iraq, I learned that he came from a family of artists: his brother was Khaled al-Jadir, and his sister was the Iraqi jewelry designer Naglaa al-Jadir. I corresponded with Khaled in Baghdad and got the address where Saad lived in Morocco. Then I wrote to him and he responded! I was happy to find that he had heard of my work and knew a little bit about me!

Toward the end of the 1980s, I planned a trip to Morocco, now that I was sure Dr. Saad was there. A group of lifelong friends accompanied me on the visit, and I hoped that this meant everyone would have a good time as they would enjoy each other's company. There was the journalist and friend Ragi Inayat; there were Abdel Ghani Abu al-Einein and his wife Ri'aya; Dr. Saad Eddin Ibrahim and his wife Aliyya.

As I was planning the itinerary and discussing the importance of getting to know the jewelry of Morocco, its designs, how it was made, and its major regions via mail with Dr. Saad, he replied with finality: "Silver means Marrakech. It's the biggest silver market in Morocco."

After a tour of Morocco, we arrived in Marrakech, where I met Dr. Saad; he had arrived there from Casablanca, where he lived. I left the group for two days, which I spent at the massive Marrakech market, famous for its silver. I would leave my hotel in the morning and only get back at night, loaded down with written information, sketches, and photographs. Dr. Saad introduced me to the major silver dealers and collectors of ancient silver in Morocco. They told me about certain techniques used only in Moroccan jewelry, as well as the major tribes and their names, what each tribe wore, and their Yemeni origins. The Shallouh is the biggest Amazigh tribe there, with their unique fashions and gorgeous jewelry, plus their outstanding woolen textiles, which they call *zurabiyat* or *kilim*, woven by the women.

I acquired a small collection representing the best of Moroccan jewelry. Always, as I was choosing, Dr. Saad would say to me: "I'm mad at you. You choose better than me, with the eye of an artist and an expert at the same time!" He now lives in London, and we are in constant contact. When I'm in London, I meet him whenever I get the chance.

My second visit to Morocco was in 2005, with an official delegation from the Egyptian Ministry of Industry to make a draft plan for developing centers for artisanal production in Egypt by learning from the Moroccan experience. The delegation consisted of Dr. Hani Barakat, head of the Technological Centers that were attached to the Ministry of Trade and Industry; professor and designer Muhammad Shakib; my sister, the artist Randa Fahmy, an expert on light fixtures and copper work; Mervat Mahmoud, of the leatherworking sector; and my friend the journalist Bahira Mokhtar from the newspaper *al-Ahram*. The Moroccans arranged an official visit for us to the major centers for traditional craft production and training—leather, the *zurabiyat* kilims, copper and brass, and jewelry. We visited Aghadir, Fez, Casablanca, and Marrakech.

My third visit was in October 2018 with a delegation of prominent Egyptian women who had had successful careers and made a difference. There was a book published about them called *Daughters of the Nile: Egyptian Women Changing Their World*, and edited by Samia Spencer, where each woman told the story of her life. It was planned that this group of women would tour the world in seminars where they could speak about their successes, and in October 2018, it was decided that the seminars should be held at universities in Morocco. I told them, "I'm coming with you!" as if I'd been just waiting for the chance.

We all met in the coastal city of Essaouira, on the Atlantic Ocean, a wonderful town dating back to the Middle Ages with a clear European influence on its architecture, the walls, and the forts there. I ate the best fresh fish I had ever had in my life on a rooftop restaurant overlooking the ocean, and I enjoyed watching the flocks of seagulls covering the houses and skies of the town as well as its squares—so much so, that in Rabat I went into a silver store and found a ring with a bird on it that I liked, and when I asked the salesman, "What region of Morocco is it from?" he responded, "Essaouira, of course!"

From Essaouira to red Marrakech we went. We visited the museum and home of famous French designer Yves St. Laurent, 400 square meters of gardens and buildings that he had bought from the artist Jacques Majorelle. Here he built his house and museum and private collection of traditional Moroccan garments and jewelry, in addition to a research library said to contain six thousand books. Of course, I understood how this red city had changed the course of this designer's work, and as a result influenced the field of fashion design in general.

From Marrakech, we headed north across the High Atlas Mountains, among towering peaks and hanging, isolated Berber villages, where we spent two nights, on our way to Ifrane—"the Switzerland of Morocco." We were only a short distance from the famous village of Ouarzazate, in southern Morocco, which I dream to visit one day. It has become the movie capital of Morocco. Unfortunately, we couldn't go at that time.

Ifrane really is a town where you feel like you're in Switzerland, with its distinctive houses and its ski slopes. We spent two days there as the guests of the wonderful al-Akhawayn University. Our next stop was Fez, the city of culture and heritage. We gave a lecture at Fez University, and we visited the famous madrasa of Bou Inania—I have never seen lovelier mosaics in all of Morocco. I took lots of pictures and added them to my archive.

From Fez to Rabat, where we held our last lecture of this cultural tour. Something really nice here that made me happy was that whenever I went into a silversmith's or a shop to buy silver, the person working there, or the salesman, would look at my jewelry and say, "You're wearing Azza Fahmy!" One time, I went into a bookshop to buy some books by the renowned Moroccan sociologist and feminist Fatema Mernissi. At the checkout counter there were two girls sitting there who caught sight of the ring with the five-fingered hand that I always wear for luck. They said, "You're wearing Azza Fahmy?"

The Flower of Cities

My contacts in Arab countries and my wide circle of friends have all helped with networking. From Jordan, Zaha Jardana (Zaha Menku, the wife of Ali Menku, a famous Palestinian businessman) became a friend and began to wear Azza Fahmy jewelry for many years. She introduced me to Mona al-Rifai (the wife of Zaid al-Rifai, prime minister of Jordan), who took to buying her gifts from me. The gifts reached Queen Noor al-Hussein, wife of King Hussein of Jordan (whom they call *Sayyidna* in Amman).

We opened a branch in Jordan in collaboration with Hala Hardana, and I began to make regular trips to Amman, either for exhibitions or to visit the queen and provide her with gifts, and gifts for the court of the king. During these visits, I got to know the great researcher Widad Kawar, who owns the largest collection of costumes and jewelry from Palestine and the West Bank. Widad and I sat for hours talking and discussing these

With Queen Noor of Jordan during a conference on women, Amman, Jordan, 1994.

two subjects: she explained the garments to me, and I told her about jewelry. She used to laugh and say to me, "Azza, I can't find a professional in the Arab world to talk to who knows as much as you on the subject!" I have many photographs in my archive of the Palestinian and Jordanian silver collections in Widad's museum. This great lady devoted her life to research and study in the field of national costume and jewelry in the Palestine–Jordan region. She wrote a major book on the garments of Jordan and Palestine, which was published in Japan, titled *Threads of Identity*. On one of my visits to Amman, Queen Noor made me a gift of a collection of books on Jerusalem in Mamluk times. "How I wish I could visit that wonderful city!" I said.

"Would you like to go tomorrow morning and come back at night?" she asked. "We can take you by helicopter." I refused, because I felt that I was going to Israel. The dream of visiting Jerusalem and Palestine was always there, but my nationalist stance always stopped me, and I dismissed the idea.

This reminds me: I was in Washington to hold an exhibition on Egypt in the Capitol, inaugurated by the Egyptian ambassador, Ali Maher. An Israeli delegation visiting the building came by the exhibition. An Israeli woman stepped forward, greeted me by name, and invited me to hold an exhibition in Tel Aviv. "How did you know my name?" I asked.

"Mrs. Fahmy!" she laughed. "You are the queen of jewelry in the region!"

Of course, I refused. But one day I got the opportunity to go. I met a woman who regularly organizes visits for Muslims and Christians to the holy places there. I thought of asking my friends what they thought about me going to Jerusalem, but then I thought, "You've got to go. It's Palestine you're going to, not Israel." So I decided to go to the Flower of Cities, as they call Jerusalem, in January 2014.

We entered Palestine from Amman via the Allenby Bridge. We spent about four hours at Israeli checkpoints, and from there by bus to Jerusalem. At last, I was in Jerusalem! Never in my life had I seen an old city as beautiful. Truly, as Fairuz sings, it is the Flower of Cities, with its famous gates—the Damascus Gate (leading directly to the Aqsa Mosque), the Lions' Gate, the Maghrabi Gate, and the Jaffa Gate. Walking through the streets wrapped in ancient stone, you constantly hear the Palestinian women raining curses down on the occupation soldiers standing guard in the city. The colors of the walls in the old city, and the stone stairs that the city streets are filled with, give you an eerie sense of time, history, and beauty. You are in the Middle Ages. I felt I would suddenly find Salah al-Din al-Ayyubi standing in front of me in this enchanting city.

I visited the Church of the Holy Sepulcher, whose keys have been in the trust of the Husseinis, a Muslim family, since the time of Salah al-Din. An Egyptian monk living there gave me bottles of the holy oil of the church, some of which I gifted to my Christian friends. Walking through the ancient city of Jerusalem, I felt unreal. I must be in some epic movie. Everything was legendary. Jerusalem is divided into the Armenian Quarter, the Christian Quarter, the Muslim Quarter, and the Jewish Quarter.

You start to feel the full weight of the oppression being practiced when you learn that Arabs are effectively prohibited by law from repairing their homes if anything happens to them. The sheer amount of papers and permits needed to fix doors and windows, for example, is a tactic engineered to encourage people to leave.

At al-Aqsa Mosque, Jerusalem, 2014.

I visited Bethlehem and the Church of the Nativity, where Christ was born. I also visited Hebron, the largest Palestinian city, divided into two—half for Muslims and half for Jews—and its Ibrahimi Mosque. I saw Ramallah, and the tomb of the great poet Mahmoud Darwish on a high hill: a lovely modern building, well cared for. I was very happy to be able to visit my Palestinian friends, authors, journalists, poets, and artists, as well as friends of my daughter Fatma that she had met on a trip made possible by a Sheikh Muhammad bin Rashed grant for young Arabs. I had lunch with them in a small restaurant overlooking the city of Ramallah. At the end of the day, they drove me back to Jerusalem.

I saw the beauty of nature in Palestine, with its hills, olive trees, and orange groves as far as the eye can see. I'm so grateful for having had the chance to see Palestine. I designed a collection of Palestine-inspired jewelry that I'm very proud and fond of.

Japan

In the mid-1990s, I was given an opportunity to visit Japan by the great Japanese Egyptologist Sakuji Yoshimura, who divided his time between Egypt and his homeland. He admired my work. I had designed the Houses on the Nile collection—all inspired by traditional Egyptian architecture—and it had been a resounding success. He organized two shows for me, plus a lecture, in Tokyo and Kyoto, the former capital. The collection sold out.

The trip was packed with visits to Japanese polytechnics, museums, and major artisans and artists. Visiting Japan changed my view of crafts and the way I approached them. I began to take an interest in what is known as the history and philosophy of crafts. The Japanese deserve the lion's share of the credit for putting crafts on the map as a type of international cultural heritage. I learned that wonderful heritage pieces, even simple pieces and ones made by modest craftsmen, most of them illiterate and nameless, have given us inspirations for arts and crafts and new contemporary jewelry with a connection to our heritage, which comes from layer upon layer of culture, heritage, and tradition.

I started to buy and read books on crafts in Japan and Korea. I learned a lot from them; they elevated craftsmanship to new heights in my mind and made me view artisans on a level with the sculptor Yanagi Soetsu

(1889–1961), the father of the folk craft movement in Japan, who wrote the most authoritative books on the subject. The Japanese and Koreans elevate and dignify crafts, which is the reverse of our attitude in the Arab world, where we look down on crafts and craftsmen. Japan made it clear to me the right way to look at crafts, which is to consider the arts learned at a polytechnic just as important as painting learned at an art school. All of this is part of the kingdom of aesthetics, work where the heart and hands share space, work that makes the piece speak to you and bring you a refined sense of joy.

Spiritual Indians say that you have a heart in the left side of your torso, and another in your hands. Skilled craftsmen in Japan and China are called national treasures! I learned from them the importance of what they call "the seeing eye." I have acquired lots of experience by now in looking at pieces of art and identifying what's wrong, if anything, with the design, and achieving the required balance in a piece. My eye has become experienced in pulling out the part that disturbs the design. That's what I've acquired in the past fifty years—the seeing eye.

I learned that the craft movement has strong ties to Buddhism, and to the professional hierarchy that led to all this wonderful craftsmanship. They also mix crafts with a philosophy of life. Japanese porcelain and ceramics is a respected art, important to the daily life of the Japanese. Think of the tea ritual there, and how the tea maker holds the pot and makes the tea and serves it to the assembly in porcelain cups—it is a process that's incredibly slow and almost a sacred ritual. They think, too, that when a ceramic piece is broken, it shouldn't be thrown away. It is pieced together and the cracks filled with gold. This gives it a new form and new uneven lines that have their own great beauty. The gold lines give so much charm to the piece. What is the philosophy behind this? It is that the difficulties of life and the hard things we go through leave deep scars on us. These are the lines of gold that bring out the beauty of the piece; these are the lessons we learn to improve the way we think and push us forward. This is what the Japanese say: "Flaunt your scars with pride. Tell people, 'These scars have made me what I am today.'"

I saw some similarity between the Japanese approach and the crafts of the Ottoman Empire in terms of training and the links between crafts and spirituality. I learned from Yanagi Soetsu that good craftsmanship starts in the heart, moves through the head, and finally to the hands. It's a finely tuned balance that produces good art, as Khalil Gibran writes in *The Prophet:* "Work is love made visible." He also says, "And when you work with love, you bind yourself to yourself, and to one another, and to God." And "Charge all things you fashion with a breath of your own spirit." I'm in no way saying this to belittle machine work and technology. What I'm talking about is the relationship, the balance, between the inner feeling of an artisan and the piece they create.

I also learned from my readings on artisanship in Asia that imitating designs from the West designs helped them understand and learn different things. I did that, too, at the start of my professional life: I copied heritage pieces that I admired and found attractive. I must have spent two or three years copying. I copied pieces from Yemen, Algeria, Morocco, and Iraq, as well as old Islamic pieces. That's how they taught us to draw in college: they put a statue or a still life in front of us to copy. The professor would stand there and correct our mistakes. Copying a well-made old piece taught me proper proportions, and I accustomed my eyes to seeing pieces that were well conceived and well scaled. Training the eye to see beauty and balance is one of the most important things a mature artist can achieve.

I also took an interest in reading about the design movement at the time of the Industrial Revolution in England. I read about Prince Albert, Queen Victoria's husband, and how the arts and crafts flourished in the nineteenth century. The Victoria and Albert Museum in London bears the best witness to the blossoming of arts and crafts during his time, being an important center for designers and artisans. Every time I'm in London, I can't help going to the V&A, which gives me new and wonderful ideas in every section I walk through. I read about British textile designer and major figure in the Arts and Crafts movement, William Morris, and saw the wonderful flowers and ornamentation he drew; one of the things that had piqued my interest in my early life was how this great designer had developed these designs, which made their way into fabrics, paper, and furniture.

I learned a great deal from ancient Indian jewelry—the marvelous Mughal period, the amazing artistry of Rajasthan, the gorgeous gold earrings of southern India. My knowledge of great Asian designers and my readings in this field, especially the Industrial Revolution in England, were my guiding light at the start of my career. I called these greats "my gurus." Not only did I learn from them, but they changed my outlook on crafts.

There is a proverb from ancient Egypt that I am fond of and believe in passionately. It was said by the vizier Ptah-Hotep (2345–2181 BC):

There is no end to learning.
There is no craftsman who has acquired full mastery.

Italy, an Open-Air Museum

I had no romantic life, except for silly little things. We were a closed-off family, and we kids were raised in kind of a traditional way. Love, to me, was talking on the phone or flirting with the boy next door: we took the same train whenever we could and looked at each other from afar while passing a hand over our hair (this was secret code for a greeting). I really laugh now to see how the world has progressed, and I see my daughters and my daughters' friends—a completely different generation! Thank goodness I can understand change. And what's more, if I were in a relationship, I couldn't go out without his permission—once I had to take permission from the boy next door to visit my uncle's house, which was right next to ours, just as I took permission from my mother to go out. One time he wouldn't let me go; my uncle was sick and I needed to go and help Aunt Tutu, my uncle's wife, with something. Well, he saw me walking in the street, and I was in for it. He stopped talking to me for a month. I got mad and asked myself, "What did I do wrong?"

In the summer of 1964, we were in Alexandria, and I received a phone call. We had to go make, and take, calls at a public telephone booth then. Every week I went to the phone booth to talk to my friends. I had heard that our college was holding a cultural exchange to Italy between students of the Faculty of Fine Arts in Cairo and the one in Rome. The trip was in a week, and everything was already in place. But I didn't have a passport! And I was in Alexandria!

I hurried back to my mother from the phone booth. I was dying to go to Italy. Italy! The land of art, creativity, and beauty. My mother agreed when she sensed my great enthusiasm and desire to go. We went back to Cairo the next day and I called my uncle (that is, my father's cousin) Abdel Azim Fahmy, who was the minister of the interior at the time. The passport and visa were issued, and in a flash my name was on the list of students going. This incident shifted the balance of power for me at the Faculty. The professors looked at me differently. I found them paying more attention to me on every level after I came back. But this isn't the time or place to talk about that.

The trip cost 150 Egyptian pounds for, I think, twenty-five or twenty-eight days, I can't remember exactly. My mother sold the diamonds she got as a wedding gift from my father—the last piece of jewelry she had left—to send me on this trip; I only found out two years later, when I asked after her diamond bracelet. My dear friend Dr. Shahida al-Baz always tells me, "You know, you chose this profession because of that bracelet of your mother's that she sold so you could go to Italy." For long years after I took up the profession and began to look at old jewelry and draw inspiration from their designs, I used to visit the stores that dealt in old diamonds. I longed to find my mother's diamond bracelet, the one my father had given her, and return it to her.

We set off by sea from Alexandria to Italy on a small Greek boat called the *Lydia*. We just barely made it to Greece; the *Lydia* listed terribly all the way, and the list only got more and more pronounced as we went on. The girls had tiny rooms down at the bottom of the boat, next to the Greek sailors' cabins. It was stiflingly hot, as the windows were very small. The cabins were next to the machine room, as well, which radiated heat, not to mention the stench of sweat from the sailors working next to the machines and sleeping in the small cabins right next to us. Most of the time, we went up on deck to recline on chaises longues. You know, this was my favorite trip in my whole life. I enjoyed myself so much and was happy all the time.

One of the professors accompanying us was Abdel Salam al-Sherif, another the artist Raouf Abdel Magid, who had studied for long years in Italy before coming back to teach us, and who spoke Italian fluently. We ate in the sailors' mess, and the food was really nothing to speak of. There were about twenty-five of us, girls and boys and professors, all told. When we arrived in Greece, our first port of call, we disembarked at Piraeus, and they took us to Athens by bus to visit the Acropolis and the famous museum there. They explained the history of Greece and Greek art to us.

When we got back to the port, the professors were leery of letting us continue the journey on to Italy in the listing *Lydia*, which seemed in real danger of sinking. There were two Egyptian boats that went on cruises in the Mediterranean to Syria and Algeria. We swapped the *Lydia* for the

Syria, which, as luck would have it, was in Greece. It took us from Piraeus in Greece to Venice in Italy.

When we boarded the *Syria* after our stay on the *Lydia*, it was like walking into Paradise. The captain, his officers, and the sailors greeted us with all the warmth of Egyptians welcoming Egyptian students! The food in the restaurant was good, which made a big difference to our comfort, and they put us up in decent cabins with good ventilation, where we could sleep.

For me, Italy was a season when my mind opened and I gained understanding and a different outlook on the world in two ways. First was my relationship with the young men with us. I now experienced a real change in the way I saw how a boy could relate to a girl with pleasant friendship. Second was the wonderful time and fruitful discussions we had with our professors on the history of art and all the fields of specialization: sculpture, painting, architecture, urban planning, temples, and museums. This marvelous lesson that I took with a wonderful group of people changed my view on human and romantic relationships, and broke me out of the box I had been trapped in. I gained so much knowledge of the wonderful art of the Renaissance in the open-air museum that is basically every town in Italy.

We visited Rome, where the Egyptian Academy was responsible for art students. It was headed by Salah Kamel, son of the great artist Yousef Kamel. We had a fabulous itinerary in Rome: we visited all the important places with works by Renaissance artists. The Vatican and, of course, the Vatican Museum, was one of our first visits, including the Sistine Chapel and Michelangelo's famous, breathtaking ceiling. When I looked up and saw this monumental work, it almost stopped my heart. There were the masterpieces by Raphael and Leonardo da Vinci, Gian Lorenzo Bernini, Michelangelo, and the masters of Renaissance sculpture.

We visited Cinecittà and toured the studios. In Rome, our teachers would walk alongside us in the streets and explain the principles of good urban planning and the relationship between streets and squares. They were wonderful practical lessons in the city of art and beauty. We visited all the landmarks of Rome and Florence, with all its squares and churches, and the great art under the patronage of the Medicis in the Renaissance. I learned that great art must be accompanied by economic wealth.

Then we went on to Venice, the fabulous floating city. From Saint Mark's Square, we took a gondola to Murano, where the incredible glass is made. Then, from Venice, we took the *Algeria* back to Egypt, in comfort.

After this trip, I decided to break free of my telephone romance and live my fun college life with simple freedom. I started a new phase in life. Unfortunately, we were already in our last year at college. While the decision might have come late, it was better late than never.

I visited Rome again in 2004, forty years after the first time I had been there in my university years. I had some business with a famous Italian menswear designer, Stefano Ricci. I had been introduced to him by Farouk Hosny, then minister of culture, and he had asked me to design a collection of cuff links for him. At the time, Hilmi Bedeir was our ambassador to Rome, and he was also the father of Rania, who worked with us in marketing, so we stayed at the ambassador's residence. Now that was a luxury trip—in addition, of course, to working with the designer.

In Rome, of course, my first visit was to the Sistine Chapel in the Vatican. I went to the church and looked up at the ceiling once more. I saw loud and bright colors, like new. I was startled, and when I asked, they told me, "They restored Michelangelo's work. This is what the colors look like after restoration." In the corner, they displayed the way it used to look, all faded. I preferred the old one, faded by time.

India, Land of Wonders

Almost all my sources of semiprecious stones in Khan al-Khalili came through my friend Hasib Yazdi, or sometimes a friend might visit me from Europe or America and say, "I have a friend who deals in gems and has this collection. Would you like to buy it?" I usually did. It was all very unprofessional.

Then, of course, I found my business growing. I couldn't do business that way anymore. I had to diversify my sources, find other countries, and discover what this outside world of ours had to offer and what it produced, and what the base prices were, of course. The first country to occur to me was India. "Girl," I said to myself, "you've got to go to India and find out the story of these stones and get to know them. India is the Land of Wonders, as the actress Soad Hosny said—the land of traditional crafts and jewelry, and precious and semiprecious gems!"

Then I said to myself, "But how will I get there?" I always have a bit of fear inside me. "Am I going to just land in India without knowing anyone there?" This was in the early 1990s. As luck would have it, my friend Atiyat al-Abnoudi was making a film with the European Union, and the grant restrictions meant that two directors from two different countries had to collaborate. Her co-director was an Indian filmmaker called Anita. She came to Egypt to meet Atiyat and work on the movie with her. It was a documentary on contrasting points of view between the old and new generations in different parts of the world, and one of the scenes in it was an interview with my daughters asking them what they thought of me. (To this day I still don't know what they said. I never saw the movie, as it was screened abroad.)

Anyway, I told Anita, "I want to go explore India."

She lived in the capital, New Delhi. She said to me, "Come sometime when I'm in town and I'll try to help you out."

After a while, I resolved to go and get to know India. I planned a time when the weather would be suitable, between the summer and the winter. Then off I went to New Delhi in 1992. Anita's father had been Jawaharlal Nehru's secretary and had a few good contacts, including the former head of the local Rotary Club. They advised me to stay at a hotel called the Imperial, in central New Delhi. They must have thought me very rich, because the hotel was super expensive, one of the nicest hotels in Delhi, built in the colonial style. I spent one night there, then met the man from Rotary. He said, "How are you even staying in that hotel? I'll book you a room in a nice bed-and-breakfast." It was in a middle-class neighborhood with a number of nice houses that were converted into little hotels, called Sundar Nagar. I stayed at a hotel there called Kalash Inn: the room was clean and the food simple, but a huge difference in price.

My exploration of India started out through this man and his acquaintances, who introduced me to contacts, some of which were useful while I was swindled by others in quality as well as price. After that, I went back to Cairo.

I kept making regular visits to India after that for about two years: most of this was exploration, discovery, and general blind bumbling around: attempts to buy gems from the stores in the markets, stepping up every time. Three years later, the Indian Embassy notified me of the start of the first official handicraft exhibition held by the Indian government in Delhi. This was in 1996. Excited and enthused, I thought it would be a large gathering where I could find out and understand a bit more about what was going on in this field. I went to India, to Delhi, staying at the Clash Inn, of course, and paid daily visits to the exhibition for five days running, getting to know the lie of the land and trying to figure out what was what.

It was a massive gathering of many artists, each with their own specialization: jewelry, precious gems and semiprecious stones, furniture, and home accessories. I met a trader there, displaying his stones, who was from Jaipur, the capital of Rajasthan. This is the major city for cutting and carving precious stones. They call it the Pink City. All the old city is pink in color, and it is a cornerstone of the Golden Triangle that you must visit when in India: Delhi, Agra (with the Taj Mahal), and Jaipur.

I bought some stones from him and went home. I kept dealing with the young man from Jaipur for about two years, each time at the fair. For two years, I bought what I needed from him and visited Delhi once a year at the time of this exhibition. One of my rituals, whenever I went to India, was to visit Anita and her family. Once while I was having dinner with them, I asked her, "Tell me about the trade in old silver in your country. It must be incredible!" Of course, this was me and my well-known nostalgia and love of traditional jewelry.

"There's only Mokeesh Jan, in Palika Bazaar," she said. "He's the best one selling old silver."

The next day, I set off for that big underground market and went to see this Mokeesh. My journey with Mokeesh Jan started from that moment on. After we became friends, Mokeesh told me, "I found a young woman coming in and starting to browse through my collection of old silver. But I noticed she was making her selections like a seasoned professional. She asked questions like a seasoned professional, too. That caught my attention."

I spent a long time in the store, surrounded by endless piles of old silver from every region in India. I might have spent four or five hours sorting through the treasures. When I spoke to Mokeesh, I could tell that he was honest and straightforward. He also understood perfectly well what he was selling, the history of each piece, and what region it was from. I felt I'd come to the right place. He ended up telling me, "Anything you need in India, I will help you with."

Mokeesh was the big man of the market. He was on good terms with all the traders around him. I could tell they respected him, and after comparing the prices I had paid in other stores before I came to deal with him, I saw a big difference!

As we were saying goodbye, he asked me, "What's your itinerary in India?"

I said, "I'm going to Jaipur tomorrow to meet a man I've been dealing with for years, and he suggested I visit the town."

"What luck," he said, "I happen to be going to Jaipur tomorrow, too, on business. What hotel did you make a reservation at?"

"I haven't yet," I said.

"Then it's settled," he said. "I'll make a reservation for you and you can come along."

I met him at the Delhi Railway Station at 6 a.m., and we took the train together to Jaipur. Seven hours later, we arrived at the Pink City, where everyone, men and women alike, wears bright colors. Everything is colorful in this charming place. A car was waiting for Mokeesh, and it took us to an old palace owned by an aristocratic family who had turned it into a wonderful hotel. Rajasthan is a very rich region of India, and it has many maharajas. The architecture and palaces have a very distinctive character. The royal palace of Rajasthan has been converted into a luxury hotel, and in the same way, all the aristocracy and most of the nobility have converted their small or medium-sized mansions into hotels, setting aside a small space for their own family to live.

I had called the young man from the exhibition, asking him to pass by my hotel in the morning so we could go to his workshop. The next morning, I went out for breakfast on the balcony of the charming hotel, overlooking the garden, and found Mokeesh sitting there with six other people around him having breakfast. They invited me to join them. This was a collection of the biggest traders and gemcutters in Jaipur (I found out later from Mokeesh). They became part of my circle from then on.

We sat there chatting while I waited for the man to arrive so we could go to work at his office. Suddenly I saw him coming in on a bicycle. I stood up to greet him and tell him to come say hello to the group. Then something happened I shall never forget. He looked at the faces of the men sitting there, whirled around, leapt onto his bicycle, and pedaled out of the hotel as if the hounds of hell were after him.

I couldn't make head or tail of it. "Why is he running?" I asked.

"He's a small artisan here," they said, "and he has a shady reputation." (Everyone knows everyone else in Rajasthan.) He saw me sitting with the biggest merchants and master craftsmen in the trade, so he decided getting the hell out was the better part of valor.

From that moment on, Mokeesh and I became like siblings, with a long business relationship together that continues to this day. I feel like I have a brother in India. The doors opened wide for me via this honest and sincere man, and I don't worry about a thing as long as he's around. As long as I'm in India, I'm in safe hands. Anything that comes to mind about a craft, industry, or raw material from India, he searches for and finds it for me at the best prices and the highest quality.

I continued to stay at the Clash Inn for fifteen years until my financial situation improved, and then I was able to stay at a four-star hotel. I went on annual trips to India to buy my stock of gems and stones. Mokeesh arranged everything: hotel reservations, a car from the airport to his office, a trip to Jaipur for sources and manufacturers, and pricing from the best suppliers.

For around thirty-five years, I made annual visits to the wonderful Indian subcontinent. I used to design my new collections and draw them up here in Cairo, then travel to source suitable stones in terms of size and color for what I included in my preliminary designs. Sometimes I timed my trips to coincide with Fatma and Amina's vacations. They visited India with me about four or five times in their childhood. For them, it wasn't that much fun, because most of the time we were sitting in an office working, and we only went back to our hotel to sleep, except for some tourist explorations around Delhi. Now, Amina has taken over the job of sourcing precious and semiprecious stones for our stock to supply our collections after she and I have designed everything the company needs in terms of new collections according to the plan that's been set out. Mokeesh is like a father to her, passing on all his experiences to her regarding the types of stones and their secrets and ins and outs. He helps her with her buying and opens all the doors of his sources to her of precious and semiprecious stones. The doors of the world of gems and stones were thrown open wide to Amina. On her visits to India four times a year, he hosts her in his home like a member of the family and calls her "my pretty little daughter." He only has two sons, Sidhar and Nirvan. They are around Amina's age, and through them, she found her way into the world of young, educated Indian people.

If you're inexperienced in the world of jewelry, you won't get far. Amina truly bears a weighty responsibility, but she's more than up to the task. The company is now fully reliant on her experience in buying and selecting stones. The help of Mokeesh and the powerful relationship we built over thirty-five years made a great difference to us in the world of gemstones, a charming and dangerous world. As for me, India has become an annual trip to the Himalayas now, to Rishikesh. I begin to see the forested mountainsides and soaring peaks as the flight is landing at Dehradun Airport. Dehradun is the capital of the state of Uttarakhand. Extensive forests cover a large part of northern India, and I go there to recharge, do yoga, and meditate with a group of my closest friends.

Working with my daughter Amina Ghaly, 2016.

My spirituality has increased and created a deeper understanding of these matters, of my day-to-day life, my happiness, and inner peace. "Be beautiful and you'll see beauty in the world." This is a true maxim that I learned from the Sufis and the Indian gurus. What you do, for good or ill, will come back to you one day. They call it karma. I drew a map of my life with the gurus there. They explained to me what stones I should wear, and that the stone needed to be touching my skin. It is very important to know the town and city where you were born, and what hour your mother delivered you. Most of these things I find hold true in my past life and my current one and in relation to my personality.

My Daughters
Fatma

I'd like to use this space to talk about my long journey's companion, my first daughter, Fatma, who was born seven years after I got married. I consider her to be the brains of the company. Ever since she was little, she's been tangled up with me one way or another. Early in our lives, Fatma and her sister were forced by circumstance to understand and accept the life of a mother unlike the other mothers all around them, especially with our lifestyle, our financial situation, and the time I got to spend with them. They often helped me with my travels abroad, and they usually had a working itinerary with me, in addition to fun and games.

To both of them I would like to dedicate this quatrain by Salah Jahin. If they hadn't been by my side, we wouldn't have succeeded this way. I consider myself lucky that they ended up loving the profession as much as I do.

> A little bitty moon like a pigeon's chick:
> Though small, its moonbeam pierced the darkness thick.
> "Oh, way to go!" I said. "Good for you! Soon
> Imagine what you'll do when you're a full moon!"

Fattoush (a kind of Lebanese salad) is the nickname I like to call Fatma, as suggested by my dear friend Mary Saad Kamel (or Na'ila Kamel, her pen name), wife of my friend Professor Saad Kamel, founder of the Mass Culture Centers, and mother of my dear friend the director Nadia Saad Kamel, who wrote a wonderful book about her mother, *The Newborn*. When Mary came

During a trip in North Sinai with my daughters, Amina (left) and Fatma (center), 2013.

to visit me after I gave birth to Fatma, and learned what I'd named her, she said, "I have a friend from Algeria, a great woman I care for very much, called Fatma, and they call her Fattoush. What do you think of Fattoush for a nickname?" I really liked it, so she became Fattoush.

When the girls were young, my work in this profession was an obvious part of their life. Since Fatma was very young, she has taken part in many visits to exhibitions abroad in Germany, Italy, and America, in addition to England for the famous craft exhibition held in Oxford, where we always represented Egypt. It was the largest collection of craftspeople from around the world, working on wood, jewelry, and leather—the top artisans from everywhere—where we made a bunch of important friends from all over the world.

During the summer vacation, it was important for me that the girls take part in the work in our Boulaq workshop. Anything to keep them busy; any small task in the workshop, to give them a feel for it, and to make them feel they belonged. I gave them tasks for training, such as how to thread a beaded necklace, or divide up and pick out the quantities of old glass village beads that I bought from Khan al-Khalili and that I was very fond of.

They divided them up by type and wrote little tags with the name on them. At the start of my career, I used various types of these old glass beads in my simpler designs.

I always liked to occupy part of their spare time with something to do with the job. I believe in teaching the value of work. People with nothing to do are different from busy people who have their interests. This is what I learned from the craftsmen of Damascus and Turkey. The crafts there succeeded and were passed down from generation to generation within families via this simple system, which became one of their continuing traditions. Small children take part in the process of production and sales—under the theory of master craftsman and apprentice, which I think is very successful and increases a child's sense of responsibility and makes them grow attached to this type of work. It also keeps them busy and away from potentially harmful habits.

Fatma has been a full member of the team since she was a little girl. She found her niche in marketing. In July 2000, she took a training course where a dear friend, Hisham Ezz al-Arab, taught her the principles of marketing. Hisham is now an international executive director for the multinational company Danone. She used to come back all excited from his class, enthused about this new thing she was learning from him. When he found out she was my daughter, he volunteered his advice to boost our sales. I believe that since then, she was set on a new path, that is, the world of marketing. Professional marketing had only a small role in our company at the start, then grew and grew until it had a substantial part to play. She gained her BA in fine arts while working; her graduation project was her own bedroom and closet. She still keeps this closet today, and has it hanging in her office at the company headquarters.

Later, Hisham Ezz al-Arab asked to meet me. We met and chatted about the importance of having a clear vision, goals, and plan for the company. On a friendly basis, he set out some preliminary points—the cornerstone, as we say. These important words became a part of our life since then, and he suggested to me—told me, really—that I had to hire someone for marketing. He recommended Rania Bedeir, who was working at a giant multinational at the time. I was terrified and shaking like a leaf because we couldn't afford high salaries at the time. (Her suggested pay was the same amount I made myself from my own company.) He said, "Meet with her anyway."

"Why not?" I said.

We met at my house. At that time I was working on my Sufi collection: al-Hallaj, Ibn Arabi, and Jalal al-Din al-Rumi. I told her a little bit about the collection I was designing, and it seems that my enthusiasm as I was talking moved something in her.

We were still in our Boulaq workshop, which had become like a sardine can for us at that point. We had just decided to rent a small office for the administrative staff in Mohandiseen. We needed a full-time accountant, and an administrative officer. After a while, we found a two-room apartment in Basra Square, the two rooms linked by a corridor.

Rania joined our staff and began to come to our little office in Mohandiseen: one room for accounts and marketing, the other for management, and a tiny office for me. Most of the time, I didn't sit there because I was running around outside doing other things. You know, for thirty years I never had an office, not until we went to the factory. In the Basra Square apartment, at last, I had—sometimes—a room of my own. I had been carrying all my documents around with me and moving from place to place; I had worked in any place that was available. I never made myself a priority in the search for office space. Even my designs, I created at a little table at home.

Fatma was just graduating from Fine Arts, but she worked with us at the company in her free time. She and Rania hit it off right away, and they made a great team. At first, Rania gave her the basic skills and rules that any company needed; as we said, a roadmap and a goal. The office was such a hive of activity, too tiny for our numbers, that I often found them standing together working in the kitchen or sitting out on the stairs by the apartment door, enthusiastically chatting with their heads together and writing pages and pages of something or other! Those girls really didn't have a place to sit.

They came to me with things they were thinking of. "Where do we want to be in five years?" It was the first time I had ever heard of a vision and a mission. After a while, they said to me, "Azza Fahmy needs to be an international brand." The sheer faith and certainty in their tones gave me no choice but to accept and agree to everything they were saying.

The workshop had grown too small for us: we needed to think about moving to a larger space. We started looking for a bigger factory and thought of looking in the industrial zones so we could really expand. By pure chance, I learned about a plot of land in a very nice area in the First Industrial Zone in 6 October City. It had been reserved for someone who couldn't pay the instalments. We managed to take his place, and we got it, paying the instalments to the 6 October City Council. Little by little, we started planning the process of building and moving. Fatma was with me at every step.

Our finances were not doing well. Every penny left over from production requirements went to building the factory. We hired what we call a "contractor in a gallabiya"—that is, someone without book-learning—from a friend! But he was good at what he did and honest, too.

We built the factory entirely with our own efforts. "Weave it for him out of his own beard!" as the folk proverb goes, which means you have to make do with whatever's available. All the doors and windows I bought from salvage dealers: village doors, old iron windows, and so on. We created a factory with its own style: a little square window with a round window next to it, a secondhand banister . . . all different things beside each other, in good taste. It turned out a charming hodgepodge with a uniquely Egyptian character.

My daughters, Fatma and Amina, and I with co-founders of Preen fashion house, Justin Thornton and Thea Bregazzi, at my workshop in 6 October City, Cairo, 2010.

With models during the launch of the first limited-edition Azza Fahmy collection in gold, Mohamed Mahmoud Khalil Palace, Giza, 2002.

Meanwhile, Fatma and Rania came up with a new project. "We have to start making products in gold," they said. "Azza Fahmy is known only for silver. We have to start changing that perception in people's minds. We want two kilograms of gold to create our first gold collection."

Well, I almost had a heart attack. I was in such a state! This was just when I was in the middle of finishing up the factory, and there wasn't a penny to spare. But their enthusiasm, and the plan they presented to me, convinced me, and I gave them the money. They suggested a fashion show with live models wearing gold jewelry, and launched into an integrated plan for the show: choosing a location, choosing the models, all the details.

In the autumn of 2002, they carried it out. The show was held at the Mohamed Mahmoud Khalil Palace in Giza, presenting the first limited-edition Azza Fahmy collection in gold. People had always thought that Azza Fahmy only made jewelry in silver. The event made a difference, and the collection sold well. People started to realize that I could make jewelry in gold.

Afterward, our name became better known. In 2003, we held another fashion show, this time at the Manastirli Palace in Manyal. It was called

The Golden Collection, and it was all inspired by old *kerdan* necklaces. A while later, a husband and wife from Khobar in the east of Saudi Arabia came to our store. For a long time, they had admired my jewelry with poetry inscribed on it. They asked us to open a branch with them in Bahrain.

This placed a weighty responsibility on the girls' shoulders: making out contracts with lawyers, details about the products to be displayed, pricing, how the store window would look, and how the people working there should look. I call this type of young, outgoing, educated young people "extra-special finishing," like we say about apartments. We started a rebranding process. We opened our first store in the Gulf, in Bahrain; they asked my consultants and went to get everything done, then show it to me for my approval. We shifted onto a higher plane on every level. With the opening of the Bahrain store, Azza Fahmy started to be in demand in the Gulf as an Arab brand.

Afterward, we opened a store in Dubai with the al-Tayer company, one of the largest companies for luxury brands. At that time, they had every brand and giant company you could think of: Jaguar, Gucci, Bottega Veneta, Yves St. Laurent, Cartier, Armani. We opened a store in Mall of the Emirates, where I added some interior design touches: an inlaid marble floor and a

At the opening of the Azza Fahmy store in Mall of the Emirates, Dubai, with Obaid al-Tayer, then UAE Minister of State for Financial Affairs, 2003.

modern Arab painting on the door, with the Azza Fahmy logo. It caused a stir in Dubai and the Arab world.

Our experience franchising with al-Tayer really made the company grow. The young team also expanded. We were now on the big regional playing field, and we needed to understand and grow. Azza Fahmy as a brand had made its way onto the scene and was on the verge of breaking into the international arena. I must say, Fatma and Rania Bedeir played the main role in convincing me of all the details of this step.

Minister Obeid al-Tayer, who managed the al-Tayer Group in Dubai, was very supportive of us and believed in us. Whenever he saw me, he gave me advice that was important for growing the business. He opened every closed door to us in his company: management, relationships, and international rules of conduct. He let us into his company's kitchen, as they say, and opened the vaults that held his secrets for us to see. We learned so much! We saw that we were an Arab brand that could be competitive worldwide, which raised the ceiling of our ambitions. Fatma and Rania needed to do all the little things that the international companies do: unifying the style of the stores; selecting staff and training them how to deal with clients; paying attention to the look of the store windows, and to packaging and its importance, and to how to present pieces to customers to view. In the end, they produced a manual for us to follow, and which is regularly developed and updated.

Rania wrote me a moving letter before she resigned. She was about to marry a young man who worked in Qatar and needed to go with him. I was so sad when she left Egypt and moved to Qatar to live. I felt like I was losing one of my daughters. I confess that I really heaped too much responsibility on her shoulders from a young age. I don't know to this day whether I did right or wrong. That's for her to say.

We hired a general manager; it didn't work out, and he left. Fatma was the one who always bore the load with me, and the consultants around me used to advise me to make her the director of the company. It's true, she had been thrown—or jumped—into the deep end very young and had had to swim. Frankly, it must have been hard for her. She has always had her nose to the grindstone.

Back then our auditor was Magdi Kamel Saleh, from the Deloitte firm, who had supported me, ever since I first knew him. I had met him through my lifelong friend Atiyat al-Abnoudi. His family are all my friends; his daughter Heba Saleh was an announcer at the BBC Arabic Service in London and is now the manager of the *Financial Times* office in Egypt. Knowing Magdi made a great difference in my career. The support he gave me while I was starting out is indescribable. At first, for years and years, he refused to accept money from me. "When you make money, I'll take money," he used to say! Faithful friends are your backbone, supporting you and lighting your way. May this wonderful, generous man rest in peace. I thank him for the support he gave me, which is indescribable. I will be grateful for what he did for me all my life. His whole family have become close friends: Kamel Magdi Saleh, his son, and the wonderful mother Nahed al-Gamal, a simultaneous interpreter at the United Nations.

I learned a great deal from Magdi. Whenever I learned something, some other problem popped up, and I would go running to him for advice. Sometimes I would be so frustrated I'd burst into tears. I didn't feel scared: I felt, "How did I not think of that? How did it not occur to me?" Management and finances were my big issue. I had no knowledge of or experience in the subject. I knew I didn't know, but that I had to know! Thank goodness, my mind was always open and ready to learn. Sometimes I told myself, "I'm an artist. I really don't want to have anything to do with these things. What is it that's forced me into them? I'm not even an accountant or any good with numbers." But I had to know something about them so I could move forward and manage the company.

There were problems that never ended. It started with thefts of raw materials and workers cheating on their quotas and selling the workshop's products elsewhere, then continued into expanding our production and how to manage it and the problems that came with that. We really needed to start implementing a system for everything: purchasing, production, and sales.

Now, looking at the different departments of the company, the accountants, the governance we apply, the policies in place, the ERP (enterprise resource planning) computer system, the unified company network—so unified you can see anything while sitting at your computer—and the technology that shows you every stage with its details and lets you quality-control it at any time, I laugh to myself and say, "Look where we were and where we are now!"

I want to tell you that nothing in the world is impossible. Everything can be achieved with willpower, determination, and love. Often I took Fatma with me when I went to the Deloitte offices to go over our budgets or business plan. One of these times, we went to go over financial stuff in their Heliopolis office. We were living far away, in Harraniya, at the time. She was driving and I was in the passenger seat. Suddenly, the car broke down in Orouba Street. I remember the exact spot to this day. And she burst into tears, floods of tears, just bawling. She said to me, "Mother, you dumped this work responsibility on my shoulders and I didn't have any choice. You made me do it, and I'm not happy. I'm miserable."

I sat there, stunned. It was like a rock had fallen onto my head. I couldn't respond. But then I said something to her I'll never forget: "Your tears are very precious to me. Nothing in this whole wide world is worth you saying you're unhappy. That's a very big thing to say. Don't worry about me or anything to do with me. Fatma, my Chinese sign is the Monkey, and monkeys are always jumping about from one thing to another, but they have a plan and they never fall. I'll arrange things so that you're not working with me. I'll manage to go it alone. Starting tomorrow, we can look for a job you'll like. We have contacts and networks everywhere in this country. We'll find something for you to do that you can love. Don't be scared. Don't worry about me. Don't bear my burdens."

"No, Mother," she said. "Wait a bit. It might be that I'm under pressure these days. Let me think about it for a while, and I'll tell you later."

"Promise?" I asked.

"Promise."

When I got home, before I went to bed, I said to myself, "Azza, calm down. It's not important to grow the company. I can work with ten workers and make the finest jewelry in the Arab world with expensive raw materials, gold, and diamonds, but I'll keep doing my work within the limits of what I can produce and manage myself and keep under control." I told myself this and went to bed.

The subject wasn't broached again. Fatma stayed on at the company and didn't come back to me with an answer. A while later, maybe six months, I asked her, "How are things? Do you still want to leave and go somewhere else?"

She laughed, my dear girl. "No, Mother. I'm happy here."

Our shift to an international market, and our participation in London Fashion Week with the international British designer Julien Macdonald in 2006, moved us onto a higher plane in the Arab world. The international media began to notice us: magazines, newspapers, and TV channels. Next came additional successful collaborations, such as the one with the international fashion house Preen in New York Fashion Week 2010. Since then, our international successes and opening up markets abroad have all been thanks to Fatma. Opening up the British market and collaborating with international museums with collections designed especially for the British Museum—all this is the work of Fatma and her team. At the start, there was always a team of consultants, mostly lifelong friends, supporting her always and from whom she got experience.

Fatma was always of the opinion that if we achieved international successes, it would reflect on us and on how the world saw us, especially in the Arab world. This is very true, and I'm convinced of it; and so it was.

Fattoush was chosen as one of the Most Important Young People of the Arab World in an initiative launched by Emirates prime minister, Sheikh Muhammed bin Rashid, titled Young Arab Leaders. The program included wonderful young people from Arab countries, one from each country with specific criteria, and they spent four months in America at ESPN University studying leadership arts, each looking carefully at a leader in their own field—for instance, Machiavelli, Margaret Thatcher, Jesus Christ, the Prophet Muhammad (prayers and peace be upon him), and so on: the strengths of each, their personality, and how they achieved their status. The young people chosen for this program were the beacons of the Arab world, the best young minds out there, a network of important connections that 100 percent benefited Fatma, raising the ceiling of regional networking.

Last year, thanks to her international network of contacts, she had the chance to study for an MA in luxury brands at an international university in Paris. I didn't hesitate for a minute to send her there to learn more. She had to grasp that opportunity no matter what. She was taught by the top executive directors of international brands—Dior, Armani, Prada, Gucci. She went

With Welsh fashion designer Julien Macdonald, 2006.

to the City of Light once a month to study for two weeks, then came back to Cairo to give us a lecture and tell us what was going on in the broader world of fashion and how things were managed there. This, too, lifted the company onto another plane. We now had a reference point with major fashion houses that had already achieved stunning success, and a better understanding of the strategies used by these massive companies that had become synonymous with luxury, and how they were run. Now we had to adhere to the strict standards of a luxury fashion house.

Fatma is executive director of the company now. When she started out, the company had forty-five employees; now our staff numbers 250. She has big dreams and bigger ambitions to put the company at the top of the heap. She's the new eyes of the business. She has a feeling for her country and for human values in every aspect of this business. I'm always asked in interviews with the press and media: "How did you achieve international recognition?" I laugh and say, "My job and Amina's is to make a quality product that stands out, a product that's competitive and that can be marketed beyond Egypt. The rest is up to Fatma and her team. She takes the product and runs with it, doing the best she can in the best way. Success is a team effort; it's not up to one person."

Now we have a board of directors and regular meetings to talk about what's happening. I attend the meetings when there's something important to discuss—reports coming in for me to understand what's going on in the company. Imagine, to this day I hate figures and finances! (I really oughtn't to say that.) At the end-of-year meetings, when they present all the numbers, it is not one of my favorite days. (I have to put up with it!) I do not like accounts and spreadsheets, but when we achieve good sales figures, that really makes me happy. In the end, they give me a brief summary of all the accounts.

Young people—new blood, new ideas, good education—are the main thing behind this company's success. Fatma now sits at the head of a group of boards of directors of young people's companies. They always learn from her experience and long years in this type of company and the issues that crop up. She often gives seminars, talks at universities, and so on, about examples of small and medium-sized companies, how they succeed and the challenges they face. These are real-life examples she has experienced day to day and problems she overcame during Azza Fahmy's long journey as a company. She helps young people who have launched new projects in art and design with the right start to their careers. Because she received a proper education, and thanks to her long experience since childhood, she has achieved a solid and laudable standard. She's now one of the important young leaders in this field in the Arab world.

Thuraya, the Light of our Lives

I can't talk about Fatma without mentioning Thuraya, my granddaughter. The two of them are a matching pair to me. Thuraya Hazem Amr Mahmoud Moussa was born on 5 January 2015 at 7:05 a.m. I was very careful to find out and take down the exact time she was delivered so as to get her personality and life direction charted. In India, they believe that the position of the stars at the precise moment we came into the world defines many things about a person's makeup. Unfortunately, when I wanted to have this chart made for myself, I had all the information except the hour of my birth. I had never felt it mattered much, and all the generation that were there at the time—maternal aunts, paternal aunts, family members—have passed away. On my first trip to India after Thuraya came into our world, I took her file to my Indian friend who makes these charts. Can you believe it, when he looked at the file and put all the information into the proper places, along with the stars' alignment at the time, he said, "What an unusual child." She was a year old at the time. "She's going to be an exceptionally eloquent speaker. She has the gift of the gab and she's very persuasive. This girl needs to go into something involving communication and speech. This side of her is very clear."

I laughed to myself and thought, "No wonder! Her grandfather is Amre Moussa, former secretary-general of the Arab League and former foreign minister of Egypt!"

This little creature, so sweet and smart, has brought me so much joy and delight. Every time I travel to a different part of the world, I buy her their traditional costume—Japan, Bahrain, Africa, the Oases. I would love to plant a seed to do with heritage and identity in her psyche. I'm also trying to teach her our famous songs by Salah Jahin. She knows them well, and recites them correctly: "The Big Night," and the old song "Get Up and Pray, Abu Za'iza'." The dearest thing I would wish for would be for Thuraya to go into the family business, which would mean we've succeeded in bringing a third generation in to preserve this inheritance.

Wordsmithing is harder than any other craft.
(The Instruction of Ptah-Hotep, 2182–2345 BC)

Amina

My daughter Amina was raised in two ways: a traditional way—the way my father and mother raised me conservatively in how to speak, family customs and family bonds, how to dress, how to respect one's elders, how late you could come back at night (which always caused fights), one's family knowing one's circle of friends and their families—and the other way, which is freedom to do what you want and take the consequences. It was Amina's choice what to do with her life. No one ever interfered with that. It was her decision alone.

When Amina was near to graduating high school—she was doing an IGCSE—she had to choose her subjects, because that was the basis on which she would go to university. It was clear in her mind that she only wanted to take art courses. After some discussion, I let her do what she wanted, and arranged with a good art teacher at her school to give her lessons in art and painting, as well as with a friend, a professor at the Faculty of Fine Arts, who also taught her painting. So the girl was really insistent on studying art! Everyone said I was crazy and was not planning for her future. "But what will she do if she doesn't get good grades in art and the Egyptian universities reject her? What'll happen then? She'll probably not be accepted anywhere!"

This is what happened. The choices were either for her to go to art school in Europe or to repeat the year. In fact, we both decided to accept the risk and went ahead. The girl was eager to go to art school and study jewelry making at a solid school in Europe. I wanted to send her to the best university in the world to learn it—something I'd never been able to do for myself.

This was when I was chosen to become a member of the World Gold Council, of which Haruko Fukuda was the CEO. She was one of the most prominent businesswomen in Japan. My relationship with this international institution broadened the circle of my international contacts and the people I knew in the jewelry field. I sat on committees that included the most prominent international fashion and jewelry designers; we met twice a year to judge international jewelry competitions. Within this institution, there are committees for learning, creative work, and technologies related to the industry. Through my contacts with the people in these committees, I learned that the leading university worldwide in the field of jewelry making and design was the University of Dundee in Scotland. Also on the list of design universities was the University of Central England in Birmingham (now Birmingham City University), famous for its silversmithing program, the best second choice as it brought together design and technology. I didn't want to choose a university in America as it was too far away. Europe, especially England, was where we were looking.

Amina had to create a strong portfolio in order to be accepted. She worked hard on it alongside the professors who taught her art. We sent in the application forms, which were accepted, and they gave us a date for the interview.

Amina wasn't even seventeen yet. She went to London and stayed with a friend of mine there. The next day, she took the early morning train to Birmingham to meet the Head of Department at the university. Back here in Cairo, I was in quite a tizzy. I knew it was a turning point and how important it was. From the time I woke up in the morning, I was praying for her to do well and be accepted. The alternative if she wasn't accepted . . . I really don't know what would have happened.

She returned from Birmingham that night and called me on the telephone to tell me what had happened at the interview. There were many applicants—I don't remember how many now—and the foundation year only accepted twenty-four. Each applicant went into the room and spent about twenty minutes there being interviewed, and when they came out, all the others would cluster around them and ask, "What did the professor ask you about?"

Amina went in and spent about forty-five minutes with him. She showed him the portfolio that she'd spent the entire past year working on. But what seemed to capture the man's attention was the story being told by this young girl. He asked her, "Why do you want to be a jewelry maker?"

Amina launched into the whole story about her mother, her profession, her collection of traditional jewelry, the designs inspired by these collections, how she and her sister had helped their mother in the business since they were little, the desert trips to remote places to collect and record this heritage, the buying trips with her mother to help with her work, and her wish to take up the profession and help grow the company.

Birmingham, a city where this industry goes way back, didn't really appeal to Amina as a place. Of course, London was more attractive to her, especially as she had applied to the famous Central St Martins College in London a while ago and been accepted. But the head of department said to her, "Have you seen the buildings and studios and laboratories here where you're going to study?" Then he took her on a tour. She saw the university buildings, the teaching studios, the level of technology, and the equipment there; then she changed her mind at once and understood that the learning facilities and the level of the university were up to the level of her ambitions.

Amina was accepted on the spot as one of the twenty-four. As I remember this now, my eyes fill with tears. My joy knew no bounds. Amina had been accepted at a good university and was fulfilling part of my dream for her of getting a good education.

There was one obstacle, though: she was only seventeen, and the university required that a student be eighteen to be accepted. She came back to Cairo for a full gap year. She had no idea what she was going to do. It wasn't feasible for her to just sit around for a year in Egypt doing nothing: I thought that was a waste of time and there would be a risk of picking up bad habits without study or interests. Well, I'd started to make some pretty strong international connections, and I'd met two jewelry makers from Italy at an exhibition who had just founded a contemporary jewelry school in Florence. I pulled out their business card, which they'd given me at the exhibition, and wrote to tell them that Amina was coming to study at their school for the next year. They responded immediately, accepting Amina at the school.

Amina was shipped off to Italy a month and a half later to study jewelry making at the Alchimia Contemporary Jewellery School in Florence—we had to really hurry. It was one of the major contemporary schools in Italy. She arrived in Italy, and for two days I heard nothing from her—there were no cell phones then. Then she told me her news.

In her first week, she had to handle the basics on her own, without me. She had to find a place to stay for that week, then longer-term lodgings; she needed to become familiar with the area around her, and navigate food, drink, and transportation. They gave her an appointment for a face-to-face interview at the school. In the morning, she arrived at the address she had taken down, and then something odd happened: the examiners had read her birthdate wrong, and thought she was ten years older—that is, twenty-seven! But she was only seventeen, and they didn't accept students that young.

The school's two directors stared wide-eyed when they found a young girl coming to study with people all over thirty-five, some over forty, some fifty. They were baffled. They couldn't very well send her packing back to Egypt! So she was accepted. She was the youngest student to be accepted at the school. Doris Manninger, the Austrian–Italian owner of the school, who has become a personal friend and a consultant to the Design Studio by Azza Fahmy in Cairo, took pity on Amina and decided to take her under her wing. She helped her settle down: all the processes of opening a bank account, finding decent lodgings, and guiding and advising her about the details of everyday life there. She was one of the greatest supporters of this young girl who had come there from Egypt all on her own. She usually invited her to spend the weekends at her house.

Doris's younger sister was married to the younger brother of footwear designer Salvatore Ferragamo. His headquarters were in a seventeenth-century building on the River Arno in Florence, and I always visit this wonderful store and the museum of this designer's long history whenever I'm in Florence. After a while, Amina told me that Doris had taken her to spend the weekend at Ferragamo's ranch outside Florence, where the designer and his family had a big farmhouse with stables of thoroughbred horses. When I heard her on the phone telling me where she'd spent the weekend with Doris, my first question was: "What kind of shoes were they wearing, Amina?"

She burst out laughing. "Mummy! They were wearing regular sandals just like everyone else!"

Sometimes, I think that nothing in this world happens by chance. Everything happens for a reason. Amina not being accepted under eighteen at the university in Birmingham; my decision to send her to Florence for the gap year; the directors misreading her date of birth and having to accept her and her spending the year there; this was all planned by a higher power. I always feel that this higher power is on my side, supporting me. Can you imagine, I never worry? I always think that everything will get done and it'll all happen for the best. I guess this is my spiritual side! And Doris and I staying friends for decades because she took care of Amina, and this great woman finally becoming our art education consultant at the Design Studio by Azza Fahmy and supporting us on the international scene! Without her, the Design Studio by Azza Fahmy would never have achieved this high standard of professional craft and artistic education.

Stories, and stories, and stories—water under the bridge! Back then I used to think to myself: "Am I crazy? Sending a seventeen-year-old girl to Europe on her own to face the world, just like that?" I really can't answer that question even now. Maybe if it happened again, I would do the same thing over again.

Amina had to live alone for a year in Florence, to find lodgings and live on her own, and to manage all the details of her daily life—food and drink and opening a bank account. I had neither the money nor the time to travel with her and supervise the process of finding a place to stay and organizing her life there. I was on a strict budget just paying for Amina's education. Truly, when I think back now on how I did it, leaving her to face all that on her own, I just don't know. Thank Heaven, everything went smoothly. All this wasn't easy for her or for me. I worried about her every day, especially at the start. How was her day going? Had she managed to open a bank account? Had she managed to find a room in a shared apartment? What were her roommates like? Was the lodging close to the school, or far away? So many everyday details this girl faced all alone over there.

We talked on the phone every Monday night after I got home so that she could tell me her news from Florence. I waited impatiently for that day, "on hot coals," as they say, to hear everything that had happened during the week. What had she done? How had she managed? What had she learned in school? Finances were just about enough to make things reasonably comfortable. There was a budget that she had to stick to.

Her time of study in Europe changed Amina. It made her stronger and more open-minded through her contact with other cultures, in her studies and in being part of this more open society. There were exhibitions, libraries, and classmates of different nationalities: Japanese, Chinese, European, and others. All this broadened her horizons in regard to the Other and how the Other lives.

The things that impressed Amina in her studies she immediately conveyed to me. In Florence, one of her teachers was the most prominent goldsmith in Italy, called Pepito. Back then, of course, I wasn't familiar with

Italian craftsmen. She came back from Italy with a book—she usually did that—by Pepito, and showed it to me. She always wanted to see new things and a different perspective and concept for different jewelry. She felt that these things needed to be viewed with respect, and that we must always see what was new, because we might learn from it. She was always bringing me books of contemporary jewelry from Japan that explained what jewelry artists in Japan were doing and what they were producing. There were a lot of Japanese students with her in school.

Amina spent an academic year in the most beautiful city in Italy—perhaps the most beautiful city in the world. It imprinted itself on her, leaving her with something beautiful. To get up in the morning and cycle to school over the historic Ponte Vecchio bridge, passing by the replica of Michelangelo's *David* on the way in the Piazza della Signoria, to see beauty and art in everything around you—in the end, this affects you, reforming your taste and vision. She learned some Italian and was thrilled that she was starting to speak a little.

There are many things Amina shared with me at a distance. The methods of teaching and pedagogy; the people and important artists she met throughout her day; what her Italian housemates did, cooked, and ate; her colleagues. But the poor dear always hid any problems she was having from me, so as not to upset me. I only learned this from her long years later, after she came back from Europe, the incidents that she sometimes faced on her own. Thank goodness I didn't learn of them back then.

All our new knowledge and opening up to contemporary jewelry was thanks to Amina. All my concentration and interests were specific: I only saw and studied traditional jewelry, whether local, regional, or international. I said to myself, "This won't do! Wake up, girl! There are other things in the world we need to understand, respect, and learn from." This new thinking, which made its way in and merged with my deep love for traditional jewelry, changed a large part of my designs, a wonderful combination that benefited me so much when I was working on my pharaonic collection. I was terrified of coming face-to-face with my ancestors the great pharaohs. Amina found the solution for me, saying, "Mother, let's make it very contemporary." And we did. We mixed ancient Egyptian motifs in a new and contemporary style. I only made the collection after about eight years of off-and-on study and discussion. We produced a contemporary pharaonic collection that was very well received both in Egypt and abroad.

Amina is my new eyes. She's good at using technology and knows about the wider world of jewelry, clothing, and fashion, using contemporary means of communication. She talks to me for ages about jewelry artisans I would really never have known otherwise, showing me what they do. All this has broadened my own horizons about what's going on in the world around us.

After her year in Italy, Amina went to the venerable city of Birmingham, the second city after London for silversmithing, and the "chocolate city" where Cadbury's got their start! But she enrolled, finally, at the University of Central England in Birmingham, as it was then called. It was a four-year course of study: one foundation year and then three years of specialization in jewelry design and execution, at the end of which she got her BA in jewelry technology and design. Our budget allowed for her to come back to Cairo once a year at the start of the summer vacation. It was hard for me to go visit her because of work and other responsibilities, not to mention it was

The Pectoral, from my pharaonic-influenced designs; it is made of sterling silver and inspired by Amarna Period (New Kingdom) faience collars.

too expensive. Two years later, I could afford to bring her back twice for vacation: once at the Christmas break, and the other for the summer. How I missed her! I so enjoyed sitting and talking with her when she came.

Amina finally came back to Cairo, having spent five years in total studying in Europe. Then for a long time—about six years—she was my ever-present shadow. She started in the production room, working with the workers on modern methods of silversmithing. The same thing happened to her that had happened with me thirty years ago: she asked one of the workers to introduce a technical modification to a piece. "It can't be done, *Bashmuhandisa!*" he said.

"Then I'll do it," she retorted, and sat down at the machine and executed it herself. I was standing on the second floor, watching her through the window. "History repeats itself," I whispered to myself, remembering the same thing happening on my return from London.

The best and happiest moments in my life are the times we're designing together. We have discussions where I try to give her the benefit of my long experience, stored in the archives of my mind, about traditional jewelry—gorgeous Egyptian village jewelry, Amazigh jewelry, the things worn by the higher- and middle-ranking Berber tribes, Indian jewelry and its influence on the Arab region, Central Asian jewelry, African jewelry and its characteristics, the magnificent jewelry of Russia and the Romanov Empire, and the jewelry of Europe and Central Europe, both old and new. I'll draw her attention to some little detail, such as how the craftsman managed to resolve the join of large and small parts in a piece. Such fun, our discussions! Both of us come out enriched. As for her, she has introduced me to contemporary jewelry design and the major artists in the field.

When Amina visited the Armitage Museum in St. Petersburg—one of the most important museums in the world—her comments to me when she got back were about the details of the Romanovs' jewelry, and how the parts of a piece were interconnected. We sat chatting about what she'd seen. This is my true joy: I feel I've implanted something important in her, bringing her into this wonderful world of craftsmanship mixed with culture. Now she knows well how to mix the contemporary and the traditional. I owe my dear daughter Amina "Nonna" a debt of gratitude for opening my eyes to the world of contemporary jewelry and major contemporary jewelry designers from both east and west.

Azza Fahmy the Mother

> "Do the one thing you think you cannot do. Fail at it. Try again. Do better the second time. The only people who never tumble are those who never mount the high wire. This is your moment. Own it."
>
> —Oprah Winfrey

Creativity and success *must* come with mistakes. I was going into a new field and I had to accept that it wouldn't all be easy. I was also prepared for the possibility of going astray a little. After all these years of living, I've learned, and my philosophy in life is that you have to accept the things you don't like along with the good things in life. The world is all a matter of balances.

The wisest thing Magdi Saleh, my godfather, said to me at the start of my career was a piece of advice I "wear like an earring," as we say in Egypt, and keep repeating at work: "Azza, the day you come to me and say, 'I have no problems' is the day I know you're not moving forward in your work." Good management in a company is the art of problem-solving. The higher the company climbs, the more obstacles come up that you must resolve.

With my dear friends Magdi Saleh and the late filmmaker Atiyat al-Abnoudi, 2008.

I feel here that I need to talk—that it's important to talk—about Azza the mother. You know, one of the hardest jobs is being a mother. You find yourself not just carrying your own self, but responsible for the lives of humans who are still taking shape, and you're supposed to play a not insignificant role in shaping who they are. It's a big thing, when you think about it, and sometimes terrifying.

The biggest problem facing a woman who works is her family. The responsibility for family and the success or failure of the whole structure hangs around her neck. If the children don't do well, people say, "Look! Their mother left them and went out to work!" You've got to succeed outside the household and within it too, which puts a great psychological and physical burden on you, especially in the early stages of starting a family and not being able to afford a team of household help—a driver, a cook, and a cleaner.

Trying to remember the start of my life now, when I began seriously making jewelry, I recall I used to wake up early, wake the girls up, get them dressed and make them breakfast, pack them lunches, go out into the street and wait for the school bus. Then there was the grocery and other shopping, then the workshop, with all the little details of the working process, what was needed today and how it was going to go. I ran to and fro from early in the morning till late at night. The house, too, had to be clean, and all our daily, weekly, and monthly needs bought, the laundry and the ironing done, and checking that everything was going well without hiccups, then helping with the homework, and getting the girls to their gym, ballet, and music classes. We also spent some time with piano lessons—what harm could it do? They had to pursue all the activities that would make them better people. Besides all this, I had to know at least a little bit about the girls' friends and their families. Do they think the way we do? Are they different from us in their beliefs and in the way they raise their children? This was important, too, for me to always pay attention to. After all, we don't want them to pick up habits that aren't part of our family tradition.

All this and more. It's you, the parent, who is their role model. You can't make any mistakes. You can't do anything silly. You have to be alert all the time to how they dress, what habits they're picking up from their circle of friends, the language they use. Once Fatma and Amina and their friends bought plastic earrings to wear. Of course, I was overcome with panic and disappointment. I was so upset! "I've failed!" I said to myself. "These habits will stick! The girls will have bad taste forever!" A short while later, when I was giving an exhibition at the Egyptian Embassy in Washington, DC, I met my friend Dr. Ayman al-Muhandes, a professor of psychiatry at George Washington University. He invited me to his home, and I poured out my heart about the plastic earrings and all my fears. How he laughed! "So you're afraid that Azza Fahmy's daughters," he chuckled, "will wear things in bad taste? Azza, the computer in their heads is saving everything you do. Don't worry about them. It'll all come out later." And it did.

I remember this now, when I see the way that Fatma and Amina behave that makes me so proud of them. So many things, and expressions they say, exactly like me: their devotion to Egypt, their culture, their heritage, their responsibility, their relationship with the company—it's all there and it's strong. I feel reassured. "Thank goodness. I succeeded, in spite of everything."

I'll try to explain what I went through all these years. I was a single mother with my own business, which required time, energy, and a physical and mental presence, especially as at that time I didn't have the financial means to hire people to do the work for me. I had to do the designing, buy the raw materials, whether wires or sheets, and prepare them, provide what the workshop needed myself, supervise the mockups that came out of the drawings—I did everything from A to Z. I tried to learn, a little bit, how to handle the finances as well and understand them so I wouldn't be robbed. And I had to meet important clients. Many different processes at the same time. Of course, I could barely keep up, and all this puts pressure on a woman's nervous system. The problem, too, is that when a mother is single and the children are with her, the general picture people see, and the ultimate appearance of the family and the children is, "Are they normal? Is their mental health affected by the split?" I tried to come out of it with as few emotional wounds and scratches as possible.

It really was overwhelming. Most separated women raising their children on their own suffer constantly from a sense of guilt. They always feel that they aren't doing enough for their children. The children have to do well! They must get good grades at school! The house has to be clean! The food prepared, the washing done, the ironing finished, all the shopping for everything the household needs . . . so many things. A long list of responsibilities that could break anyone. I couldn't slack off on anything, and nothing could be half-baked. This was in addition to the responsibilities of work. The business had to stand on its own two feet, it had to do well, it had to go smoothly.

Now, when I am interviewed on TV or in the press, they ask me about the hardest things I faced in my career. I respond with all confidence and frankness, "The family. The success or failure of a family is always blamed on the mother, and society sees it as the mother's responsibility alone." It was a terrifying responsibility for me. I didn't ever want to have not done my duty by the girls and in the household, and at the same time, my work, my small business, had to keep going. The difficulties you encounter at work and with the workers include production issues, lack of money on occasion (for instance, the workers *have* to be paid at the end of the week, and the workshop's raw materials can never be allowed to run out), listening to the customers' complaints and resolving them and working toward ensuring they don't happen again: a long list, daily, weekly, monthly. In the end, I had to come home at the end of the day and take care of the girls and find out how things were going, and then plan for the next day. I truly don't remember now what state I was in at the end of the day. I swear, in all honesty, what I know and remember is that I had my shoulder to the wheel and my nose to the grindstone all the time. Truly, from the heart, after all the years that have gone by for us as a family, now that's water under the bridge, I want to ask them: Was I really the mother they had in mind? Oh, how I hope I've done right by them! If I've left anything undone, I swear I didn't mean it.

I want to confess here: it's true that I was frazzled and exhausted, but I was never weak. I was exhausted and strong. I could see the path clear before me, and I believed in it wholeheartedly. This was very important to me.

I broke up with my husband, their father, when Fatma was ten and Amina was seven. The decision wasn't easy, nor was it an easy time for me. Even if you're already sure it's the right thing to do, it's still hard. Sometimes I had very dark times when I didn't know what to do. An example: before we separated, we'd taken out a loan from the bank and decided to build a factory, and I was the first guarantor. Naturally, the project failed due to the divorce. I can't describe to you the years I spent paying off the debt, and the compound interest. Ten years working like a mule to pay off the debt! And on another front, I had to keep things running. Years of worry and fear. I cried so much in my terrified fretting that often, before I fell asleep, it seemed I had filled the pillow with my tears!

Sometimes, my world narrowed to the eye of a needle. I didn't know what to do, especially when it came time to pay the instalments on the loan. Back then, the only thing that could pull me out of my darkness and misery was to sit down and design a piece I loved. Sometimes I would do it on paper, and often, if there wasn't a pen and paper, I imagined and drew it in my head. At once, I would find myself transported to another plane, thinking of artistic solutions to the pieces I was making, and starting to calm down and feel cheerful, and feeling that things would be okay. Like flying. Jalal al-Din al-Rumi says, "You are born with wings."

When I remember this now, I remember my dear friend, the Tunisian intellectual Habib Atiya, may he rest in peace. He used to tell me, back when he was involved in politics, that he was jailed for a time because of being a leftist. Sitting in his cell, depressed and lonely, and sometimes even tortured, he told me, "Azza, I flew away in my imagination and walked with a friend through the Jardins des Tuileries in Paris, chatting about things we liked." Jewelry is happiness and joy for me. It got me through my darkest times. It always kept me going, happy, with a certainty that things would be okay, and that everything would eventually turn out right. The main thing was to not lose hope and to keep doing the thing that gave me joy and lifted me onto another plane. I want to tell you something else, too: Everything passes. And as Gamal al-Ghitani says, "The suffering is equal to the joy."

The issue of the girls and getting them through the divorce with the least possible negative impact was always on my mind. No matter how civilized the breakup, it still affects the children's lives. I tried to do what was right and practical. I started to go to a psychologist and plan with him how I would achieve this balance in my life with the girls. He always said to me: "Immerse them in love. Love them as much as you can. Love is healing." Have I succeeded? I really don't know, I swear. Was I the mother who did everything she ought to do, and fulfilled all her duties? Truly, they are the ones who must answer. I did all I could with what I had—especially with my situation and the heavy responsibility I had to carry and keep walking, whether professionally or personally. Did I—as the doctor told me to—give them the love they expected of me? I don't know. Again, the answer lies with them. I did all I could, and it was the most I could do at the time.

I attended every parents' meeting to find out how they were doing at school. Fatma has been very smart all her life, and all the teachers attest to it. But one time I was at a parents' meeting and Amina's teacher told me that her progress and performance weren't good. I went home in a terrible state! The guilt complex multiplied. I always woke up early with them at 6 a.m., and we had breakfast together and I made their lunches, and we chatted about this and that. My mother had taught me that breakfast was the most important meal, and you shouldn't buy ready-made food: all the sandwiches and food were homemade. Amina was sitting opposite me at table; I burst out crying and said to her, "Amina, please! I can't go over your homework and your lessons for you every day! You can see how tired I am when I come back from the workshop! You have to bear the responsibility of studying and doing your homework on your own! It's your responsibility! Homework and studying aren't my job!"

I was babbling and my tears were falling, I was really worked up. Poor Amina was so startled! She stared at me wide-eyed and didn't know what to say. She ended up not saying anything, and we didn't speak of it again. The nice thing, though, is that two or three months later, there was another follow-up parents' meeting, and when I met the same teacher, she was delighted. "What happened?" she asked me. "Amina's moving forward by leaps and bounds! She's the third-highest-scoring student in the class!"

There were so many things to do and daily duties and to-do lists to check off that I absolutely had to plan and organize all the time to keep things going. There needed to be more hours in the day, I thought, to get everything done. I had to do everything quickly: I didn't even have time to sit down quietly at mealtimes and eat. I bolted my food standing up, as I had things to do and the day wasn't long enough. Of course, this habit ruined my digestion and I have chronic ulcerative colitis to this day, although I am a little better since starting yoga and meditation, and taking annual trips to the Himalayas to unplug and disconnect from the world.

One of the things I was just trying to remember now is that the girls sometimes came home from school saying, "We only have two pairs of jeans each, three sweaters, and two jackets." They could see what the other students were wearing and the amount of clothing they had. Their school didn't have a uniform, and the children who went there were all from affluent families and changed their clothes often. I sat down and explained to them that our circumstances were different from theirs, that we had obligations: school fees, schoolbooks, other books for general knowledge that I liked them to read. We had a limited budget for clothes, which we had to stick to. I have to give them credit, they never asked me for anything extra after that, and when they wanted something, they asked, "Mummy, can we afford this?"

We took many trips to see my friends in England and America. We would stay there a while and I'd put on exhibitions, and of course it was an opportunity to buy nice clothes at prices that wouldn't break my budget. The girls used to come back with a few clothes, and they looked pretty and well turned out.

Honestly, these two girls lived through some hard times when we had to scrimp and save, and they were always so good about understanding our financial situation compared to all the people around us, what we could and couldn't afford, and what we could ask for and what we couldn't. They helped me when I needed them. They were always the greatest help in showing Azza Fahmy pieces at international exhibitions or Egyptian embassies abroad. Every little detail, starting with making sure of the look of a piece, the display, pricing, and arranging the exhibition, down to helping with sales—important things I couldn't have done by myself.

When I sent Amina to study in Italy and then England, when we had a bit more money, she always had a budget. It's true that we were doing better financially, but we still had to plan our expenditures carefully: university fees, rent, transportation, food, warm winter jackets so she didn't get sick, and so on. She and I used to sit down and write out our expected spending in two copies, one for her and one for me—each of us with her own sheet of paper. And the dear girl used to review the sheet regularly, and she always stuck to her budget and never broke our financial agreement. I remember one time she called me when she wanted to buy pajamas. "I found two pairs of pajamas," she told me over the phone. I don't remember what the first one cost, but she said, "I like the other one better, but it's five pounds (sterling) more. Can I buy it?" This kind of thing touched me deeply. I felt that I had succeeded in making them money-conscious and aware of their budget. (Of course, I told her, "Buy the one you like best.")

When our financial situation improved, this reflected on our spending, and I felt I could loosen up a bit. Still, this tendency to be careful with money stayed a habit of mine after thirty years of being on a strict budget. To this day, I calculate everything. Sometimes it becomes annoying—sometimes I get frustrated with myself! But it seems to have become part of my DNA, stuck in my genetic makeup. It has even reflected on my use of expensive raw materials in my work. To this day, I am scared to make a piece in an expensive material like gold! I even have a fear of creating pieces with a lot of diamonds, rubies, or emeralds, although I'm artistically capable of crafting them well and professionally. Honestly, this is something I don't like about myself. I need to put it aside. You know, all the pieces with gold, diamonds, and jewels are what Amina pushed me to create. "Don't be scared," she kept telling me. And they really made a big difference to our work. I was always "the silver lady." But then gold came in, alongside the silver.

I got into spirituality, meditation, and yoga on the advice of my dear friend Fawqiya Shahata when she saw my mental state and how I lived, rushing along like an express train, and my frequent attacks of palpitations. Her advice really saved my life, and I am eternally grateful to her. After that, I developed and moved onto a different path: I learned how to reconnect with myself and also to become aware of negative thinking about daily life and the mental issues that face me. Negative thinking is very powerful and it has to be jettisoned, because it is extremely destructive. There are moments of peace you need to incorporate throughout your day for balance. Ever since, I've been determined to work hard on myself, to try and change and work on my flaws before complaining about people and circumstances, and to realize that happiness comes from oneself, from within, not from others. The other person will never make you happy. You make yourself happy. The yin/yang philosophy is correct: there is a spot of white in the black, and a spot of black in the white. You must accept it. I must be good on the inside so as to see the world as good. This is why I've incorporated the proverb "Be beautiful and you'll see beauty in the world" into many of my collections, because of how fond I am of it, and how much I believe in it.

My relationship with yoga and meditation has grown stronger. I feel that spiritual and Sufi readings, too, have made a great difference in my life. My visits to India and the Himalayas are something I insist on doing every year.

They are sacred and essential to my physical and mental health. The courses on spirituality I took have changed how I see the world. So has my belief that everything happens for a reason—even the stumbling blocks that can put a stop to plans or projects—and that it is all for the best.

The major thing I achieved is being at peace with myself. I am calm. Things don't upset me like they used to, and I don't throw a tantrum when a project doesn't go through or our plans are messed up. It is all good; it didn't work out because it probably wasn't "written." If it had been "written," it would have happened. And always, in the end, I find out, and am grateful, that it didn't happen because it wasn't in my fate.

All the knowledge I took away from this has changed my life and lifted me onto a better plane of understanding and accepting the Other. As Einstein said, "Information is not knowledge. The only source of knowledge is experience." Another thing that makes me happy, which I learned in India as well, is my relationship with birds. I love to feed the birds. I wake up in the morning to find them perching on my balcony, waiting for me to put out their seed. They look at me through the glass and chirp as if to say, "Put out the food and water!" The first thing I do is put out the birdseed and water, and then I sit there, watching them: moments of overwhelming happiness to start my day and give me joy.

> "Do you want to do a good deed? Water the plants and give the birds some seed."
>
> —Egyptian proverb

> "Life doesn't give lessons for free to anyone. So when I say that life has taught me, you can be sure that I paid the price."
>
> —Naguib Mahfouz

EPILOGUE

"But do not hurry the journey at all.
Better if it lasts for years."

—"Ithaka," C.P. Cavafy

I think I've pretty much reached the end. I've said almost everything, and it's time to end the book now. Don't think fifty years is a long time. They've flown by. I don't know when or how they flashed by. You know, I've really enjoyed writing this, because I saw all of my life in one piece, right here in front of me.

It's really been a rich, full life—a combination of many lives. A happy childhood with a wonderful father and mother; a youth that was, for me, a time of opening up to new cultural worlds, unfamiliar adventures, and unconventional discoveries; so many trips to most of the countries in the world that are known for things related to my profession, some of which I have written about (but not all). It hasn't been an easy life, and circumstances were overwhelming occasionally, but I lived it as I wanted to, and in the way I felt, believed, and saw to be right. As my favorite Sinatra song goes, "I did it my way."

"Everything that seems to us like coincidence is carefully planned."
—Gamal al-Ghitani

I've truly reached the conviction that nothing in all this happened by chance. My silversmith ancestors in Sudan; my mother's diamond bracelet, which she sold so that I could go to Italy and have my eyes opened; the book I bought when I was not well off; the girls becoming an important part of this creation, and being happy and enthusiastic to be there—all this happened because it was planned for me, and written that I should be here. It wasn't chance.

I know now, and I have a strong belief, that to succeed and know where we're going, we must also know where we come from.

I know myself better on the personal level, and I understand where the things planted inside me—good or bad—came from. I've seen my life, the bitter and the sweet, and I don't exaggerate when I say that I cried, and cried a lot, as I wrote down my story. It all came out, the bitter and the sweet. But this has been a healing process for me, a kind of self-discovery. I want the final scene to end well, with a good achievement.

Can I tell you something? I really don't feel that I'm older—although I guess, technically, I am an old woman. Inside, I'm still a young girl of twenty. My problem is that I have endless dreams. I'm always dreaming of new things that I love, always accompanied by a firm conviction and faith that they can be achieved and an enthusiasm that brings happiness with it. This is living a wonderful life, where no sooner do I calm down and find peace and stillness than a new circle starts—a circle of thinking, preoccupation, work, and happiness.

I don't want to depart this life before I draw the final scene. (I won't tell you about it so as not to spoil the surprise.) I have a feeling that this is my new life, just about to start!

My mind is at ease about the company, the girls, and the young people: my daughters, my own blood, who bear the responsibility with love, enthusiasm, and commitment; and the young people that I call "my work family," who aren't of my blood, but whose love and passion for the company reassure me. Now let me conclude the story by dedicating the following lines by the poet Ahmad Fouad Nigm to them:

> Our Egypt is the best of girls.
> She wants you to make her pretty.
> You are the people of noble character.

I feel that the patriotic bird, which was spoken of by the great poet Mahmoud Darwish, has laid eggs and given us a lot of chicks. I see flocks of young birds flying high in Egypt's beloved skies.

GLOSSARY

Abdel Halim Hafez: Popular romantic singer and movie star of the 1950s and 1960s.

Ablaq: An Islamic architectural feature, used in Egypt and the Levant, where white and black or white and red stone alternate in rectangular or ornamental shapes.

American College (Asyut): The most famous school in Upper Egypt. Founded in 1865 by missionaries, it contains an important historical library comprising twenty thousand books and its own museum of ancient Egyptian, Islamic, Roman, and Coptic artifacts, as well as museums of biology and geology. It has produced generations of Egyptians fluent in foreign languages, and has played an important role in the promotion of Upper Egyptians who have achieved high positions in government.

Bashmuhandisa: A title of respect for (in this case, a female) engineer, architect, or designer, from the Turkish *bash*, "chief/head," and Arabic *muhandis*, "engineer."

Cicurel: A chain of upscale department stores founded by Jewish–Italian owner Morino Cicurel in 1877. The name Cicurel was associated with the Egyptian royal family and aristocratic families in Egypt throughout the first half of the twentieth century.

Feddan: A unit of land measurement, roughly equal to an acre.

Hagg: Title for a Muslim man who has performed the pilgrimage to Mecca; it is also used as a title of respect for older men regardless of whether or not they have actually been on the pilgrimage.

Harat al-Yahoud: "Jews' Alley," a district of Gammaliya in the historic old city of Cairo. It is said that the neighborhood was originally divided into two parts: one for the Rabbinic Jews and one for the Karaite Jews, and had thirteen synagogues, of which only three remain.

Imru' al-Qays: Celebrated pre-Islamic Arab poet, author of one of The Suspended Odes (see *al-Mu'allaqat*).

Khanqah: Structure built specifically for spiritual gatherings of a Sufi group known as a *tariqa*. Usually has a central hall and smaller rooms off it.

Kishk: Egyptian savory pudding, essentially like cream of chicken soup with a much thicker consistency, using starch in addition to flour. Like cream of chicken soup, it can have chicken pieces in it.

Ma'allim: Like *usta*, a title of respect for a master craftsman, but with added status, usually if a man is wealthy and owns his own shop or business. For a woman, it is *ma'allima*.)

Ma'mur: an attribute added on the name of a mosque to mean "always full of believers."

Mashrabiya: Traditional Arabian art of making wooden window screens with intricately interlocking pieces. The goal is to look out of the window and see without being seen.

Milaya laff: Literally "wraparound sheet," it refers to the flirtatiously modest garment worn by urban and Northern Egyptian women over their colorful gallabiyas, a rectangle of cloth about one meter across by two meters long, worn wrapped around the body (hence *laff*, "wrapping") in a specific style.

Millieme: Unit of currency equal to one-tenth of one piaster, one-thousandth of an Egyptian pound.

al-Mu'allaqat: "The Suspended Odes," the most famous poems by pre-Islamic Arab poets, so called because they used to be inscribed in gold lettering and hung up around the Kaaba in Mecca.

Omar Effendi: A chain store originally established in 1856 and nationalized in the 1950s.

Pocket Theater: An avant-garde theater, now closed down, so named for its small size. It was located next to the Andalus Gardens on the island of Gezira in Cairo.

Qalawun Complex: A thirteenth-century mausoleum, mosque, school, and hospital on al-Nahhasin Street, founded by al-Mansour Qalawun, who was one of the most famous Bahri Mamluk sultans.

Qasaba: A commercial thoroughfare, from the word for "reed" (because of its long, straight nature). The English word "casbah" is derived from *qasaba*.

Qaysariya: A covered market of a type widespread since early Islamic times in the Upper Egyptian towns of Sohag, Girga, Minya, Asyut, Qous, and Qift.

Rabʿ: In Islamic architecture, a craftsmen's center, divided into small rooms where the craftsmen ply their trades, above which are living quarters.

Sednaoui: Chain store founded by Syrian brothers Selim and Samaan Sednaoui, specializing in Egyptian fabrics and textiles.

Shamm al-Nasim: Egyptian Easter. Dating back from ancient Egyptian times, the occasion involves excursions to gardens and parks, coloring eggs, and eating salt fish.

Shamsi **bread**: Traditional bread of Upper Egypt, made with dough left to rise in the sun *(shams)*.

Tarabin: The largest Bedouin tribe in the Sinai Peninsula, named for the place they originally came from, Wadi Turba, east of Mecca.

Toub: Traditional draped garment worn by Sudanese, African, and Bedouin women; a length of cloth wrapped around the wearer's body several times, not dissimilar to the Indian sari.

Wikala: A center for trade, consisting of a central courtyard with rooms all around, in which dealers of goods such as cotton and dates would congregate either weekly or seasonally. The lower rooms were for buying and selling, and the upper ones were accommodations for the people from out of town.

Zar: Religious ritual of African origin where God's name is invoked to the rhythmic beat of tambours and participants engage in a swaying group dance. Thought to exorcise evil spirits, it also functions as entertainment of a sort for poorer or more conservative women.

REFERENCES

al-'Abidin, Ali Zein. *al-Huliy al-sha'biya al-nubiya*. Cairo: General Egyptian Book Organization, 1981.

Ali Mubarak (Pasha), *al-Khitat al-tawfiqiya al-jadida li-Misr al-Qahira wa-muduniha wa-biladiha al-qadima wa-l-shahira*. Cairo: n.p., AH 1306.

Fakhry, Ahmed. *Siwa Oasis*. Cairo: The American University in Cairo Press, 1973.

Gunn, Battiscombe G. The Project Gutenberg EBook of The Instruction of Ptah-Hotep and the Instruction of Ke'Gemni, https://www.gutenberg.org/files/30508/30508-h/30508-h.htm

Haridi, Salah Ahmad. *al-Hiraf wa-l-sina'at fi 'ahd Muhammad 'Ali*. Cairo: Dar Al Maaref, 1985.

INDEX

In the index *AF* is Azza Fahmy. Craftsmen, shopkeepers, and others who are given a title are indexed by their title *(hagg, khawaga, maʻallim, uncle, usta)* even when a surname is given in the text. The actual uncles of Azza Fahmy are indexed by their surname.

al-Abbas ibn al-Ahnaf 222
Abbas Hilmi I, Khedive 73
Abbasi family (goldsmiths) 122
Abdel Magid, Raouf 242
Abdel Sabour, Salah 222
Abdel Zaher, Professor 31–32
al-Abnoudi, Abdel Rahman 45, 59, 175
al-Abnoudi, Atiyat 13, 164, 168, 183, 230, 245, 257
Abu al-Einein, Abdel Ghani 173, 174, 232
Abu Gabal house (Helwan) 70–71
Abu Suliman, Eid 193–97
Abydos (al-Arraba Madfouna) 24–31
Advestian, Edward (gem setter) 106–107
al-Afarizi, William (silversmith) 128
al-Afrang, Yousef (gold dealer) 117
Aga Khan Foundation 220

Agha Zada family (gem dealers) 111–12
Aghurmi (town) 203
Ahmad (dealer from Bahariya Oasis) 210
Al-Ain Gallery 14, 59, 209
Aisha ("Auntie") 147, 148
Akhmim (town) 14
Alchimia Contemporary Jewellery School (Florence) 178, 265–69
Aleppo 219–21
Alexandria: Manshiya shopping district 41–42; summer holidays 34–43
Ali, Amr 185–87, 192
al-Allaqi, Farida 228
American University in Cairo 181
amulets 50, 128, 177, 191, 208
Angele, Madame 60, 163
Anita (Indian film director) 245, 246
al-Ansari, Ibtisam 71

Antiquities Authority 144–45
Arab–Israeli War (1967) 72
Araxie, Madame 221
architecture: Abha, Saudi Arabia 224–25; Dakhla Oasis 213; Iraq 231; Mamluk 88–89, 92–94, 97–98, 114; Siwa 202, 203
Armant (town) 23
al-Arraba Madfouna (Abydos) 24–31
Ashmolean Museum (Oxford) 28
al-Ashqar, Nidal 214–19, 221
Atiya, Habib 275
Aziz, George (antiques dealer) 107
Aziz, Naguib (silversmith) 128
Azza Fahmy Archive 199–200
Azza Fahmy company: Al-Ain Gallery 14, 59, 209; Bahrain branch 256; Dubai branch 256–57; fiftieth anniversary 1, 94; growth 252–55; international market 259–60; Jordan branch 235; management 257–61. *See also* Azza Fahmy designs; Design Studio by Azza Fahmy, The; Fahmy, Azza
Azza Fahmy designs: aha moment (career epiphany) 81–85; architectural inspiration 92–94; Badari patterns 21; bridle-inspired 98; contemporary designs 268–69, 270; Desert collection 209; exportation laws 145–46; in gold 255–56; Houses on the Nile 238; Mamluk Collection 93–94; medieval era–inspired 164–65; patriotic expression 86–87; pharaonic collections 27–29, 185–86; "Poems around Your Neck" 221–22; poetic verses on jewelry 66, 175–77, 219, 221–22; for *Shafiqa and Metwalli* 110–11; Symbols collection 177. *See also* Azza Fahmy company; Design Studio by Azza Fahmy, The; Fahmy, Azza; jewelry, traditional

Badari civilization 21
Baghi, Abdallah 204–205, 206, 209
Barrada, Fatma 81–82
Barsoum house (Helwan) 69–70
Baruch the dust dealer 134
Basta, Sanad ("Uncle") 46
bathhouse 104–107
al-Baz, Shahida 242
beads 13, 107–110, 128, 195–96, 212–13
Bedeir, Hilmi 244
Bedeir, Rania 252–53, 255, 257
Bedouin 109, 111, 119, 124–25, 187–91, 194–95, 227
Bell cotton company 8–10, 13–16, 60
Benzion family 28
Bibliotheca Alexandrina 175
Bicar, Hussein 174
books: AF's research and writing of 183–85; children's books design 79–80; collecting 165–67, 199–200; publishing and distribution 80–82
Boulaq al-Dakrour workshop 167–68
brass workers 113–16; Muhammad Samaka 110–11; Uncle Mustafa the Engraver 109–10

British Council 168–69
Bulbul (goldsmith) 54

Cairo Book Fair 81–82
Cavafy, C.P. 281
ceramics 80, 212
Chahine, Youssef 172
Christie's auction company 28
City of London Polytechnic 168–73
clothing, traditional: Bedouin 191, 194–95, 227; burqas 128, 173, 194–95; gallabiyas 173–75, 210; Libyan 228–29; *milaya laff* 96; from oases 212; Omani 224; Siwan 207–209. *See also* Egyptian culture; embroidery; jewelry, traditional; textiles
clothing choices in workshops 159–63
College of Applied Arts (Cairo) 87–88
copper merchants. *See* brass workers
coral 112, 186, 228, 229
costume design 216–18
cotton mattresses and quilts 34
cotton production 8–16, 106; and gold sales 12–13, 122–24
crafts hierarchies 131–32, 140–41
crafts research 199–200. *See also* Fahmy, Azza, travel and inspiration
craftwork, attitudes toward 238–40

daggers 224
Damascus 217–19
Damdam, Eli (engraver) 134
Daniel, Norman 168–69, 171
Daniel, Ruth 168, 171
Darwish, Mahmoud 86, 177
Daughters of the Nile (Spencer, ed.) 233

al-Daw, Hawa' (paternal grandmother of AF) 49–55
Dekheila (village) 39
Design Studio by Azza Fahmy, The 178–83, 266–67. *See also* Azza Fahmy company; Azza Fahmy designs
Dupke, Christa 184, 209

Eady, Dorothy (Umm Seti) 26–27, 29–31
Egyptian culture: agriculture 44–45; amulets 128, 177, 191, 208; *'angarib* (woven straw) beds 47–48; ballet 81; bandits 37; bathhouse 104–107; book publishing and distribution 80–82; camels 190, 192–93; cheese making 62; children's activities 12, 20, 22, 31, 34, 40, 41; class divide 162; consumption patterns 8; cookbooks 43; copper whitener 43; cotton mattresses and quilts 34; cotton production 8–16, 106, 122–24; dog breeding 23; donkeys 136, 154–56; entertaining guests 16–17; family lunch 10; folk art 173–75; food gifts 35–36, 57; foods 10, 32–33, 62–63, 97, 101, 161–62; *haggana* (mounted police) 15, 37; headscarves 32; hygiene 33–34; leather wallets 12–13; *makhrouta* (dessert) 35–36; marriage customs 123, 205; *milaya laff* 96; *moulid*s 70, 97; Nile floods 20; 1970s arts 175–77; opium use 104; public transportation 60, 74–76; romantic relationships 241; sewing and

mending 8, 64, 67; *shabka* (marriage gift) 123; *shamsi* bread 36; shopping 8, 38–39, 41–42, 63, 90–91, 96; silk textiles 14; slaves 25–26; snake charming 17–20; street food 32–33; sugar and sweets 97; Suwara festival 193–94; sycomore figs 10; telephones 241; television programs 74–75; traffic authority checkpoints 202, 203; Umm Kulthum 69; water carriers 43; women of Upper Egypt 22. *See also* clothing, traditional; jewelry, traditional; Sudanese culture; tribes
Einstein, Albert 279
Eisa, Soheir 81–82
embroidery: gold thread 134–35, 228; Libyan 228; in Sinai tribes 194–95; in Siwan clothes 207–209; Syrian 217. *See also* clothing, traditional
England 156, 168–73
engravers 109–10, 134, 136, 163
European Union grant 178
Ezz al-Arab, Hisham 252
Ezzat family 55. *See also* Mahmoud as surname

Faber family 67–68
Faculty of Fine Arts 75–77, 150, 201–204, 241–44
Fadda, Muhammad (silversmith) 128
Fahmy, Abdel Azim (cousin of AF's father) 241
Fahmy, Abdel Azim (uncle of AF) 37
Fahmy, Abdel Farrag (uncle of AF) 165
Fahmy, Abdel Wahab (uncle of AF) 47

Fahmy, Ahmad (uncle of AF) 36, 49
Fahmy, Azza: reflections on life and career 1–3, 281–83. *See also* Azza Fahmy company; Azza Fahmy designs; Azza Fahmy Design Studio; Ghaly, Amina (daughter of AF); Ghaly, Fatma (daughter of AF); Mahmoud, Zubeida (mother of AF); al-Subki, Abdel Moneim (father of AF)
—, early years: books and culture 45–47; childhood house 16–20; education 31–33, 61; at Faculty of Fine Arts 75–77, 150, 201–204, 241–44; family roots 5; father 5–8, 10, 16, 22–24, 37, 41–42, 44–47; father's death 52–53, 59; father's work 8–10, 13–16, 60; grandfather 10–11, 47–50; grandmother (Habbouba) 49–55; Helwan society 67–74; home life 33–34, 43–45, 60–67; mother 17, 43, 55–59, 61–67; pets 23, 51; in Sohag 20–25; Sohag Preparatory School for Girls 31–33; summer holidays at beach 39–40; summer holidays preparations 34–36; summer holidays travel 37–39
—, learning the craft: beginning training 88–91; brass workers 109–11, 113–16; career search 79–88; Gamal gold plate 117–22; gold and traditional jewelry 12–13, 122–24; Hagg Sayed's workshop 98–104; Hallmark, Weights, and Measures Authority 125, 141–46; *Hosh Qadam*

(Khashqadam) 96–98; Khan al-Khalili 91–95; Malatili Bathhouse 104–107; Nubian jewelers 136–39; old beads 107–110; Sagha (gold- and silversmiths' district) 116–17, 122–24, 127–30, 133; *Shafiqa and Metwalli* (film) 110–12; silver merchants 124–33, 161, 195, 227; *wikala*s 133–36; workshop dust and *shashangi*s 134, 140–41

—, business and motherhood: Azza Fahmy Design Studio 178–83, 266–67; Boulaq al-Dakrour workshop 167–68; first book 183–92; first workshop 163–68; Harraniya years 152–58; London scholarship 168–73; marriage and children 147–52; the 1970s arts 175–77; protective clothing 159–63; Ri'aya and folk art 173–75; Sinai travels 192–97

—, travel and inspiration: AF as mother 271–79; crafts research 199–200; daughter Amina 263–70; daughter Fatma 250–62; England 156, 168–73; granddaughter Thuraya 63, 175, 262–63; India 244–50; Iraq 230–32; Italy 150, 180–81, 241–44; Japan 1, 238–41; Jerusalem 236–38; Jordan 177, 235–36; Lebanon 214–16; Libya 228–29; Morocco 205–206, 232–35; Nepal 76; North Africa 227–28; oases 209–14; Oman 222–24; Saudi Arabia 224–27; Sinai 192–97; Siwa Oasis 201–209; Sudan 53–54; Syria 217–22; Tunisia 229–30; UN Conference on Women (Beijing) 182–83; United States 167, 236

Fahmy, Farah (aunt of AF) 48, 54, 69
Fahmy, Farrag (uncle of AF) 49
Fahmy, Fatma (aunt of AF) 48, 49
Fahmy, Ibrahim (great-uncle of AF) 15
Fahmy, Mustafa (AF's father's cousin) 75
Fahmy, Randa (sister of AF) 200, 233
Fahmy, Safiya (aunt of AF) 49–50, 68, 72–73
Fahmy, Samira (aunt of AF) 37, 47
Fahmy Bey, Muhammad (grandfather of AF) 10–11, 47–50, 67–68
Fahmy family 37, 55. *See also* al-Subki, Abdel Moneim (father of AF)
Fakhry, Ahmed 26–27
Farouk, King of Egypt 42
Fatimid era 97, 164–65
Fayoum 80
Ferragamo, Salvatore 266
filigree 102–103, 110–11, 184–85
folk art 173–75

Gabgab (silversmith) 206–207
al-Galla, Hassan (plater) 135
gallabiyas 173–75
al-Galla family 134–35
al-Gamal gold plate 117–22
Gasser, Awad (goldsmith, silversmith) 137–39
gem dealers 107, 111–12, 133–34, 244–50

296 INDEX

gem setters 106–107, 161
General Information Authority 76–77
Geographical Society Museum (Ethnographic Museum) 98, 123
Ghali, Anna 107–109
Ghali family (goldsmiths) 122
Ghaly, Amina (daughter of AF): childhood 33, 152, 154–56, 276–77; designing 270, 278; education 263–69; gem buying 248–49; travels 182, 214, 218–19
Ghaly, Fatma (daughter of AF): award and training 260–61; childhood 33, 152, 154–56, 250–52, 276–77; executive director 261–62; marketing 252–60; marriage gift from AF 216; as model for jewelry 209; travels 182, 214, 248
al-Ghanem, Badriya 160
al-Ghazali, Nadhim 231
al-Ghitani, Gamal 275, 281
Gibran, Khalil 240
al-Gindi, Magda 71
gold and traditional jewelry 12–13, 122–24. *See also* jewelry, traditional
gold mines 189
gold plate/platers 117–22, 134, 135, 161
goldsmiths: Abdin district (Nubian) 136–39; of Aleppo 220–21; of Baghdad 231; Greek 144; guilds and hierarchies 131–32, 140–41; Italian 267–68; Sagha district 116–17, 122–24, 127–30, 133; in Sudan 54–55
gold thread embroidery 134–35, 228

Gordon College (Khartoum) 52
Green, Christine 28–29, 156
guilds 131–32, 140–41

Haddad, Fouad 158
Hafez, Aisha Hanem (maternal grandmother of AF) 55, 74
Hagg Abbas al-Talli ("the plater") 134
Hagg Abdou Saber (antiques trader) 106
Hagg Farag al-Aqra' (silversmith) 127–28
Hagg Farouk Abdel Khaliq (gem dealer) 107
Hagg Halwagi 161–62
Hagg Hassan Yaqout (craftsman) 102–103
Hagg Ibrahim al-Sunni (craftsman) 106
Hagg Muhammad al-Mikkawi (silver merchant) 124–33, 161, 195, 227
Hagg Sayed (craftsman) 98–104, 165
Hakkak Fayrouz Sinawi (craftsman) 102
Hala, Madame 143–44
Hallmark, Weights, and Measures Authority 125, 141–46
Hamdi, Baligh 147–49
Hamdi, Husam 147
Hamed, Shazli (goldsmith, silversmith) 137
Hardana, Hala 235
Harraniya years 152–58
Haruko Fukuda 263
Hassan, Abdou Ahmad "Abdoun" (goldsmith, silversmith) 137
Hassan, Selim 26–27
Hassan the Engraver 163

Helwan: family visits 37; first workshop 163–68; home life 60–67; hotels 68–69; hot springs 72–73; Japanese Garden 67; rail transportation 60, 74–75; schools 61, 71–72, 163–64; society 67–74, 163–64
Helwan Secondary School 61, 163–64
Henein, Adam 178
Henein, Erian (plater) 161
Henry (goldsmith) 133
Hifni, Abla 147
Hifni, Tareq 184, 185
Higab, Sayed 15, 80, 175
Hosh Qadam (Khashqadam) 96–98
House of Iraqi Fashion 230
Hussein, Hisham 53
Hussein, Saddam 230

Ibn Khaldun 110
Ibn Zaydoun 222
Ibrahim, Fatma (first wife of AF's grandfather) 47
Idris, Mahmoud (husband of AF's aunt) 40
Imru' al-Qays 216
Inayat, Ragi 175–76
India 244–50
industrial waste 140–41
Iraq 230–32
Ismail, Khedive 42, 60, 74
Israel 236
Israelis, turquoise mining 111
Istanbouli family (goldsmiths) 221
Italy 150, 180–81, 241–44
Iverson, Barry 184, 209

al-Jadir, Saad 232–33
Jahin, Salah 20, 70, 176–77, 250
Jan, Mokeesh (silver dealer) 246–48
January Revolution (2011) 117
Japan 1, 238–41
Jardana, Zaha (Zaha Menku) 235
Jerusalem 236–38
jewelry, traditional: Algerian 227–28; amulets 50, 128, 177, 191, 208; beads 13, 107–110, 128, 195, 212–13; Bedouin 109, 119, 124–25, 187–91, 194–95, 227; coral 112, 186, 228, 229; countryside style 12–13, 118–24; desertification and silver sales 133; filigree 102–103, 110–11, 184–85; gems 106–107, 111–12, 133–34, 244–50; gold and traditional jewelry 12–13, 122–24; gold plate 117–22, 134, 135, 161; Indian work in Saudi Arabia 226; Iraqi 231; Libyan 228–29; Moroccan 233; North African 229; nose rings 188, 210–11, 212, 214; Nubian 136–39; from oases 210–13, 214; Omani 223–24; Siwan 204, 206–207, 208, 209; skilled craftsman vs. artisanal artist 115–16; Sudanese 124–25; Syrian 220–21; Tuareg 227; turquoise 111. *See also* Azza Fahmy designs; clothing, traditional; Egyptian culture; jewelry making
jewelry making: coded language 141; gold thread 134–35; Hallmark, Weights, and Measures Authority 125, 141–46; licensing exam 141–42; protective clothing 159–63;

silversmithing techniques 99–101. *See also* Azza Fahmy designs; jewelry, traditional
Jordac, George 3
Jordan 177, 235–36
Jumblatt, May 215

Kamal, Soheir 156
Kamel, Mary Saad (Na'ila Kamel) 250–51
Karnak Temple 28–29
Kawamel (village) 21
Kawar, Widad 235–36
Khalifa, Kamal 176
Khan al-Khalili: architecture 91–95; early years of designing 159–63; first training 88–91
Khartoum University 53–54
Khatib family (handweavers) 14
Khawaga Fawzi Mikhail 117
Khawaga William 107
Khawaga Yousef Matatia 128
Khorassani's 112
Klidar, Abla 230
Kniou, Mona 216
Kordofan 49

Lalaounis, Ilias (goldsmith) 144
Lamin, Sheikh (silversmith) 124–25
Lebanon 214–16
Lehnert & Landrock 43–44
Lesha, Mounir 72
Libya 228–29
literature and jewelry 175–77
Luxor 28–29

Ma'allim Atiya Baqi 128
Ma'allim Yaqoub Salib 128
Macdonald, Julien 259
Mahdi Revolution 39, 49

Mahfouz, Naguib 111, 279
Mahmoud, Samir (uncle of AF) 55
Mahmoud, Zubaida (mother of AF): cooking 43; domestic life 57–59, 61–67; end of life 65, 66; family roots 5, 55–56; financing AF's travel 242; marriage 56–57; reactions to AF's marriage proposals 148, 151; reactions to AF's work 89, 90
Mahmoud family (maternal relatives of AF) 37, 55
Mahroussa (royal yacht) 42
Malatili Bathhouse 104–107
Mamluk art and architecture 88–89, 92–94, 97–98, 114, 165
Manku, Ali 215
Manninger, Doris 266–67
al-Mansouri (antique dealer) 107, 108, 124
Marrakech 232–33
al-Mashad, Mustafa 24–25, 59
al-Masri, Suzanne 99
Mehrez, Shahira 174, 210
al-Messiri, Nawal 216
al-Mikkawi, Hagg Muhammad (silver merchant). *See* Hagg Muhammad al-Mikkawi (silver merchant)
al-Mikkawi, Ibrahim (silver merchant) 124–25
Ministry of Culture 79–80, 165, 229–30
Ministry of Industry 233
monasteries 24
Morocco 205–206, 232–35
Most Important Young People of the Arab World 260
motherhood 271–75
al-Mougi, Sara 88

Moulid al-Erian (saint's birthday) 70
Moussa, Thuraya (granddaughter of AF) 63, 175, 262–63
al-Mughazi, Fayeq 72
Muhammad, Hassan Ali (goldsmith, silversmith) 137
Muhammed bin Rashid, Sheikh 260
Muhammad Samaka (craftsman) 110–11
al-Muhandes, Ayman 273
Murad family (platers) 118, 121–22
Murtada, Ahmad 136
al-Mustansir bi-Allah, Caliph 97
al-Mutanabbi 219

Nada, Hamed 201–202
Nada, Ihsan 150
Nasser, Gamal Abdel 33
Nasser era 80–81
Nehru, Jawaharlal 46
Nepal 76
Nigm, Ahmad Fouad 282
al-Nimr, Ri'aya 173–75, 230, 232
Noor al-Hussein, Queen of Jordan 235, 236
North Africa 227–28
Noubar (goldsmith) 133
Noura bint Abdel Rahman, Princess 224, 226
Nubian jewelry 136–39
al-Nugoumi, Abdallah 39

oases 209–14
Oman 222–24
Omar ibn Abu Rabie 222

Palestine 236–38
Palestinian jewelry and costumes 223, 235–36
Pepito (goldsmith) 267–68

plating/platers. *See* gold plate/platers
Porret, Evelyna 80
pottery 80, 212
prayer beads 112
Ptah-Hotep 241, 263

Qaboos, Sultan of Oman 224
Qadi family (gem dealers) 112
Qasabgi family (goldsmiths) 134
Qattan's (trader) 111
*qaysariya*s (roofed markets) 22, 124
Quos (city) 124

Ramadan, Walid 192–93
Rami, Ahmad 222
Ricci, Stefano 244
al-Rifai, Mona 235
Rifa'is (snake charmers) 17–20
Rizq, Aziz (silversmith) 128
Rochas, M. 22–23
rosaries 112
al-Rubi (metal pressing) 135
al-Rumi, Jalal al-Din 275

Saad (workshop boss) 104
Saad al-Din, Mursi 147, 149
Sadeq, Said (plater) 118–19, 121
Sagha (gold- and silversmiths' district): of Aleppo 220–21; of Baghdad 231; of Cairo 116–17, 122–24, 133, 160–63. *See also* goldsmiths
Sahel Selim (town) 21
Sainte Famille School 71–72
Saleh, Magdi Kamel 257–58, 271
Salem, Nehad 90, 184
Salih, Tayeb 34–35
al-Samaka gold plate 121
Sarhan, Samir 214–15

Saudi Arabia 224–27
Sawiris family 13
al-Sayyab, Badr Shaker 219
scrap dealership 126
Segal company (gold plate) 118, 121–22
Selim, Zeinab 90–91
Severian, Avedis (gem setter) 106–107
Shaalan, Zeinab 160
al-Shabi, Abu al-Qasem 176
Shafiq, Samira 79–80
Shafiqa and Metwalli (film) 110–12
Shahata, Fawqiya 278
Shaker, Ihab 79–80
Shaker, Nagi 110–11, 176
*shashangi*s (assayers) 140–41
al-Sherif, Abdel Salam 76, 242
Sherif, Dina 1–2
Shiha, Eid (craftsman) 102–103
al-Shubukshi family (gold dealers) 117
Silk Road 109
silver merchants: in India 246–48; sheikh of 124–33, 161, 195, 227
silversmithing techniques 99–101
silversmiths: in Abdin district (Nubian) 136–39; guilds and hierarchies 131–32, 140–41; in Khan al-Khalili 88–91; in Sagha district 115, 127–30; Siwan jewelry 204, 206–207; of Sudan 124–25
Sinai 192–97
Sirgani family (goldsmiths) 122
Sir John Cass College of Arts and Sciences 168–73
Siwa Oasis 201–209
Sohag 20–25

Sohag Preparatory School for Girls 31–33
South Red Sea 187–92
Soviet Union 81
St. Laurent, Yves 234
al-Subki, Abdel Moneim (father of AF): childhood 49, 50, 52; cultural excursions 24–25; death 52–53, 59; education 52; family roots 5; family ties 37; networks of 22–27, 29–31; personality and taste 7–8, 10, 16, 41, 44–47, 50, 57; as storyteller 5–7, 41–42; work 8–10, 13–16, 60. *See also* Fahmy as surname
Sudan 53–54
Sudanese culture 50–52. *See also* Egyptian culture
Sudanese jewelry 124–25
sugar 44–45, 97
al-Sunbati, Samir 187, 190
al-Sunna, Gamal (craftsman) 102–103
Syria 217–22

al-Tabrizi, Shams 77
Tahawi family 120
al-Tamman, Nevin 208–209
Tawfiq, Bibawi (gold dealer) 117
al-Tayer, Obeid 257
al-Tayer company 256–57
al-Tazi family (gold dealers) 117
Tewfik, Khedive 68
textiles: *kastour* fabric 38–39; silk 14. *See also* clothing, traditional
al-Touni, Helmi 85–86
tribes: Ababda and Bishari 189–90; Algerian 227–28; Amazigh

233; Bedouin 109, 111, 119, 124–25, 187–91, 194–95, 227; desertification and movement 133; Eastern Desert and southern Red Sea 187–92; Hawwara 25; Rashaida 133, 187–89; Sinai 192–97; Sudanese 48, 51, 54; Tarabin 193–94; Tuareg 227; Western Desert 227; Zandi 48. *See also* Egyptian culture; jewelry, traditional
Tunis (town in Fayoum) 80
Tunisia 229–30
turquoise 111

Umm Hashem (*makhrouta* maker) 35–36
Umm Kulthum 69, 148–49
Umm Seti (Dorothy Eady) 26–27, 29–31
Uncle Ahmad (polisher) 160–61
Uncle Amin (silversmith) 204
Uncle Hussein Abdel Sayed (tribesman) 189
Uncle Kittana (snake charmer) 18–20
Uncle Mustafa the Engraver 109–10
UN Conference on Women (Beijing) 182–83
UNIDO (United Nations Industrial Development Organization) 53–54
United States 167, 236
University of Central England (Birmingham) 264–65, 269–70
University of London Museum 28
UN Women Tokyo conference 1
Upper Egypt: bandits 37; dialect 60; gold jewelry purchases 122–24; slaves 25–26; Sohag 20–25; women 22. *See also* Egyptian culture
Usta Abdel Hamid (family cook) 57, 62
Usta Erfan (goldsmith) 130
Usta Ramadan (silversmith) 88–91
Uways, Hajj Omar 21
Uways, Sayed 21
Uweida, Kamel (craftsman) 128

Victoria and Albert Museum (London) 240
Victory College (Alexandria) 61
Vita Mia (shop) 90–91

Wadi al-Gemal festival 192–93
Wahbi, Zahi 66
Walker, Mr. ("Uncle") 16, 23
Wassef, Atef (antique dealer) 133
*wikala*s 133–36
Winfrey, Oprah 271
workshop dust and *shashangi*s 134, 140–41
World Gold Council 263–64

Yanagi Soetsu 238–39
Yaqout, Hani (craftsman) 103
Yazdi, Hasib (gem dealer) 111, 244
Yoshimura, Sakuji 238
Yousef, Salah (jewelry equipment seller) 140–41, 161

Zein al-Abidin, Ali 139
Ziyad, Tawfiq 177